MA

THE MEASURE O

SRI KRISHNA PREM
and
SRI MADHAVA ASHISH

MAN, THE MEASURE OF ALL THINGS

In the Stanzas of Dzyan

THE THEOSOPHICAL PUBLISHING HOUSE
WHEATON, ILL., U.S.A.
MADRAS, INDIA, LONDON, ENGLAND

First U.S. edition 1969
QuestBooks

Published by The Theosophical Publishing House
Wheaton, Ill., U.S.A.
www.questbooks.com

Library of Congress Catalog Card No. 74–87256

A Publication supported by The Kern Foundation

© Sri Krishna Prem and Sri Madhava Ashish 1966

Printed in the United States of America
978-8356-0944-9

Cover by Kirsten Pott

Who is it knows? Who here can tell us surely
  From what and how this universe has risen?
And whether not till after it the gods lived?
  Who then can know from what it has arisen?
                                        Rig Veda X. 129 (Kaegi)

As one that looks up to the heavens and sees the
splendour of the stars, thinks of the Maker and searches,
so whoever has contemplated the Intellectual
Universe and known it must search after its Maker too.
What Being has raised so noble a fabric, and how?
Who has begotten such a child, this Divine Mind, this
lovely abundance so abundantly endowed?
                    PLOTINUS. *Enneads* III, viii. 10 (Turnbull)

Surely in the heavens and the earth there are signs
for the faithful; in your own creation, and in the
beasts that are scattered far and near, signs for true
believers; in the alternations of night and day, in the
sustenance Allah sends down from heaven with which
He revives the earth after its death, and in the marshalling
of the winds, signs for men of understanding.
                        Qu'rān Sūrah XLV (Dawood)

PREFACE

'Hear a plain fact,' said the mystic Blake, 'Swedenborg has not written one new truth. Now hear another, He has written all the old falsehoods.' Yet he seems to have studied Swedenborg with interest and respect.

But what does it profit to replace the heavenly Jerusalem of the Christians, with its harps and thrones, or the golden Vaikunth of the Hindus, with its fans and fly-flaps, by the 'summer lands' of the Spiritualists and the astral planes, etc., of conventional occultism?

Repetition of the same old lies!

And yet there is Truth behind them all. If this study of the *Stanzas of Dzyan* can help to remove even a few of those glittering veils with which 'the face of Truth is covered over', it will have served its purpose. The Truth is what we seek, and he who seeks, not just believes or doubts, shall find.

It may be we have failed; it must be so in parts at least. But let us remain, 'dizzy, lost, yet unbewailing', seeking for that state where:

> 'The soul of Adonais like a star
> Beacons from the Abode where the Eternal are'.[1]

The *Stanzas of Dzyan* are known only as the text of H. P. Blavatsky's cosmogonic commentary *The Secret Doctrine*.

[1] Down to this point the preface is taken from that written for the Adyar edition by Sri Krishna Prem.

Though Sri Krishna Prem was once, I have never been a member of the Theosophical Society founded by Blavatsky. Our boldness in offering an independent commentary on the Stanzas was based on the facts that neither is theosophy as such any man's property, nor did Blavatsky regard the *Stanzas of Dzyan* as her own.

The ancient Cosmogonies and Creation Myths were, in effect, affirmations of the divine nature of all things, giving significance to human life and validity to the moral and social codes formulated on the patterns of what they represented man to be, or rather, what he should become. The *Stanzas of Dzyan* represent such an affirmation.

Sri Krishna Prem recognised the value of the Stanzas, but felt that Blavatsky had left room for further enquiry into their meaning. With the encouragement of Bertram Keightley, a personal disciple of Blavatsky's who had helped her in the preparation of *The Secret Doctrine*, and helped by the deep insight of his disciple Sri Krishnarpita Mai, he wrote an independent commentary some time in the late thirties. Dissatisfied with what he had written, he put it aside, to be read only occasionally by friends, until the middle fifties when he suggested I try my hand at completing it. In the intervening years of spiritual discipline his nature had changed and developed so markedly that he told a friend who was pressing him to publish: 'I cannot finish it. The man who wrote it no longer exists. But,' he added, 'I might rewrite it.' Although he insisted my name appear as co-author, the book is his. If I have contributed anything of value, it is because he has guided me in all things since I first met him.

The first edition of this volume,[1] which deals with the Stanzas on cosmic evolution, was in the press at the time of Sri Krishna Prem's death. A similar rewriting of his commentary on the second set of Stanzas, dealing with the evolution of man, may soon be completed.

Sri Krishna Prem (Ronald Henry Nixon, 1898–1965) was

[1] Theosophical Publishing House, Adyar, Madras, 1966.

one of those rare men who combine a passionate and single-pointed devotion with an enlightened clarity of intellect. Born in Cheltenham, England, he went to Taunton School and then saw active service as a subaltern in the Royal Flying Corps in 1917. As an undergraduate at Cambridge he was deeply stirred by Buddhism and Theosophy, and this brought him to India in 1921 where he taught English at Lucknow and Banaras Universities while searching for a living Guru. He fell in love with India, her people, her philosophy, and her way of life, becoming a much loved and almost adopted member in the family of Dr G. N. Chakravarti, who was then Vice Chancellor of Lucknow University, a close friend of Annie Besant, and sometime Secretary to the Indian branch of the Theosophical Society. Though the Chakravarties did not conceal their commitment to the spiritual path, it was several years before 'Professor Nixon', as he was then called, came to see that behind Mrs Chakravarti's social façade was a woman of outstanding mystical experience. He became her disciple, and when, in pursual of her path, she took holy orders as a Sanyasin with the name of Sri Yashoda Mai and left home as a mendicant, he, too, left his university post and followed his Guru to the Himalayas. Together they built a temple consecrated to Sri Krishna, and there Sri Krishna Prem remained in his Guru's service, following the austere life of the Sanyasi for the rest of his days. As if to compensate for his intellectual brilliance, his Guru led him along the traditional path of devotion to Sri Krishna, performing ritual worship and adhering to the detailed code of behaviour associated with Hindu orthodoxy.

Sri Yashoda Mai had died two years before I first met Sri Krishna Prem in 1946, and he was running the small ashram they had founded. I was not at first wholly sure that I liked him, though I had to admire his searching clarity of mind and to respect his intense devotion. It was as if his shining intellect was also an armour that kept one from entering the magic circle of his dedication to Sri Krishna and his Guru. Only when I pressed a personal question did he let me see something of the real man behind the shield, and that glimpse won my heart.

Unlike the ordinary intellectual who likes to demolish human illusions, but has nothing to offer in their place, Sri Krishna Prem would never attempt to shake a man's inadequately based faith unless he could give something of his own certainty in its place. He could be ruthlessly destructive in the intellectual field, particularly with regard to dependence on authority, and with his wide knowledge of both Western and Eastern philosophical and theological systems he was a formidable opponent in argument, but in his view faith should be rooted in the eternal, not in the disputable authority of texts and historical events. Whereas most men bolster their positions with vehement arguments that are really directed against their own hidden doubts, so that they spend energy to support their faith, he drew strength from his calm certainty.

But the discipline had done its work. The greater depth of inner experience which came to him was reflected in a universality of outlook, quite different from the apparent sectarianism of his earlier years. His intellectual armour softened, and feeling and intellect now flowed together, the former losing its fear of involvement and becoming ready to embrace all comers, while the latter, no longer needed for defence, became a surer and more balanced instrument. He became an integral man. And though I can point to no particular moment to mark the event, it slowly became clear that he was no longer a seeker but one who had found.

The changes to his nature were expressed in changes in his way of life. When he saw that the orthodoxy of the Krishna cult had been a safe channel for his feelings, rather than a necessary adjunct to the truth, he simplified the whole paraphernalia of specifically Vaishnava religion with which he had been surrounded. Guided from within, he deliberately broke away from the sacred structure of sectarian do's and don'ts;

yet none of it was aggressive in the way that such structure breaking is apt to be. The more whole he became, the more simple and wholly loveable he was. His old attitude of 'I care for nobody. No, not I' was gone. Previously he had left one with one's admiration rather chilled by a suspicion that he really would not care what happened to the disciples he barely tolerated when he could at last turn his back on the world for ever. Now there could be no question of his not caring. He had come not merely to tolerate but even to encourage an increasing crowd of cosmopolitan friends and disciples (the distinction was not always very clear) whose constant demands taxed his strength to exhaustion. And while there was still an undercurrent of Radha-Krishna devotional modes of expression, his teaching of the inner path was shorn of traditional and mythological trappings. For the most part he spoke directly of human problems and of man's place in the cosmic evolution.

It was not as a sometime ritualist and author of books that he won the love and respect of his many intimate friends and followers who sought the path he had trodden, for people drew strength more from his presence than from what he said. All treasure the memory of his radiant personality, his blue eyes that seemed to see right through one, his humour, his disconcerting questions before which falsities crumbled to dust, the love he gave so freely, and, above all, the fire of spiritual certainty whose central flame gave significance to the many facets of his nature.

He had become what a man should be: rooted in the eternal, guiding his actions from direct perception of the truth, fearing nothing, and evading no human responsibilities. After his death in November, 1965, a friend wrote to me: 'To me he was the tangible proof of the intangible, and gave a perspective and dignity to life.' To him who showed me the Way I dedicate this edition.

SRI MADHAVA ASHISH
Mirtola

ACKNOWLEDGEMENTS

The authors gratefully acknowledge permission given
by the copyright holders of the undermentioned works
for quotations included in this book.

The Secret Doctrine (incorporating the *Stanzas of Dzyan*).
1938 edition. H. P. Blavatsky. The Theosophical
Publishing House, Adyar. Also, by permission of the late Sri
B. P. Wadia, the facsimile of the 1888 edition produced by the
Theosophy Co., California.

The Voice of the Silence. H. P. Blavatsky. The Theosophical
Publishing House, Adyar.

Transactions of the Blavatsky Lodge; Theosophical Glossary.
H. P. Blavatsky. The Theosophical Publishing House,
London.

Thrice Greatest Hermes. G. R. S. Mead; *Meister Eckhart.*
Pfeiffer. Translated by C. de B. Evans; *The Works of
Thomas Vaughan.* A. E. Waite; *Sepher Yetzirah and Aesch
Mezereph.* Wynn Westcott. John M. Watkins.

The Enneads of Plotinus. Stephen Mackenna. Faber & Faber.

The Essence of Plotinus. Grace Turnbull. Oxford University
Press, New York.

The Thirteen Principal Upanishads. Hume. Oxford
University Press, Bombay.

The Tibetan Book of the Dead. W. Y. Evans-Wentz.
Oxford University Press, London.

Dialogues of Plato. Jowett; *Hermetica.* Walter Scott.
Clarendon Press, Oxford.
Prolegomena to the Study of Greek Religion. Jane Harrison;
Selected Poems from the Diwani Shamsi Tabriz. R. A.
Nicholson. Cambridge University Press.
Mathnavi of Jalalu'ddin Rumi. R. A. Nicholson. The
Gibb Memorial Trust & Messrs Luzac.
A New Approach to the Vedas. A. K. Coomaraswamy. Luzac.
The Sūfi Path of Love. Margaret Smith.
Dialogues of the Buddha. Rhys Davids; *Majhima Nikaya.*
Lord Chalmers. The Pali Text Society & Luzac.
Complete Psychological Works. Sigmund Freud. Standard
edition. Edited by James Strachey. The Hogarth Press,
London, and W. W. Norton, U.S.A.
Psychology and Religion. C. G. Jung; *The Light of Asia.*
Sir Edwin Arnold. Routledge & Kegan Paul.
Dionysius the Areopagite. C. E. Rolt. The Society for
Promoting Christian Knowledge.
The Signature of All Things. Jacob Boehme. Everyman's
edition. J. M. Dent.
The Awakening of Faith in the Mahāyāna. Suzuki. Open
Court Publishing Co.
Doctrine and Ritual of Transcendental Magic. Elephas Levi.
Translated by A. E. Waite. Rider.
The Koran. Dawood. Penguin Books Ltd.
The Garden of Vision. Adams Beck. Ernest Benn.
The Lotus Eaters; Ulysses. Lord Tennyson. Macmillan,
London.
Process and Reality. A. N. Whitehead. Copyright 1929
by Macmillan Co., renewed 1957 by Evelyn Whitehead.
Macmillan, New York.
Adventures of Ideas. A. N. Whitehead, Macmillan & Co.,
New York & Cambridge University Press. Copyright by
Macmillan Co., 1933, renewed 1961 by Evelyn Whitehead.
The Nature of the Physical World. Eddington. Macmillan
& Co., New York, and Cambridge University Press.

CONTENTS

INTRODUCTION

From the beginning of time men have sought the solution to a three-faced mystery: the mystery of origins, the mystery of present being, and the mystery of destiny. Usually their search has been directed outwards amongst the data of sense experience; backwards into the apparent certainty of the accomplished past, forwards in speculation into the indeterminate future. Only very rarely 'some wise man seeking Deathlessness, with reversed gaze has seen the inner Self',[1] the Self who is 'Lord of what has been and is to be'.[2]

This, however, is the real purpose of all the ancient cosmogonies: to invite us to turn our gaze inwards to the source and origin both of the 'outer' universe of phenomena and of the 'inner' universe of consciousness, to find there the ever-present and eternal simultaneity of what is here seen as a flow of separate events in time; and above all, to fathom the ultimate mystery of our selfhood.

But what has the Self, the mysterious root of human consciousness, got to do with a cosmogony, an account of the origination of the material universe? Such a question can only arise when, as most of us do, we explicitly or implicitly draw distinctions between ourselves and the things (phenomena of sense experience) around us: things we desire or fear to possess;

[1] *Kaṭhopanishad*, IV. 1.
[2] *Ibid.*, IV. 5.

B

events we desire or fear will happen; qualities of mind or feeling that add to or subtract from our self-opinion; things we value as adding to our pleasure, power or importance; things that crowd in oppressively upon us, restricting our freedom of action and absorbing our energies with their mute demands for attention.

We evaluate certain aspects of experience as good, and in gaining possession of these 'goods' we feel we have added to ourselves. By possessing more we become more. It is this evaluation of phenomena that truly constitutes materialism, this, and not any scientific theory about the nature of energy structures in space.

If we make an effort to isolate our selfhood from the phenomena of sense, one of the things we see is that, apart from the conventions of ownership, we do not really possess anything, not even our bodies. We are usually in the position of observers, often against our will, of a flow of 'external' or 'internal' events, and we are led to question whether those events have independent reality apart from an observer.

This is where the problem of the self meets the problem of matter. We have to find an integral understanding of all experience which will resolve the dilemma in the interdependence of conscious observer and content of experience.

The teachings of the conventional religions are of little help to us here as they lack the synthesis we need. The material sciences seem inclined to ignore the whole problem, and to regard consciousness as a property of certain complex material structures. Philosophers propound theories, but never seem able to demonstrate their validity even to their own satisfaction. Only when we turn to the evidence of mystical vision do we find accounts written by men in whose experience the duality of self and matter was resolved.

Nāgārjuna, the great *Mahāyāna* Buddhist, said, 'There is no difference at all between *Nirvāṇa* and *Samsāra* (the world ocean), that which is the limit of *Nirvāṇa* is also the limit of the world. Between the two we cannot find the slightest shade of difference.'[1]

The manner in which such men formulate the ineffable truth of their vision into teachings for others varies; and the task is so difficult that even the Buddha is said to have hesitated to teach at all. The *Stanzas of Dzyan* along with other better known cosmogonies constitute one such type of teaching, deriving ultimately from the vision of a Seer. In these Stanzas the duality between self and matter is resolved by showing how both poles of being—the conscious experiencer and the objects experienced—arise from a single source. The universe as we know it has thus the same origin as have we who experience it. We and the universe are interdependent elements of psychic process in consciousness. Looking outwards we fill the universe with values taken from within ourselves. Looking inwards we find that the patterns of the psyche correspond to the patterns of the outer world. Through the understanding of these symbolic correspondences we are enabled to reach a deeper understanding both of ourselves and of the universe, of the relationship between the two, and of our common source.

But what great Seer wrote this particular cosmogony? We do not know, any more than we know who wrote the first chapter of the Hebrew book of Genesis, who first told the myths later related in the Quiche *Popul Vuh,* or who first chanted the Vedic hymns. These Stanzas were first made known to the modern world as the *Stanzas of Dzyan* by H. P. Blavatsky in her book,[2] *The Secret Doctrine.*

Many people might suppose that, if one was going to write a commentary on a cosmogonic myth, it would have been wiser to choose something of less controversial origin as one's text. Our purpose, however, was not to comment on *a* cosmogony but on this particular collection of verses behind whose obscurity we had sensed a profundity of meaning and a universality of application beyond anything sanctified by the

---

[1] *Mādhyamika Kārika,* XXV. 19 and 20.
[2] *The Secret Doctrine,* H. P. Blavatsky, London, 1888.

joint approval of orthodox scholarship and orthodox religion.

By whom the original Stanzas were written, where they were found, how H. P. Blavatsky[1] came to record and translate them, and the methods she used to do so, are questions outside the scope of this work. When one cannot have scholastic proof of the origins of the orally transmitted Vedic hymns or of the historicity of the sayings of Jesus of Nazareth—both sanctified by ancientry and religious fervour—what 'proof' is going to help us here?

The Stanzas have been criticised as quite unknown to learning, either of the scholarly or of the orthodox religious variety; also for using an eclectic mixture of technical terms drawn from all manner of heterogeneous sources. Buddhist terms are found in them, but in a setting such as is found in no extant Buddhist book; Hindu terms also, but in a sense scarcely occurring in any standard works on Hindu philosophy.

On internal evidence, as the professors would say, there is much to discredit the Stanzas; that is, on internal evidence of the usual sort. But there is an internal evidence of another sort, one which is not bandied about in dusty lecture rooms but which speaks in silence in the heart, and, on that evidence, the *Stanzas of Dzyan* stand out as a unique and intensely valuable document which will repay our careful study. As a matter of fact, for those of us who are not archaeological fanciers, that is the only sort of evidence or importance that attaches to any document whatever. Even such a book as the *Bhagavad Gītā* draws its authority not from the fact that Sri Krishna is supposed to have spoken it, nor from the fact that Śankarāchārya wrote a commentary on it, nor from the fact that many men have revered it, but from its own inherent truth as a description of and guide to the inner life, a truth which is testified to and guaranteed by our own hearts and our own hearts alone. This is true of all the great religious scriptures of the world, and it is the same with the *Stanzas of Dzyan*; they stand upon their own feet and are their own authority. No

[1] We shall hereafter refer to H. P. Blavatsky by the initials she made famous—H.P.B.

romantic origin in secret rock-cut libraries, no supernormal provenance of any sort, can add one scrap to the authority which they possess by virtue of the meanings they unfold within the heart that tries in patience to understand them.

Suppose we receive teachings from a presumptive Mahātma whether in Tibet or anywhere else, unless we have access to the well of truth in our own hearts, how could we recognise him for what he is? Is it really supposed that such beings are authoritatively labelled like museum pieces? No, it is quite useless to base one's faith in these or any other teachings on the manner of their appearance. That is a path which, in the end, leads not to wisdom but to the pit of unimaginable follies. The possession of occult powers in no way guarantees their possessor's philosophy; and there are, and always were, frauds and deluded people in unfrequented corners of the world even as there are in cities.

It is not with such individualised Mahātmas that we are concerned, for not even a true Mahātma can impart the wisdom save to him who has found its seeds within himself. Our business is not to speculate about what we would do if we were privileged to meet such a great Being, but to turn resolutely away from earth-born ignorance and listen to the truths of the wisdom that, whatever anyone may say, are sounding within us at this very moment. If we can hear something of their fiery voices within us, then the study of these Stanzas will be of use and we shall come to know for ourselves the truth about their origin. If not, they had better go back to whatever libraries they came from before we add further fantasies to our already large stock.

The basic situation would not have been changed, either had an ancient manuscript been produced, or had H.P.B. claimed to have written them herself. Someone, a remarkable someone, composed these verses; our concern is with their content.

From this point of view, then, these comments have been written. In order to avoid possible misunderstandings it will be as well to state at the outset that the sense in which they have been interpreted is sometimes, perhaps, a different one from that followed by H.P.B. herself. This neither means that the writers are ignorant of what she has said, nor necessarily that they disagree. The symbols of occultism are such that any number of different readings may be given, each of them true in its own sphere, and the writers have chosen those most suited to the general plan of their exposition.

Readers who find certain familiar terms being used in an unfamiliar sense are referred to H.P.B.'s statement that these Stanzas will open to more than one key. Most of us have either made for ourselves, or taken as ready-made, a map of what we think the universe ought to be like. This is quite as it should be, but unfortunately, our own map is apt to keep getting in the way of our understanding of other people's maps. If we dismiss the other man's picture of things because it is not expressed in accustomed terms or because his terminology applied to our map would make nonsense, our lack of sympathetic flexibility will limit the range of knowledge to which we can turn for guidance or encouragement on our path. It would, for instance, lead to hopeless confusion if one tried to follow events of English history with reference to the same place names on the map of America.

This attitude towards the subject will be quite unacceptable to those who have neither sufficient confidence in their power of perception to judge the inner value of the Stanzas for themselves, nor the temerity to venture outside the restricted boundaries of knowledge approved by orthodox scholars, scientists, theologians, and sectarian dogmatisers. All such are well advised to leave the secret teachings and this commentary alone.

Knowledge of the inner worlds is necessarily beyond the domain of those whose learning is avowedly mundane; and anyone seeking inner knowledge will be faced with facts incredible by ordinary standards. If the seeker of inner knowledge does not open himself to these facts he will learn nothing, yet, if he believes them, the outer world will sneer at his credulity. Only if he is ready to prefer his inner aim beyond all other considerations, even to the extent of thinking it better to believe something wrong rather than to hang back from believing what should be believed, is he fit to travel the inner path.

It was in this sense that Agrippa said 'He who would be a Magus (a master of the Secret Wisdom) must be credulous', and Thomas Vaughan 'Now, for my part I have always honoured the Magi, their philosophy being both rational and majestic, dwelling not upon notions but effects, and those such as confirm both the wisdom and the power of the Creator. When I was a mere errant in their books I did believe them. Time rewarded my faith and paid my credulity with know-ledge. In the interim I suffered many bitter calumnies, and this by some envious adversaries who had nothing of a scholar but their own gowns and a little language for vent to their nonsense. But these could not remove me; with Spartan patience I concocted my injuries and found at last that nature was magical, not peripatetical.'[1]

To be fit to travel the path of the Spirit a man must have the sort of courage that sustains him unshaken in the certainty of his inner aim even though the censure of others rocks his outer world. He who hesitates on the brink of the dangerous waters of this knowledge, wishing for assurance of his safety before plunging, will never achieve inner certainty. One cannot learn to swim without swallowing much water.

What, in fact, is the Secret Doctrine, seemingly connected with the *Stanzas of Dzyan* through the title of H.P.B.'s book? It is the Eternal Wisdom underlying the teachings of all religions, the actual facts, of which we can never have more than interpretations unless we ourselves gain experience of them. For this reason it is secret. Every religion claims the Wisdom for its own; each tries to encompass it within the framework of a systematised expression; and each then claims for its

[1] *Coelum Terrae* (A. E. Waite).

interpretation a divine infallibility that can belong, not to any systematised interpretation, but only to the eternal and ineffable truth beyond all frameworks. Into these regions the mystics of all religions have adventured and have seen the one great light, but those who are concerned with the framework see only the differentiations of that light, the stained-glass windows of their particular sects.

If we wish to see that unitary light, the standard religious teachings can only take us to a certain point on our journey, the limits of the exoteric frameworks. Beyond that point the road enters a wild and dangerous country where we can get no support from those organisations and precautions that society devises for its greater safety.

It is not that the organised religions know nothing of the universal truths, for without that knowledge their teachings would attract no one. Their teachings are interpretations of the divine wisdom; nice, safe interpretations for the most part, presented in the socially approved manner. The truths are there for all to see, if anyone would but look, but most people do not look, or they look without intelligence, and it is not in the interests of priesthoods to open their eyes for them to perceptions that would show them the universal truth beyond sectarian differences. Here lies the trouble. Putting aside theories, we find in practice there are no religions and no sects, only men with human aspirations and human failings. Priestly hierarchies, priestly castes, and sectarian organisations inevitably find their temporal interests clashing with their understanding of the eternal verities. They are the official interpreters of the truth, and into their interpretations creep concealments and distortions favouring their worldly positions. In India the Brahmans have too often wished to exploit their knowledge to the exclusive advantage of their caste. Any Buddhist may no doubt become a monk, but the primary duty of the laity seems to be the support of the monks. Throughout the East, and particularly in Confucianism and Shintoism, the fear of the angry extinct ancestors is exploited to the advantage of church and state. In Christianity and Judaism the distortions follow the pattern of the angry God myth: upstairs in heaven is an irascible, domineering patriarch ready to rain down punishments on men's heads. And all in the interests of the local scheme of morals—and of the priesthood.

On the one hand are the threats of punishment, on the other the promises of rewards—liberation, deliverance, seats in heaven. Each race and each religion contrives in turn its own versions of these fables, fables that have just enough truth behind them to call out a response from the psyche of man.

One of the reasons why the modern psychological approach to the fundamental problems of life is so disliked by the prelates of orthodox religions is that it places within reach of every man a key to unlock the mysteries of the psyche and so of religion. Priesthoods like to keep the secret of their power to themselves.

Spirituality is the prerogative of no one race, no superior caste, and no particular religion. It is the birthright, whether claimed or not, of man as man. The Spirit is the very core of our being, our life, our consciousness, and it is the knowledge of this fact that is our passport to that unmapped land of truth from which all religions have drawn the teachings they so grudgingly divulge.[1]

Let us then study an independent account of the universal truth; an account unknown to religions and unchilled by the cold touch of academies. For that is what these cosmogonic Stanzas are, a rough map of the divine cosmos by means of which we may be able to set our course on the inner pilgrimage of discovery. We shall not be able to dispense entirely with frameworks, for without some sort of system we cannot organise or express our thoughts. Nevertheless, we must try to avoid not only the well worn distortions of orthodoxy, but also the influences

[1] Meister Eckhart '. . . was accused of preaching to the people in their own language things that might lead to heresy, and this led to his excommunication . . . on the general grounds of preaching to the laity the secrets of the Church.' *Meister Eckhart* by Franz Pfeiffer.

of our personal hopes, fears, habitual thought patterns, and prejudices, all of which would tend to distort our vision.

In the commentary we have neither been concerned to relate the Stanzas to the physical sciences of today, nor to provide one of those easily-remembered schematisations that in religious societies commonly replace intelligent enquiry. We have attempted to trace in the Stanzas the story of the emergence of the content of consciousness from its source, and the divine descent of man seen as a symbolic though none the less true account in terms of the concrete universe. That these two ways of looking at one and one only reality—that of the emergence of all things as the content of divine consciousness, and that of the material evolution of worlds—form almost exact parallels should be, but seldom is, obvious. We have tried, therefore, to bridge the gap for those who are looking for a means to relate this world of hard material objects with the world of spiritual values, the world of science with the world of the soul.

The powerful and widespread roots of the scientific tree are intensely selective. They draw from the soil only those elements which will help the growth of that particular tree. To go no higher, almost all the emotional elements of the psyche are rejected: science recks little of human emotions except as factors that disturb its accuracy. Even the rich manifold of sense experience finds small place in the structure of that tree. The very world of sense which science sets out to explain is, in the end, explained away altogether. For, consider the universe that science sets before us, a universe devoid not only of colour, sound, and warmth, but of all the sense qualities that make up the world of actual experience.

The world of science is not *the* world, but merely an abstraction from it. We must emphatically state that the real world is a tissue of psychic experience. 'Apart from the experiences of subjects there is nothing, nothing, bare nothingness.'[1] Grass *is* green and the sky blue. The wind *does* sough among

[1] Whitehead: *Process and Reality*.

the pine trees and the waves of the sea thunder in dazzling clouds of spray along rocky shores. These are the elemental facts of the world, and a science that explains them away in the pretence of explaining them can never be finally satisfactory.

Nor, in fact, is science able to tell us anything in answer to the questions we really want to ask. A loose brick on the top of a high building is displaced by the wind and happens to fall on the head of my friend in a crowd below. As a direct result my heart is filled with a deep and vivid experience: Why, why, why? Science, as nowadays understood, can give no answer. It can tell me about the impact of molecules of gas happening to fall upon an aggregate of (by courtesy) solid atoms in unstable equilibrium; about the subsequent acceleration of the freely falling body and its impact on the occipital sutures of my friend's skull which happened to be just in its line of fall. But, O God, what a mockery it all is. Happened! Why did all those 'happenings' happen just then and not a moment later when the impact would have been upon the pavement or even on someone else's skull, which would have been an entirely different event as far as I am concerned? If electrons are 'waves of probability' and nothing ever comes into contact with anything else, then what are these impacts, these shatterings that change the whole course of life for me? Ages ago we had the same mocking sophistry from the lips of Pakudha Kaccāyana: 'When one with a sharp sword cleaves a head in twain, no one thereby deprives anyone of life, a sword has only penetrated into the intervals between seven elementary substances.'[1]

And where is my friend? That thing you took away on a stretcher was not him. Where is that sun-like heart that warmed the whole of life, those thoughts that wandered through infinity? You who talk so much about the conservation of matter and energy, tell me what has happened to that world-illuminating energy of Spirit? Don't tell me that you know nothing about spiritual energy, that the Spirit is something

[1] *Dialogues of the Buddha*, I. p. 74.

nobody has ever seen. Which of you have ever seen these
electrons, this energy that was 'potential' in the brick? I have
seen the stuff of feeling take form before my very eyes and
known the living energy of spirit go forth from many a heart
to change the world. Shall there be no conservation there?

No, the 'universal laws' of science cannot tell me why my
bootlace broke that day, making me miss my train and my
appointment, nor why I and my family just 'happened' to be
out, the evening my house was destroyed by a bomb.

These questions are not irrelevant cobwebs to be brushed
aside as of no account. They are the living questions to which
men seek an answer, and it is the failure of science, academic
philosophy, and orthodox religion to give any answer that is
causing men's hearts to turn away and seek for light elsewhere.

However, many people still feel that the scientific method
has proved itself so successful a mode of enquiry into the nature
of being that other methods of enquiry must be inferior, or
even that there are no other real methods. The cosmogonic
myths of the ancients have thus become to be regarded as the
first lisping of child humanity, man's first questionings into
the nature of being, the first attempts at a scientific enquiry.
This attitude is mistaken, for as A. K. Coomaraswamy has
pointed out, '. . . endeavours to interpret "scientifically" are
beside the mark: the "science" here is not astronomical, but
psychological and ontological. Nothing can be *less* scientific
than to assume for Vedic liturgists an interest in natural facts
of the same kind as our own.'[1]

Plato held much the same view, though for him 'science'
had different connotations: '. . . whether a man gapes at the
heavens or blinks on the ground, seeking to learn some
particular of sense, I would deny that he can learn, for nothing
of that sort is matter of science; his soul is looking, not upwards,
but downwards, whether his way to knowledge is by water
or by land, and he may float on his back in either element.[2]

[1] *A New Approach to the Vedas*, note 65.
[2] *Republic*, Bk. VII. 529.

It is not part of our purpose to criticise the findings of science in its own field—the field of relative or contingent truth—but we must realise that human successes in that field have by no means solved our human problems; indeed, some even go so far as to think our difficulties have been exacerbated by the exploitation of the findings of science. No evaluation of life that gives almost exclusive importance to the understanding of the organisation of sense phenomena, but hardly concerns itself at all with the problem of the unobjectifiable consciousness of the perceiver of those phenomena, can ever give us more than a portion of the integral truth.

In fact it is not against any kind of 'science' that our criticism is directed; sciences, like religions, are the products of the minds of men. The progress of modern science comes from the application of clear analytic thought; but the abstract symbols used in such thinking, for all their accuracy and flexibility in certain fields, have limitations that make them unsuitable for the understanding of other modes of thought, for instance, the text of these Stanzas with their concrete symbolism.

Jane Harrison, who was perhaps one of the first to appreciate the inapplicability of analytic thought to mythology, writes:

'There is no greater bar to that realism of mythology which is the first condition of its being understood, than our modern habit of clear analytic thought. The very terms we use are sharpened to an over-nice discrimination. The first necessity is that by an effort of the sympathetic imagination we should think back to the "many" we have so sharply and strenuously divided, into the haze of the primitive "one".

'Nor must we regard this haze of the early morning as a deleterious mental fog, as a sign of disorder, weakness, oscillation. It is not confusion or even synthesis; rather it is as it were a protoplasmic fullness and forcefulness not yet articulate into the forms of its ultimate births. . . . . . It is necessary to bear in mind this primary fusion, though not confusion, of ideas.'[1]

[1] Jane Harrison. *Prolegomena to the Study of Greek Religion*, p. 164.

The clarity of analytic thought upon its own purely mental level is gained at the cost of ignoring the non-intellectual elements of reality which are essential to its full comprehension. The knowledge which our Stanzas seek to impart is not the analytic knowledge of the discursive mind (*manas*), but the feeling-knowledge of the intuitive mind (*buddhi*). The aspirant to such synthetic knowledge must learn to leave the earth and master, as it were, another element in which the laws of stability are quite different. The intellectualist logic of 'B is either A or not A' must be transcended if reality is to be grasped in its entirety. For this purpose the archaic symbolic thought, with all its fluidity and seeming vagueness, will be found an invaluable instrument. The modern man may have to fight at first to overcome his distrust of something so different from all that seems to him accurate and precise, but if he perseveres he will find that the undoubted truth of the results he gains thereby will serve to guarantee the validity of the method through which he has reached them, just as the practical results of science guarantee the validity, in its own field, of the scientific.

Here the attempt is being made to relate the ancient concrete symbols to the abstract language of the present. The use of alternative images from all over the world may sometimes make the reader feel that the unknown is being explained by the yet more unknown, or that the exchange of terms has landed him within a welter of symbols whose maze-like interconnectedness leaves his mind bewildered instead of enlightened. But not for nothing has Jalalu'ddin Rumi praised 'bewilderment' as superior to discursive reason. A wide range of alternative readings of the symbolic relationships becomes possible which, though it may lead to a number of apparent contradictions, is yet invaluable for the apprehension of synthetic truth. All the great scriptures of the world contain these apparent contradictions which later writers have devoted themselves to smoothing out. The so-called contradictions are not, however, disposed of so easily, and they re-appear as irreconcilable differences between the various cosmologies and mythologies of the world, as may be seen for instance in the differing symbolic genders ascribed to what are plainly the same principles of being. Faced with such a situation we have to throw aside our preconceived logical deductions if we wish to achieve any greater degree of perception than that of a merely sectarian orthodoxy.

This archaic symbolism is somewhat rich food for those accustomed to the over-refined white flour and over-polished rice of abstract philosophic discourse; but it is not, and, one may say, was never in its raw form intended to be food for pedants. It is rich in the sense that the fat soil of a compost heap is rich in well rotted matter of past life now ready to help build life anew. Into such rich soil the trees of knowledge and of life send their roots, feeling their way down into the dark matrix of the subsoil, afterwards to flower and fruit in the sunshine above. Our life does not move according to a precisely apprehended intellectual schematisation, but by the deep and dark emotive forces of all that side of our beings to which we refer when we use the word feeling in preference to thinking.

Now, as at all times, these concrete symbols are the real and actual language of our psyches, and, whether our search is for knowledge of the macrocosmic universe or of the microcosmic self, we have to turn to our mistress Psyche for knowledge of the feeling half of life. Without this, our cogitations will be as unbalanced as a world that should know no night, no dark fortnight of the moon and no southward path of the sun in winter, but only the shadowless light of an equatorial noon.

We must not approach texts of this sort with the academic sense that any practical interest in such teachings, any suggestion that they might be realisable in actual life, savours a little of the vulgar. Thus approached they will never reveal their true meaning. Even an experimental attitude towards a symbol will tend to prevent the evocation of images from the psyche. Only real questions, rooted deeply in the core of our being, can call forth replies from the deeper layers of knowledge.

Such texts are not the sterile postulates of the laboratory, but teachings for the soul, based on mystical experience and intended to be corroborated by mystical experience. The truths of the soul are to be experienced, not just speculated about, and there is a vast body of non-academic evidence affirming, not only their validity, but their all-transcending value.

A characteristic which these Stanzas have in common with many, if not all, ancient texts—the Vedas and Upanishads for instance, and also with the symbolism of dreams—is that statements already made are repeated again in different symbols. The ideal of the merely logical type of mind is to express itself once in the most appropriate abstract symbols and then pass on. But those who wrote down these archaic texts were too keenly aware of the inadequacy of any given set of symbols, however carefully used, to fall under the delusion that there could be such a thing as imparting a meaning in the best possible words once and for all. Accordingly, they sought less after economy of expression than after achieving adequacy by piling up a number of symbolic statements, so that what was inevitably missed in one rendering might be gained in another, each time drawing our attention to different aspects of the one truth.

The average modern mind, however, has almost lost the power to read concrete symbols. It takes them as illustrations, metaphors, poetry, or even allegory, and persists in holding that such a text as our present one needs only to be translated into the abstract symbolism of modern science or philosophy for its meaning to be adequately rendered. But this is not so. The reader must learn to use his intuition and grasp the meaning of the symbols directly. Mere translations into abstract terms will no more reveal the heart of the mystery than wax impressions of its surfaces will give the essence of a solid body. No solution is possible in intellectual terms since all such presuppose duality and so beg the question from the outset. Nevertheless the solution *is* hidden in the cryptic symbols of the Stanzas 'as butter in milk, as oil in sesamum seeds, as fire in wood'.[1] He who seeks it must do his own churning since none can do it for him: when he has found it, he will perforce be silent.

One of the advantages in using the concrete symbols of sense experience when describing non-physical levels of being is that they are imbued with a feeling of reality. The ability to think in terms of abstract concepts has its importance, but such thought is apt to become divorced from actuality, so that we find, for instance, the philosophy of the western schools losing contact both with the mystical life on the one hand and with material necessity on the other. That transcendent Being from which this sphere of experience has arisen is not an abstraction, it is the Real; and such reality as we feel ourselves to experience here is a derivative of that central Reality, compared to which all this appears illusory to those who have known it.

If we are to achieve more than vague ideas and noble thoughts about divinity, we have to avoid falling into the error of feeling that reality is a quality chiefly, if not solely, inherent in physical sense experience, and correspondingly feeling that mental concepts have no actuality in themselves. That sort of thinking, or more properly feeling, leads to the belief that the world is made up of grossly concrete things, separate tangible masses whose objective being is the criterion of reality: rocks, trees, houses, radios, neighbours and Banks.

Certainly, the word 'real' derives from the Latin *res*, a thing; but a *thing* in its primary sense is any object of perception, whether sense perception or mental perception. The Universal Mind of the Stanzas (*Mahat Ātman*) is in this sense the first thing because it is the first level of manifestation. It is both itself and the contents of its own thought, the first reality. We can also draw a parallel with the *logos* of Christian theology which is both the thought and the manifestation of that thought. 'In the beginning was the Word (*logos*), and the Word was with God, and the Word was God.'[2]

[1] Śvetāśvatara. Upanishad, I 15.
[2] Gospel of St. John, I. 1.

C

It is to help ourselves heal this split between the oppressive 'thingness' of things and a rarefied divinity we do not feel to be actual that we take aid from the feeling content of concrete symbols in the effort to transfer their associated values into regions that are too apt to be devoid of 'tangible' reality.

Throughout the work it will be found that images drawn from the form of man and the patterns of his psyche have been used as analogues of cosmic events and of the patterns of divine consciousness. Some may think this to be a ridiculous anthropomorphism, but the ancient seers would not have been of their party or they would not have used such symbols. It is, in fact, not anthropomorphism but the age-old correspondence of the microcosm with the macrocosm, the Hermetic axiom of 'as above, so below'. The great Cosmos, like the little cosmos of man's daily life, is psychic through and through.

To say that all we know is necessarily known in terms of our experience is a truism, but it draws attention to the fact that it is the sum total of our experience and not merely abstracts of intellectual or emotional parts of it that constitutes our knowledge both of cosmic events and of divine consciousness. There is no part of man, as there is no part of the cosmos, which has not emerged from the unitary source. Within us and around us we experience nothing but aspects of divine consciousness; but, if we wish to arrive at a knowledge of the source of all things, we have to search in the one place where we can have knowledge at first hand, and that is within ourselves. Around us is the macrocosm, within us is the microcosm, each in its own way gives us knowledge of the other in that divine interplay of subject and object which is the source of all knowing and all being.

Every system of thought has its advantages and its disadvantages. The danger of thinking in terms of concrete symbols lies in the human tendency to mistake the symbol for the reality, the means for the end, and so to be led away by the false will-o'-the-wisp of substitute secrets. We think it a matter of consequence to determine our position amongst the 'globes' and 'races'; the next higher Masonic degree always holds out delusive promise of a real knowledge; the right breathing exercise or the right yogic posture (*āsana*), if only we could find it out and master it, would certainly send our *Kundalini* spouting up like a fountain of fire. These and a thousand other substitutes, some less and some more harmful, hold us feverishly searching for the lost child that all the time is sitting on our own laps. The source of that glamorous will-o'-the-wisp glow is in ourselves, and its power to attract us lies in our attachment to the gratification of outward turned desires. First we must withdraw our projections from the desire life, then only shall we begin to perceive those divine powers and patterns that by their immanence in the symbolic objects both of thought and of the material world fill those externalities with an inner light.

Just as in the interpretation of ancient texts it is wise to prefer the more difficult of alternative readings, so in the study of symbols it is wise to prefer the more inward meaning. In spite, however, of this warning, many will inevitably suppose the purport of a cosmogony to be a matter of astronomical and historical events. We reiterate that no matter how much we use, and legitimately use, the symbols of cosmology and of daily life to evoke images in illustration of our contentions, we are in fact speaking of psychic movements in consciousness and of these alone. This is not to suggest that outward turned experience is a mere nothing. The objects of sense are not only symbols of the divine archetypes but are also the manifest bodies of those inner realities.

'Every element has its source from a higher form, and all things have their common origin from the Word (*logos*) the Holy Spirit. . . . So God is at once, in the highest sense, both the matter and the form of the universe. Yet He is not *only* that form; for nothing can or does exist outside of Himself; His substance is the foundation of all, and all things bear His imprint and are symbols of His intelligence.'[1]

[1] Adolphe Franck: *La Kabbale.*

Throughout, we are speaking of movement in consciousness; other than consciousness there is nothing whatsoever. In the last fifty years, however, we have heard a lot about 'unconscious' mental processes and, while it is not intended to suggest that the phenomena so *described* by psychologists do not exist, the use of the English word 'unconscious' to describe them is open to criticism. When psychologists say that a certain psychic content is unconscious they really mean that *we* are not normally conscious of it, a meaning which comes out in Freud's original term *unbewusst* which signifies the *unconscioussed* or that of which *we* are not aware.

Actually the whole manifested universe is pervaded by and floats in consciousness, but that is by no means to say that the whole universe is synthesised in the systems of content which make up our personal egos. If one aspect of the unmanifest is here described as unconscious, it is done to negate the thought that that consciousness can in any way be equated with our normal experiencing which is never without content and never without self-reference, even in what for us is deep sleep; the unmanifest is beyond the reach of any formulable thought, for it is 'without form and void'. Here, the word unconscious denotes the polar opposite of the self-related subjectivity we normally assume to be abstract consciousness. It is the consciousness of that which delights in being known, in being experienced.

> 'David said: "O Lord since thou hast no need of us say, then, what wisdom was there in creating us." God said to him, "O temporal man, I was a hidden treasure; I sought that that treasure . . . . should be revealed".'[1]

A word of warning must be added about the use of the word Spirit. It is an ambiguous term applied variously to the subtle vehicle of man's after-death being, to the opposite of matter, and to that Divinity, at once inner and transcendent, which is the goal of all mystics. The first is a mere misuse of the word,

[1] Jalalu'ddin Rumi: *Diwān.*

the second is a useful philosophical abstraction, and the third refers to the very root of our being. But because the root of our being and the root of the cosmos are ultimately the same, and because the experience of the cosmos is 'within' us, just as we are 'within' the Cosmos, the ambiguity is inescapable and cannot be banished by a mere adjustment of terms. It is this ambiguity that causes people to confuse the spirituality of the mystic with what is called the 'spiritualising' of the universe. If there are such things as the 'spiritualising' of mankind and the awakening of 'higher principles' on a racial scale, independent of human effort, they are movements in time and space and, as such, come and go in time and space. Men may gain or lose any number of higher sense powers, may live in etherealised bodies or be born by the apparitional birth, but so long as these events owe their appearance to the natural movements of the universe they are themselves bound under the compulsion of time, and have no power to liberate men from the bondage to their egotistical desires. We may prepare ourselves for the coming of such events, and even assist their coming, but only in the sense that a growing boy may assist his physical growth by exercising his body; without conscious effort to assist that flow of life which is ultimately beyond his control he cannot 'add one cubit to his stature'.

As is inevitable, the terminology has raised a number of questions and will no doubt give rise to more. In such a work as this, if one is trying to get away from the well-worn ruts of standard cosmological systems, one has either to invent a new set of terms which besides putting an additional strain on one's readers deprives them of helpful resonances of association, or to use the old terms in such unusual senses that their associated resonances are misleading.

Again, one cannot afford to be deprived of useful and meaningful words just because they have become devalued in ordinary speech. The colloquial associations of 'mental', for instance, must not be allowed to obtrude when we speak of Mind with its proper associations of intellectual brilliance, clarity, power, range, activity and single-pointedness in contexts where it is parallel to *Nous, Mahat Ātman*, or Great Soul. Another such word is Imagination.

Our choice of terms has been somewhat eclectic. Sanskrit equivalents have been given as an aid to those accustomed to Hindu philosophical terms, but this does not imply that we have taken any one of the many Hindu systems as the norm or basis of the exposition. Nor should it be thought that the use of one parallel from any given system of terms supposes the whole system to be parallel. Nor again that though the majority of terms used in the Stanzas themselves are 'Buddhistic' it implies that they are setting forth any extant Buddhist system as such.

Lastly it must be added that the interpretation which follows arrogates no authority and makes no claims to originality. If it be asked by what right it is put forward, the answer is that it is by the right which every man has to set forth as well as he can whatever he understands of the words of the teacher who dwells within the hearts of all men. If the book helps any other to understand those words it is justified. If not, then the attempt has failed or the words have been incorrectly apprehended. One thing is certain: whatever *truth* this book may be found to contain has the same ultimate origin as the Stanzas themselves, for all truth is one and comes from the same Source.

To that Source it is offered in reverence.

Commentary on
the Stanzas of Dzyan

SUMMARY

The first three Stanzas are concerned with the gradual awakening of the entirely unmanifest and transcendent cosmic principles which stand behind and give birth to the manifest universe.

Stanza I describes, as far as any description is possible, the condition in the Cosmic Night of Cosmic Deep Sleep.

Stanza II depicts the state of Cosmic Dream and hints at events taking place within the Darkness in preparation for the coming Dawn.

Stanza III describes the Dawn as it brightens to the full sunrise of that Divine Mind whose content is the manifest universe.

The later movements which give rise to this present type of experience are all in some sense secondary in importance to the principles outlined in these three Stanzas, for the patterns of the first principles govern all subsequent levels of existence. All that the later Stanzas have to say is implicitly contained in what has already been said. The great theme of the universe has been sounded; the subsequent Stanzas do but develop it in various ways.

They show how the one flowing tide of life brings into existence the individual foci which form the conscious selves of every existent being. Through these foci are then brought the psychic content of the lower levels, culminating in the type of experience which we term the physical world and which some are blind enough to consider the only reality.

Stanza IV describes the assembly of differentiated powers and elements which make up the archetypal pattern of the Cosmos, and it shows their place in the hierarchy of being. It relates the inner and causative patterns both to the transcendent principles and to their counterparts in form.

Stanza V describes the means by which the inner patterns begin to be exteriorised, and Stanza VI describes their establishment as material worlds.

Stanza VII traces the descent of the living, conscious powers which culminates in the birth of man.

The subject under discussion is not an easy one in any of its aspects, and we necessarily start at the most obscure point, the unmanifest origins of the whole Cosmos. But before we begin on this journey of discovery, let us recollect what it is we are setting out to find. This is not an impersonal enquiry into the origins of sticks and stones, broken pottery and fossilised skulls, nor is it a dry structure of philosophical abstractions, nor a comparative study of cosmological systems to be filed away in the archives of our mechanical brains. We are engaging in an active search for our very Self, Man, the most elusive and most wonderful creature of the universe. These Stanzas are about us, our origins, our development, our conscious selves and our bodily forms. No matter how obscure the ideas that are presented, nor how strange the vocabulary that has been used, the effort to grasp their meaning can lead us to an understanding both of ourselves and of our relation to the world around us in terms of values which will give a purpose to our lives and an incentive to find within ourselves the perfection we so conspicuously lack.

We ourselves, with all our petty meannesses, our brutal and insane cruelties, our obscenities, our pursuit of trivial pleasures,

and our misguided ambitions, bear within us the seeds of that
perfection.

Around us in the world an assortment of voices deny the
premises for such a statement. Materialists call us epipheno-
mena of matter; the operational theory of truth says that our
thesis has no meaning; biologists have referred to us as minor
crustal phenomena. Actively or by suggestion the world seems
bent on denying all but material values. Man *shall* live by
bread alone. Man *shall* seek nothing but merriment, when he
isn't working. Man *shall* be dust. This work is for those who
do not accept such denigrations of man and are attempting to
make their way against the downward, pleasure and power
seeking currents of life.

This cosmogony, as will be seen, is not intended as a substitute for the best scientific views of cosmic and human origins.
Still less is it an attempt to 'put Science right' about concrete
happenings that are within the latter's competency to describe.
Rather, these Stanzas, like all such, whether ancient or modern,
are concerned with one thing and one thing only: the place of
Man in the Cosmos and the place of the Cosmos in Man.

The reader will find no astronomy and geology, no planets,
nebulae and rocks, none of the apparatus of a 'real' cosmogony.
We repeat that this commentary is dealing with cosmogenesis
from a psychic point of view. We are considering the universe
as a tissue of psychic experience: our categories are psychic
ones, and with their help we have attempted to show that the
process of cosmic manifestation is entirely a movement within
the unity of conscious being towards the achievement of
self-conscious experience.

STANZA ONE

Being the first of seven Stanzas from
The Book of Dzyan
Translated by H. P. Blavatsky in her book
The Secret Doctrine, Book I, Part 1
'Cosmic Evolution'

1. *The Eternal Parent, wrapped in her ever-invisible Robes, had slumbered once again for Seven Eternities.*

2. *Time was not, for it lay asleep in the infinite bosom of duration.*

3. *Universal Mind was not, for there were no Ah-hi to contain it.*

4. *The seven ways to bliss were not. The great causes of misery were not, for there was no one to produce and get ensnared by them.*

5. *Darkness alone filled the boundless all, for Father, Mother, and Son were once more one, and the Son had not yet awakened for the new wheel and his pilgrimage thereon.*

6. *The seven sublime Lords and the seven Truths had ceased to be, and the Universe, the son of Necessity, was immersed in Paranishpanna, to be outbreathed by that which is and yet is not. Naught was.*

7. *The causes of existence had been done away with; the visible that was, and the invisible that is, rested in eternal non-being—the one being.*

8. *Alone, the one form of existence stretched boundless, infinite, causeless in dreamless sleep; and life pulsated unconscious in universal space, throughout that All-Presence which is sensed by the opened eye of the Dangma.*

9. *But where was the Dangma when the Ālaya of the Universe was in Paramārtha and the great wheel was Anupādaka?*

BEING IN LATENCY

The first Stanza begins with the unmanifest origins of all things. It seeks to describe what cannot be described, and therefore has to proceed by a series of negations. These serve at the same time to introduce us to some of the terms that are to take their place in the scheme unfolded in subsequent verses.

The manifestation of a universe is considered as a cyclic event which has occurred before and will occur again. Between manifestations all is withdrawn into the Darkness of non-existence. This is the point at which the story opens.

From one point of view the new universe will be an *ab initio* new creation; from another it will be a repetition of countless previous creations. Contradictory though these two themes may seem in theory, they are reconciled by our experience of life. To each one of us life is forever new, notwithstanding that we know it to be an endless repetition of well established patterns.

'So the dawn wind of creation must be thought of as of a double origin: one of the Spirit, moving without motion or any why, the other actuated by and because of past events.'[1]

The one view places the origin of phenomena in eternal principles; the other in infinitely extended time. Neither view in itself can tell the whole story, for Time and Eternity are mutually dependent terms.

We have to perceive the possibility of each creation being an entirely new event without relationship to the past, otherwise the problem is merely pushed off into an infinite regression. Yet, because it has to be seen as metaphysically possible, that is not the same as saying that it necessarily is so.

[1] A. K. Coomaraswamy, *A New Approach to the Vedas.*

(1) *The Eternal Parent, wrapped in her ever-invisible Robes, had slumbered once again for Seven Eternities.*[1]

This Eternal Parent is the great Matrix, the great Mother, Universal Nature, known to Hindu philosophy as *Mūlaprakriti* and to Spinoza as *Natura naturans*. She is the Womb out of which is born all that will be born in the Universe. Her being must not, however, be conceived as an ocean of 'matter', though it is often symbolised as the great dark Waters, the waters of chaos—in Greek mythology the goddess Rhea, the 'flow'. Matter she is not, even by courtesy, for 'matter' does not yet exist; yet she is that out of which *what is called* matter will emerge and is, so to speak, the ontological basis of what seems to us 'stuff'. It is useless to try and describe her in neat intellectual counters for, even when not 'slumbering', *i.e.* even when a cosmos is manifested, she is still what Hindu thought terms *avyakta*, unmanifest. She is also known as *Avidyā*, a word which plays on the double meaning of the root *vid*, to know and to be, for *Avidyā* is the great non-knowing as well as the great non-being. She is the great non-knowing because she is the 'content' side of the unitary and ultimate Reality referred to in this verse as the Ever-Invisible Robes. She is non-being because in her is nothing definite, nothing that exists in the root sense of that word, *i.e.* to stand forth.

She *is* not, for all existences are born from her, while she herself is *Ajā*[2], the great unborn. She knows not, for her whole Being throbs with a passionate yearning to be *known*. If she is sometimes termed unconscious, it is only in the sense that she is not the bright forthshining awareness of the Father, the Light of lights, who is her opposite pole; yet it must always be

[1] There are slight variations in the wording of the Stanza texts as published in different editions of *The Secret Doctrine* and in the *Transactions of the Blavatsky Lodge*. In preparing this commentary the various texts have been compared. Attention has also been given to the version of the Stanzas from the 1886 manuscript, included in the Adyar edition of 1938.

References to S.D. I and II are to the first edition of *The Secret Doctrine* or to photographic reprints of the same. References to S. D. III are to the third volume, now the fifth in the Adyar edition of 1938.

[2] *Śvetāśvatara Upanishad*, I. 9.

remembered that it is she who, in her dark being, draws forth that Light. But for her, that light would not shine forth, and the tides that surge within her massive depths are tides of Life, without which there would be no life at all. Devoid of form, empty of forms, she holds within her darkly living heart the potentiality of all forms. To consider her 'dead', as was done by the later, intellectualised *Sānkhya* in India and, tacitly, by much scientific thought, is an entire mistake. If it is she who sends us forth in finitude, it is also she to whom that finitude returns to rest, and the ever-living universe around us is, as we shall see, a Web of which She is one of the Weavers.

The conception is a similar one to Plato's Receptacle;[1] devoid of any geometrical form, it is 'the foster mother of all becoming'. Whitehead summarises as follows: 'It is there as a natural matrix for all transitions of life and it is changed and variously figured by the things that enter it; so that it differs in its character at different times. Since it receives all manner of experiences into its own unity, it must itself be bare of all forms. We shall not be wrong if we describe it as invisible, formless and all-receptive. It is a *locus* which persists and forms an emplacement for all occasions of experience. That which happens in it is conditioned by the compulsion of its own past[2] and by the persuasion of its immanent ideas.'[3] Whitehead also states that it imposes a common relationship on all that happens and is the source of the 'immanence of Law derived from the mutual immanence of actualities'.

It may be of interest to note that Whitehead says of the Platonic Receptacle that 'It seems to be a more subtle notion that Aristotle's "matter" which of course is not the "matter" of Galileo and Newton',[4] thus implying that the Aristotelian 'matter' refers to the same fundamental principle, though in a less subtle manner.

Many readers of early Theosophical literature have been

[1] Plato's *Timaeus*.
[2] See also verse 6.
[3] Whitehead: *Adventures of Ideas*, p. 240.
[4] *ibid.*, p. 192.

puzzled and some have scoffed openly at the statements found therein about 'matter' as the one Eternal.[1] Perhaps they will now realise that the scoffs were premature and arose through insufficient thought about what the word matter meant to *ancient* thinkers as opposed to Galileo and Newton. Those who persist in thinking in terms of nineteenth century billiard balls or even in terms of twentieth century electronic systems have only themselves to thank if the archaic teachings appear to them ridiculous.

To get any image of it, one should turn to psychological processes and imagine it as like the matrix of dark dreamless sleep in which potentially exist, and out of which emerge, the bright images of a dream. Abstractly considered, it is the root of all objectivity, though not in itself an 'object' in the sense in which we are accustomed to use the term.

The Eternal Parent at this stage is not isolated from its source, the unitary Root of consciousness and form alike. This Source is known to Hindu thought as the *Parābrahman* in which knower, known and knowledge are all one unity, and to Buddhist thought as *Shūnya* the 'Void', or as the *Tathāgata Garbha*, the Womb of Buddhahood; sometimes also as the *Bhūtakoti*, the Limit of Being. That unitary Source is here referred to as the Ever-Invisible Robes in which the Eternal Parent lay wrapped in slumber. That One is forever a mystery. Never under any circumstances can It become 'visible' even to the eye of thought. Neither 'gods' nor men can or will ever see It, as Hindu books have repeatedly told us, for it is beyond the differentiation of seer and seen. Of It nothing is said for nothing can be said. But words are not the only symbols by which meaning is conveyed, and it is by attending to the direct feeling perception of concrete symbols and not by the logical intellect alone that a sense of the meaning of such glyphs of transcendent principles is to be obtained. Such at least has been the practice of Seers who doubtless knew their own business better than those who have criticised them without having

[1] *e.g. The Mahātma Letters*, pp. 55 and 56.

shared their experience. Indeed, whenever exponents have attempted too much in this connection, the inevitable substitution of the symbol for the reality and the consequent confusion has led to a debasement of the conception of the supreme Principle by allocating to it qualities that truly belong to manifest worlds.

The term Eternities as used in these Stanzas is not that Eternity which is defined by Boethius, 'Eternity is the simultaneous and complete possession of infinite life',[1] and by Plotinus as 'That which neither has been nor will be, but simply possesses ever-being.'[2] This latter Eternity or 'ever-being' is here termed Duration, evidently with the intention of evoking the associated idea of that which endures as opposed to that which changes.

The Eternities of the Stanzas are age-long cycles, the *aeons* of the Greeks, the *kalpas* of the Hindus. Although this usage is apparently contrary to that of other writers it has been retained in the commentary.

The real difficulty is in imagining how any reckoning of 'ages' could exist in what is utterly beyond all manifestation, especially as we are explicitly told in the next verse that 'Time was not'. We have to do here with the ancient Hindu teaching of the Days and Nights of *Brahmā*, the teaching that after the ages during which the universe is in manifestation there is an equally long period during which nothing is manifest, all having been reabsorbed into the Ultimate One.

Our Stanzas divide the period of cosmic manifestation, the Day of *Brahmā*, into seven great ages, so great that the psychological associations of the term eternities have to be invoked to give any idea of their extent. The Cosmic Night of *pralaya* is symbolised as being of the same extent, even though 'time was not', to preserve its equivalence to the Day. This is an occasion when the facile 'Why? Why seven?', followed, in the case of most critics, by the irritated sense that what is not

[1] *Consolations of Philosophy,* Book iv.
[2] Plotinus, En. III. vii. 3. Time and Eternity (Turnbull).

D

susceptible to logical analysis is nonsense, must be put aside if anything more real than intellectual abstraction is to be touched. It is so well known that seven was a mystical number with most, if not all, ancient peoples that there is no need to repeat all that has been written to show the widespread use of this number. Later on an attempt will be made to indicate why this particular number should have a fundamental significance for our cosmogony.[1] For the present it may simply be taken as the number of the perfect cycle. As an example of its use in ancient teachings we quote from the Kabbalistic *Sepher Yetzirah*:[2] 'These Seven Double Letters He designed produced and combined, and formed with them the Planets of this Universe, the Days of the Week, and the Gates of the soul in Man. From these Seven He hath produced the Seven Heavens, the Seven Earths, the Seven Sabbaths: for this cause He has loved and blessed the number Seven, more than all things under Heaven.'

Notice, however, that in the words 'once again' the conception is introduced of the alternation of Cosmic Day and Night as a repeated, indeed an endlessly repeated, process. This process is the metaphysical foundation of all those rhythms which we see in this world, the rhythms of summer and winter, day and night, seed time and harvest, inbreath and outbreath, systole and diastole, birth and death, waking and sleeping, introversion and extroversion. The same pattern would apply to those alternate expansions and contractions of the universe which some physicists have conjectured. Everywhere in fact, throughout the whole realm of nature, physical or psychic, from 'atoms' to universes, this rhythm will be found to be established: a period of expansion is followed by one of contraction, a period of running down by one of winding up.[3] This alternation is indeed the very breath of Life, and all the examples we have quoted, as well as countless others, have their

[1] *Infra*, p. 59.
[2] *Sepher Yetzirah*, 14. 3.
[3] The *vivarta kalpa* and *samvarta kalpa* of the Buddhists.

root in the beating of the great Cosmic Heart of which our symbols are trying to tell us.

The cosmos is thus not a dead mechanical process as conceived by many scientists, but living being—we will not say *a* living being. Explanations of anything whatever in terms of mechanism are abstractions, useful for certain purposes, but fundamentally inadequate. Every heart beat, human or subhuman, in the universe, every vibration of so-called matter, is based on that cosmic Heart or Breath. Just as the contemplation of a visual symbolic image passes beyond it to the archetypes of form, so he who listens to the inner rhythm of his heart passes beyond it to the rhythm of the universe because the latter is the basis and root of the former. It is for this reason that such inner listening is capable of being a part of yoga, capable, that is, of giving genuine knowledge of the cosmic process and its unmanifested root.[1]

(2) *Time was not, for it lay asleep in the infinite bosom of duration.*[2]

Here, we are face to face with the contradiction already referred to. Time did not exist, yet seven eternities were flowing past. Time obviously did not exist for there was nothing to mark its passage, neither the revolutions of celestial bodies which serve us as the measure of objective time, nor the obscure psycho-physical events which give us our feeling of subjective time, nor of course was there any one to feel the time pass. Nevertheless Time had not vanished 'into nothing' but into that Timelessness of which Time is the moving image, and which our Stanza terms Duration—that which forever is, as opposed to that which forever becomes. Just as in really dreamless sleep time vanishes for us, so in the Cosmic Night time as succession vanishes with the events whose successive

[1] 'Others expound the Sound (Brahma) in a different way. By closing the ears with the thumbs they hear the sound of the space within the heart. . . . Passing beyond this variously characterised sound (*shabda-Brahman*), men disappear in the supreme, the non-sound, the unmanifest Brahma. . . .' *Maitri Upanishad*, VI. 22.

[2] Cf. Plotinus, III. vii. 11: 'Time lay, self-concentrated, within the Authentic Existent; it was not yet time; it was merged in the Authentic and motionless with it.' (Stephen Mackenna).

nature it marked. The succession of events, physical or psychical, that are the experience of time had ceased; the experience
of time was therefore no more. Yet something remained, for
the One is no mere blank abstraction, even though in denying
its similarity to common experience many Seers have described
it in negatives. Even the Hindu affirmative statement, that the
Brahman is Being, Consciousness and Bliss (*Sat, Chit, Ānanda*),
may well be regarded only as contradicting an absolute
negation.

'Time', says Plato, 'was created with the heaven, in order
that being created together they might be dissolved together.'[1]
And Plotinus develops the thought further. He defines time as
the life of the Soul in movement as it passes from one stage of
experience to another, and adds: 'If then, Soul withdraws,
sinking again into its primal unity, Time would disappear; the
origin of Time clearly is to be traced to the first stir of Soul's
tendency towards the production of the sensible universe. Soul
begot at once the universe and Time.'[2]

Even in the Cosmic Night, Time is not absolutely non-
existent. It lies 'asleep' because it is utterly unmanifest, but its
archetypal root is still there in the Divine Breath that ceases
not even in *pralaya*.[3] We read in the Upanishads that there are
two modes of Time, the formed and the formless. These two
are assimilated to the two forms of the *Brahman* termed Time
and the Timeless. 'That which is "prior" to the Sun (here the
Universal Mind is meant) is the Timeless, without parts. But
that which begins with the Sun is Time which has parts.'[4]
Elsewhere we read of divided time (*khanda kāla*) and undivided
time (*akhanda kāla*). This latter, which may be considered as
the noumenal form of the time we know or can imagine, is
the same as the Duration of our Stanza. Its 'temporality' eludes
all description, yet somehow it is there and supports the symbolic passing of the Seven Eternities.

[1] *Timaeus*, 38b.
[2] Plotinus, III. vii. 12 (Turnbull).
[3] *Pralaya*: The dissolution or reabsorption of a world or of a universe.
[4] *Maitri Upanishad*, VI. 15.

In this connection there is a significant passage in one of Sigmund Freud's later books. Speaking of the impersonal regions of the psyche that are not synthesised into or accessible to the personal ego and which are termed by him the 'Id', he says: '. . . . we perceive with surprise an exception to the philosophical theorem that space and time are necessary forms of our mental acts. There is nothing in the id that corresponds to the idea of time; there is no recognition of the passage of time, and—a thing that is most remarkable and awaits consideration in philosophical thought—no alteration in its mental processes is produced by the passage of time. Wishful impulses which have never passed beyond the id, but impressions, too, which have been sunk into the id by repression, are virtually immortal; after the passage of decades they behave as though they had just occurred. . . . This seems to offer an approach to the most profound discoveries. Nor, unfortunately have I myself made any progress here.'[1]

Certainly it is difficult, if not impossible, for the reason to make much progress here, and those who are indissolubly wedded to the method of rational thought are likely to turn away from the whole enquiry. They will come down upon us with the scissors of dialectic and will have no difficulty in demonstrating, to their own satisfaction at least, that we are talking nonsense.

Intuitive thought, however, is capable of taking us further and of showing that there is a condition in which time, so to speak, becomes introverted and enters into itself, and in so doing loses all its manifest temporal qualities. It becomes dark, massive and infinitely concentrated; yet it remains itself, and from it overt time will manifest again. An analogy may be found in the way in which a spatial curve, say a hyperbola, may be made to enter into a non-spatial mathematical expression but it is only an analogy and the real process must be grasped by intuition.

[1] Freud's *Complete Psychological Works*. Standard Edition. Revised and Edited by James Strachey. Vol. XXII, Page 74, Lecture XXXI 'Dissection of the Personality'.

If we attempt to enter in still further, we can dimly perceive that on 'the other side' of the central massive point there extends a negative shadow. Time has entered into and gone through itself. On the 'other side' something extends, or perhaps 'in-tends', something which exactly balances the cyclic extension which we know as outer time. There too are images of cycles and eternities. There too the duration is spread out into the curve of time, but, though poets have spoken of 'Day the shadow of Night and Life the shadow of Death', to us it is all negative. We cannot understand it, still less can we express it, but there, no less than here, is 'Time the moving image of Eternity', and in the Night no less than in the Day the cyclic eagles wheel within the Void.

We should also remember that we are not here concerned with a time in the past when 'time was not'. The massive Duration and the negative, 'introverted' Time exist 'now' just as much as at any other 'time'. Turn time inward upon itself with sufficient intensity and even now we are in the midst of the Cosmic Night. The Levels of being, the passage of the cycles, all vanish and, in the words of a later verse, 'Darkness alone fills the boundless All, for Father, Mother and Son are once more one.' This is no mere theorising. The indrawn state of the cosmos (*nitya pralaya*) is as perceptible to the Seer now as is the cosmic day.

The Cosmic Days and Nights are, in fact, not processes *in* time but modes *of* time, and though it is convenient and natural to think of the Cosmic Night as something that occurred long ages ago and will take place again in an equally distant future, yet, remembering our analogy of the spatial curve and its mathematical expression, it is truer to think of the whole process with its almost infinitely remote pasts and futures as drawn out 'at this very moment' by an outward-turning from a processless Reality. The graph of time has been, is being, drawn out from the equation of duration. We plot it out and mark on it our own position. And yet the whole process is but a symbolic statement, and it is as true to say that we are never in time at all, since even now we are in Eternity.[1]

Can we then ourselves choose Day or Night at will? That is a question which depends on what we mean by 'we'. Certainly our empirical selves, our minds, cannot make any such choice for they themselves are parts of the process of the Day. Nevertheless there is That in us which can, for at the very heart of our being is That which is beyond all space and time, That which was, is and will forever be, the opening of whose Eyes brings forth the long processions of the Day, whose closing Eyelids are the curtains of the Night. Say what we will, we cannot go further than the words of the verse: 'Time was not, for it *lay asleep* in the bosom of Duration.'

(3) *Universal Mind was not, for there were no Ah-hi to contain it.*

Gradually, as the text proceeds, we are being introduced to the principles that will be used in the explanation of the Cosmic manifestation.

The Universal Mind is the all-embracing Consciousness which enfolds the universe within its grasp. Viewed from below, it may be regarded as the synthesis of all the individual minds within the cosmos, but it is more than a synthesis, being rather the prior existence from which they have developed by differentiation. Its existence during manifestation is not something to be established by speculative thought, but something which is directly experienced by the Seer. Speculative philosophy can do no more than correlate such experience with the partial experiences of the world, which are gained by individual selves.

The Hindu tradition knows this Mind under a variety of

[1] The following example may perhaps be of help to some readers. If the equation $xy=a$ is plotted out for positive and negative values we get a curve known as a hyperbola which falls into two halves, meeting, as mathematicians say, at infinity. The upper half representing the positive values can symbolise the Cosmic Day while the lower or negative half symbolises the Night. Yet all the positions on both halves of the curve are included in the non-spatial expression $xy=a$ and may be considered as having issued from the central zero point.

names. It is the formed (*mūrta*), temporal (*sakāla*), and partite (*sakalā*) Brahma,[1] the total Lord or Ruling Power (*Ishwara*) who synthesises in his being the three powers of projection, upholding, and withdrawal, which were later personalised as the Brahmā, Vishnu, Rudra trinity. Again it is the Great Intelligence (*Mahat-Buddhi*) of the *Sānkhya*, the Great Self (*Mahān Ātman*) of the *Kaṭhopanishad*.

The Universal Mind is the first manifested principle, the farthest shore of the Cosmos. In Vedic times it was symbolised as the god Varuna, the over-arching sky which embraces all that is. It is the Store Consciousness (*Ālaya Vijñāna*) of the Yogāchāra Buddhists, the Universal Intelligence (*Aql-i-Kul*) of the Sūfis, and also the Noëtic World, the Spiritual Cosmos of Plotinus. Perhaps the Extensive Continuum of Professor Whitehead is also connected with this, though here one speaks with great caution. In any case, it is a unitary and all-embracing consciousness which has as content the Divine Archetypes, the so-called Divine Ideas of Plato, from partici-pation in which arise all the concrete forms within the cosmos.

Ah-hi is the same word as the Sanskrit *ahi*, a serpent. Here the symbol of the serpent is used in its connotation of a constricting power, a power that embraces or limits and thus contains. Without limitation or demarcation of the area of operation there can be no manifestation. 'No man,' says Hegel, 'ever achieved anything until he had first limited himself,' nor, we may add, did the powers that created man. In endless space there are no directions, no inside and outside, no here and there, nor is there foundation on which to build. Many creation myths begin with the search for a firm basis or a limit to space, without which there can be no concentration of energy and so no means of producing effects.

The serpent emerges from its egg as does a line from a point. When the head and tail meet, it forms a circle; linear expansion is thus limited and becomes measurable, whether in terms of time or space. The unlimited expansive power of creation is

[1] *Brihadāraṇyaka Upanishad*, II. 3. 1.

embraced, and thereby the content becomes knowable. Mythology is full of such symbols: Ouroboros, the devourer of his own tail (the eternally recurrent cycle); the wriggling serpent of the ecliptic: Hapi, the Egyptian Nile God in his serpent-enclosed cavern: the Constrictor about the Mithraic Kronos; Nārāyana in the folds of the cyclic serpent *Shesha-Nāga*; the snake-garlanded Shiva.

There can be no all-embracing consciousness without that which is embraced, nor can there be any beginning unrelated to an ending. *Ahi*, the serpent, is the vehicle of that all-embracing consciousness at the junction of whose head and tail is the momentary 'now' which is becoming.

At the stage now being described, consciousness is inturned, introverted, absorbed in the innate (*sahaja*) contemplation of its own inner processes, like a child sucking its own toe with that blank, withdrawn expression of the small baby—the child Nārāyana as he floats on a leaf on the waters of *pralaya*, in whose yawning mouth the Rishi Mārkandeya finds the entire universe.[1]

In another context later in the Stanzas, the serpents appear as representing the Divine Creative desires that spiral their way outwards and downwards through the levels of the universe, the forces of *pravritti* or forthgoing.

(4) *The seven ways to bliss were not. The great causes of misery were not, for there was no one to produce and get ensnared by them.*

Readers may feel this negation of details in each verse could have been dispensed with by a single sweeping denial of everything which would render all else redundant. The state of the withdrawn Absolute (*pralaya*) is not so easily described.

Our minds are not truly capable of grasping the import of an absolute denial even if it were made, and were we to examine ourselves closely we should find that we were emotionally reluctant to face the negation of the independent being we assume to be ours. In clinging to our egotistic desire for indi-

[1] *Srimad Bhāgavata*, XII. 9.

vidual survival we find support in assuming that elements of our personality also remain.

The naming of these principles in the introductory verses conveys to us some sense of the gradual building up of a tension within the darkness of non-being, the feeling of expectancy that precedes the rising of the curtain on a stage. These verses are the setting of the stage.

'The Way Up is the same as the Way Down', said Heracleitus. In the terms of our verse we may say that the seven ways to bliss are the same as the great causes of misery, for the former are the way up, the Ladder of the Soul, and the latter are the way down. The actual ladder is the same in both cases.

The ladder is made up of the levels of cosmic experience or grades of 'outwardness' of which our physical sense world is the outermost or lowest. As a knowledge of these levels is of the utmost importance in understanding the Stanzas it is desirable to give a brief outline sketch of them here, while the details must be gradually filled in as the Stanzas proceed.

In the first place we should note that they all spring from the fundamental polarity of the One Reality. The subjective and objective aspects of that One are known symbolically as the Father and Mother respectively. There is, however, a third factor to be reckoned with, and that is the underlying unity of the two which manifests itself as the tension by which the one acts upon the other.

It is as though the two sides of an elastic body were pulled apart. The result will be a tension between them which, if suitably handled, will be capable of manifesting various phenomena before the two sides finally come together again and the tension vanishes.

The essentially creative act is the dissociation of subjectivity and objectivity out of the primal unity. Self and not-Self then come into being, though not into independent being, for each is bound to the other by the unity of which both are polar aspects. That binding together is the power by which the whole universe acts, Not-Self acting upon Self and Self reacting again upon Not-Self. We have thus three factors, Self, Not-Self and Power, and out of these three the web of the universe is woven.

The general scheme of the creation is now clear. The world of experience deriving from the two polar aspects of one source can neither be a world of pure subjectivity, nor a world of purely objective material. We shall not be asked to believe that each one of us (if there are more than one) lives like a paranoiac in a private world of subjective fantasy, nor that American skyscrapers are nothing but ideas in the mind of God. Nor, on the other hand, shall we be asked to abrogate our humanity in favour of an entirely material analysis of the nature of consciousness. Whatever is manifest to thought, feeling, or sensation, will be understood as being a blend of subjective and objective elements. The remaining stanzas will deal with the development of the complex structures, the seven ways to bliss, that derive from these simplex beginnings, but the keynote of the system has been sounded.

From the mutual interaction of the three primal factors arise four and only four simple combinations.[1] These, taken together with the original three, give the seven which make up the major framework of the cosmic scheme of seven levels of being or grades of experience. Within this framework the infinity of mutations are produced. There are, of course, other systems of symbolic thought which divide the unity into different sections. No matter how many or how few, the unity remains. No one system of division is ultimately better than another, for all better and worse is relative to time, place, and person. The Stanzas expound the universe in terms of sevens, and the commentary necessarily follows them. For instance, the twelveness of the heavens expressed in the signs of the zodiac can be said to arise from the interplay of sun, moon and stars. Other worlds with other planetary periodicities could have other numerologies.

---

[1] We can take these factors one at a time: a, b, and c; two at a time: ab, ac, bc; and three at a time: abc—making seven.

'But if any one hath placed these things in another order, I shall not contend with him in as much as all systems tend to the one truth.'[1]

A diagram of these seven levels together with some of the various names by which they are referred to is given below, though it is not expected that it will be fully intelligible at this stage.

TABLE OF THE SEVEN COSMIC LEVELS

0.	Ever-Darkness	Oeaohoo		*Parabrahman*
1.	Father-Light	Father	*Svabhāvat*	*Shānta Ātman*
				Purusha
2.	Matrix	Mother	The Eternal	Root Matter
			Parent	*Mūla-Prakriti*
		Unmanifest		

		Manifest		
3.	Universal Mind	Son	Great Self.	*Mahat Ātman*
			Oeaohoo, the	
			Younger	
4.	Higher Mind	Level of Individuation		
		Monad or *Jīva*		*Shuddha Manas*
5.	Lower Mind	Level of Differentiation		*Ashuddha Manas*
6.	Desire Nature	Formative Level		*Kāma Bhāva*
7.	Physical level of shared and relatively			*Sthūla Jagat*
	stable continuity of objective reference			

The meaning of the saying of Heracleitus quoted at the beginning of this section now becomes clear. The Way Up is the same as the Way Down because in both cases the ladder is made up of these seven levels. Viewed as the Way Up they are the seven ways to bliss; as the Way Down they are the great causes of misery. This cosmos is the course of the soul, and the course of the soul is the cosmos. All is movement,

[1] *Aesch Mezareph.*

in consciousness and of consciousness. There are no levels of the cosmos which are not levels of consciousness, and no levels of consciousness that are not stages of the soul. The ways of bliss and the causes of misery are therefore as well expressed in terms of the cosmos as they are in terms of the psyche, for there is not the slightest difference between them.

The seven ways to bliss are in fact the means by which the aspirant masters each of the seven successively. As such they are identical with the seven *pāramitās* or 'perfections' of which an account is given in the third tractate in *The Voice of the Silence*.[1] The 'seven ways' are really the seven stages on one Way, the text following in this the ancient Buddhist usage which speaks of the four stages on the Path as the Four Paths.

Just as the practice of the *pāramitās* is the Way Up, so the practice of attachment to the subtle or gross forms on the various levels constitutes the Way Down. Since all forms on all levels are inevitably transient, attachment to them is a source of sorrow or misery. This was taught by the Buddha who followed up his declaration that all compounded things are transient with the corollary that all are causes of sorrow. The Way Down is essentially a way of sorrow, since it is the way of progressive attachment to ever grosser forms.

H.P.B. refers here to the twelve *nidānas*[2] as the causes of misery, but in so doing she is only saying the same thing from a slightly different angle, for the *nidānas* are the causal connections which govern the appearance and disappearance of all forms whatsoever.

At this stage, of course, there being no cosmic levels in manifestation, there was no Ladder of the Soul; and, there being no individual centres or Selves, there was no one to

---

[1] *The Voice of Silence* (H. P. Blavatsky). The ordinary enumeration counts six *pāramitās*, though another four are sometimes added making a total of ten. The six usually described are *dāna* (charity), *shīla* (harmonious action), *kshānti* (patience, forbearance, endurance), *vīrya* (effort, energy), *dhyāna* (meditation) and *prajnā* (wisdom). *The Voice of the Silence* inserts a seventh, *vairāgya* or non-attachment between *kshānti* and *vīrya*. The above are all highly technical terms and must not be supposed to be identical with their ordinary everyday meanings.

[2] The standard list of twelve *nidānas* can be found in any work on Buddhism.

get entangled in the web of attraction and repulsion to forms that were not yet existent. In short, the verse states that the two great Ways, the Way of Forthgoing and the Way of Return, had not begun to manifest.

(5) *Darkness alone filled the boundless all, for Father, Mother and Son were once more one, and the Son had not yet awakened for the new wheel and his pilgrimage thereon.*

In the oldest traditions to which we have access the Ultimate Reality, what in Hinduism is termed the *Parabrahman*, was symbolised as Darkness. In the Rig Veda[1] we read, 'Darkness there was; at first hidden in the Darkness all this was undiscriminated Waters.' This same symbolism is to be found in ancient Egyptian cosmogony and also in those verses of Genesis that tell how Darkness was on the face of the Waters. We may also note that Sūfis sometimes use the term *ama*—blindness—for the same purpose.

The use of such a symbol was not due, as some have supposed, to a naive agnosticism on the part of those primaeval Seers, but to the realisation that the state of the Unitary Reality before its polarisation into Light and Forms, subject and object, if it is to be referred to at all (and, indeed, most were reluctant to do so), must be symbolised as Darkness since no words or thoughts of ours can compass its being.

At some period, however, on the edge of recorded history, newer generations of Seers seem to have felt that the symbol, appropriate as it was in itself, was liable to mislead by suggesting to men of lesser insight that the Ultimate Reality was a blank night of nothingness. Accordingly, we find in later traditions, such as that of the Gita, the symbolism is changed and we get the *Parabrahman* referred to as the Light of lights, the Sun beyond the Darkness.[2] The Stanzas of Dzyan, following the earlier tradition, preserve the symbol of Darkness; and it will be found as we proceed, and should be borne in

[1] *Rig Veda*, X. 129. 3.
[2] *Bhagavad Gītā*, VIII. 9 and XIII. 17.

mind throughout, that terms of light, radiance, *etc.*, always imply an at least relative decline from the Ultimate.

The disadvantage of the use of light as a symbol in this context is that visual associations make us think both of a percipient and of a source of radiance, with the objects illuminated distinguishable by virtue of contrasting degrees of light, shade and colour. Here, a state is being described in which no distinctions are possible. To us, therefore, the sense is better conveyed by the image of all-pervasive darkness. Where light is equated with knowledge and darkness with ignorance, implicit in the distinction is the idea that that 'knowledge', however divine, is not the all-inclusive consciousness of the transcendent One.

We may compare what Dionysius the Areopagite says in *The Mystical Theology* II:[1]

'Unto this Darkness which is beyond light we pray that we may come, and may attain unto vision through the loss of sight and knowledge . . . that we may begin to see that super-essential Darkness which is hidden by all the light that is in existent things.'

At this period, then, Darkness, the ever-unmanifested *Parabrahman*, was all that was. It 'filled the All' for there was naught but It.

Father, Mother, and Son, were once more (after the preceding manifestation) one within Its bosom. Who are these three in whom we can easily recognise the primordial Gods of so many cosmogonies? The Mother is that Eternal Parent of whom we have already spoken, the Great Mother of so many religions in the ancient world, She who, philosophically conceived, appears as the *Matrix*, the eternal root of all objectivity and womb of creation. That, at least, is the Mother as viewed from below. From above She is the content or objective aspect of the Darkness.

The Father, on the other hand, is the subjective aspect of

[1] Translated by C. E. Rolt.

the same Reality, the invisible Light of which we have spoken before and which is destined to impregnate, *i.e.* illuminate, the dark Mother, and so, by uniting with Her, to produce the offspring who is sometimes described as androgynous, the Universal Mind mentioned in verse 3. In the Rig Veda, the same primal pair are named the *Rita* and *Satya* which can be equated with the two forms of truth, *veritas in rei* and *veritas in essendo*, contingent truth and essential truth. These are like the two ruling powers of which Socrates speaks, 'one set over the intellectual world, the other over the visible'.[1]

At this stage, however, those separate aspects symbolised as Father and Mother were not separate, but united in their Source, the Darkness. The Son, or Universal Mind, had not therefore 'awakened', but existed only as an abstract possibility and so could not bring forth the wheel of the new cycle in which he himself would be the Pilgrim. The Son is goer, traveller, pilgrim, in the sense that it is he who travels to the furthest shore of the manifestation and returns to his home, for he is himself the manifestation as it moves from its most subtle phase to its most gross, and back to the subtle, in the cyclic forthgoing and returning that is the pattern of his endless movement.

(6) *The seven sublime Lords and the seven Truths had ceased to be, and the Universe, the son of Necessity, was immersed in Paranishpanna, to be outbreathed by that which is and yet is not. Naught was.*

We have already referred (in verse 4) to the fact that the universe, when manifest, is here regarded as being made up of seven levels of experience. These seven levels appear and re-appear in these Stanzas under various names. There are perhaps some who will wonder what is the necessity for such variety in terminology and why one term should not suffice for all purposes. The answer is that one term would evoke only one set of associated images and would express only one aspect of

[1] *Republic*, Bk. VI. 509

the level, whereas each level has many aspects and therefore
many names.

The seven sublime Lords are the seven levels of the Cosmos.
But when we have made this equation we have not said all
that is to be said. The seven levels are levels of consciousness,
and the consciousness of any given level has a unitary or
collective as well as a distributive aspect. It is not merely the
sum of so many individual consciousnesses, but a unitary whole
out of which those individual aspects have been differentiated.
It is therefore not inappropriately symbolised as a Sublime
Lord, a being which holds in its grasp the entire content of the
level in question; in fact, as ancient writers would have said,
it is the god of that level. If it is added that the seven sacred
planets of antiquity are also used as symbols for the levels, we
can see that the sublime Lords are the same as what have sometimes been termed planetary spirits or angels. In terming them
gods, however, we must not suppose that they are anthropomorphic or even personal, at least, as we usually understand
the word. They are living, conscious powers or beings,
probably most easily thought of as impersonal. Mythologies
have doubtless symbolised them in personal form, but it
should always be remembered that such personality is not the
bundle of idiosyncrasies that we know here. They are not men,
but gods. And let us not come down here with our 'we cannot
conceive' and 'we are forced to think'. If we cannot conceive,
then we must try to intuit. Those who have ever known a god
will know how different he or it is from a man.

Since the seven levels are also the very structure of the
cosmos, the very bed-plate on which it is built, and since they
remain throughout the manifestation, however much the
forms therein may change and pass, they are also referred to as
the seven Truths. All forms may pass away, but the levels of
consciousness in which those forms float remain for ever
throughout the Cosmic Day. 'All is perishing except His
Face.'[1] The existence of the Truths was such a commonplace

[1] *Qu'rān.*

E

to those for whom these Stanzas were originally written that their cessation could not be left to be taken for granted. The modern man is usually so ignorant of the meaning both of their existence and of their cessation that by a curious inversion he feels himself superior to those who might have been ignorant only of the meaning of the latter.

The Necessity, of which the universe is here said to be the son, is the Eternal Parent, the Matrix. Psychologists have shown how the feeling of fate, of dire necessity, arises from what they term the unconscious, that is, from those regions of the psyche that are not integrated into our normal consciousness or personal ego and, as such, work compulsively upon us from within the darkness. Within that darkness are hidden structures, the *kārmic* resultants of our own past actions and experience, and, though we have allowed them to vanish from our conscious memory, they are still active, and sometimes force us to act in a way we should never have wished. They can pursue us, for instance, in the form of a fate which makes us always 'too late' on critical occasions, or which afflicts us with ill-health just at those times when our conscious purposes most need all our bodily energies; though it is not intended to suggest that their action is always of this unfavourable sort.

In much the same way the Matrix, with all its buried potentialities and its implicit structures, acts as a 'cycle of necessity'. In the Gita, also, the Matrix, 'the emanation which gives rise to the birth of beings',[1] is referred to as *karma*, action and its compelling fruits. From this point of view, and bearing in mind what has been said about 'the gods', we can understand what is meant by the Greek saying that even the gods are subject to Necessity.

The Universe, then, and its mother, Necessity, are still immersed in *Paranishpanna*, the ultimate Darkness, to be (later) out-breathed by the transcendent Subject or Light pole of the latter when it comes into operation. That Light, the root of what we shall later recognise as consciousness, both 'is' and 'is

[1] *Bhagavad Gītā*, VIII. 3.

not'. It 'is', because, like its opposite pole, the Matrix, it is eternal, and, as we read in the Gita, 'Know thou, that *Prakriti* and *Purusha* are both beginningless.'[1] Even in the state of *pralaya* which we are now considering, that Light exists, because it is an eternal aspect of the one Reality. At the same time it 'is not', because it is not yet differentiated from the primal unity.

Even when differentiated it still 'is not', for it is not 'manifest'; the first manifest level of existence being the Universal Mind of verse 3, which is the same as the Son of verse 5, here called the son of Necessity. One term of the Subject-Object relationship cannot by itself constitute a manifest level, and this Light is, as it were, an abstract of pure subjectivity. When the Son is born he unites in his own being the qualities of his Father, of his Mother, and of the unitary source from which both Parents sprang. The Father as a separate entity only lived for, and died at, the conception so that the Son is the Widow's Son. The Father as a half-way term between the manifest and the unmanifest, between being and non-being, both 'is' and 'is not'.

Paranishpanna or rather *parinishpanna* is a term belonging to the Yogāchāra school of Buddhists, who used it to signify the highest and only ultimate truth.[2] They recognised three such grades of truth.[3] The first is *parikalpita* or merely apparent truth, the truth of common everyday experience, which, from a higher point of view, is illusory. The second is *paratantra*, dependent truth, the truth that comes from seeing the world, not as so many mixed things or substances, but as an ever-changing flux, coming and going with entire dependence upon causal laws; this is the truth of science or philosophy. The third or *parinishpanna* alone is real truth, the absolute truth

[1] *Ibid.*, XIII. 19.

[2] *Parinishpanna* is a Sanskrit term. The corresponding Tibetan word is *yong-grub* as mentioned by H.P.B. or *yons su grub*. The literal meaning is 'supremely accomplished' or 'effected'.

[3] In this they differed from the *Mādyhamika* school which recognised only two: *samvritti*, or relative truth, and *paramārtha*, or absolute truth. Plotinus, like the Yogāchārins, taught three grades.

reached by mystic meditation; it is the seeing of all things *sub specie aeternitatis*. H.P.B. has used the word here to signify the ultimate Reality, the Darkness.

In this connection it will be as well to forestall possible criticisms by stating that such terms as this, when employed in the Stanzas, are not the original terms (which were in what H.P.B. referred to as 'Senzar') but Sanskrit terms used as their equivalents by her and taken from here and there as her catholic but somewhat unorganised acquaintance with the translations of Sanskrit books suggested to her. This fact, plainly stated by her, explains the somewhat miscellaneous collection of terms used—unfriendly critics have termed it a hotch-potch. The 'hotch-potch', if such it is to be called, is that of H.P.B.'s exoteric reading, not that of the Stanzas themselves, nor, it may be added, of her real knowledge of their meaning.

It should also be remembered that H.P.B. was not writing for the small group of Orientalist scholars, and so did not care to observe the rules of their game. Scholars like to have consistency in the usage of terms so that they can refer them to their appropriate affiliations, and to have exact references, *etc.*, so that they can check the work that has been done. From their own point of view they are doubtless right, but so, from hers, was H.P.B. The affiliations of the Stanzas cannot be easily classified for they extend to every system of genuine mystical thought that the world has known; and as for checking the work, that can be done only by intuition. Those who are able to use this latter faculty have methods of their own for 'checking', methods which stand in no need of the *apparatus criticus* of ordinary scholarship.

(7) *The causes of existence had been done away with; the visible that was, and the invisible that is, rested in eternal non-being—the one being.*

In this verse we are introduced to the idea, which we have somewhat anticipated in the comments, that this process of cosmic manifestation has definite causes. It might seem that this is quite an obvious idea and one which is assumed by all people, but in fact the majority of the religious cosmogonies of the world have very little, if anything, to say on the subject. The Christians invoke an inscrutable volition of their extra-cosmic God, while the Vedantins invoke an equally inexplicable *Māyā*, something which is neither the *Parabrahman* nor yet something separate from it, an eternal falsehood (*mithyā-bhūtā sanātani*), a magical illusion which operates on—whom? The Buddhists with their famous *ye dharmā hetuprabhavā*[1] lay indeed great emphasis on causation, but of their various schools only the Yogāchārins make any effort to discuss the causation of the cosmos as a whole, the other schools being content to regard the problem as one of the topics not to be thought about. For this silence there is indeed much to be said, since, as the Buddha taught, the treading of the Path 'is not contingent on the truth of the theories that the world either is or is not eternal'[2] and he who will not follow the Path until he knows how the universe originally came into being is like a man who will not have a poisoned arrow extracted from his body until he knows by whom and why it was shot.

Nevertheless, though the Stanzas do, in their symbolic way, give some account of the origin of the cosmic manifestation, this verse does not do more than enunciate the proposition that there are in fact causes for the periodical manifestation of a universe. Those 'causes of existence' are the two poles into which the one Reality divides. The Darkness (*Parabrahman*) is not a blank unity out of which nothing ever could emerge, but a living—one could almost say organic—unity of which subjectivity and objectivity, Father and Mother, are the two polar aspects which never vanish into nothingness, but even in *pralaya* only become latent in mutual union. An inner tension within the one Reality, the nature of which will be discussed in connection with the next verse, causes the differentiation or standing apart of the two poles which by

---

[1] 'Of all things that arise causally, the Buddha has shown the cause.'
[2] *Majjhima Nikāya*, 63.

their interaction give rise to the whole manifested universe and so are said to be 'the causes of existence'.

In the present stage these causes were still only latent and the subject-object division had not occurred. The Light of sub-jectivity or awareness that had once been visible or manifest in a previous universe is now invisible. It is united with the Matrix within the Darkness of the one Being that yet, because it is not and can never be an object for any consciousness, is also termed Non-being. This last word, like all others in the Stanzas, is used symbolically and must not be identified with nothingness. The word 'being' was evolved to describe the most abstract quality belonging to all the objects of our experi-ence, a certain overtness or manifestness which, because it pervades all our experience, is impossible to isolate in thought or to define except by saying that *being* is what characterises all manifest experience, that by which things 'stand forth'. We need some other word to characterise the condition during the cosmic night, a condition in which there is no standing forth at all. The verse calls it non-being, and it is best conceived as a kind of negative being. Perhaps we also might term it an *intensive* being as opposed to the *extensive* being of the Day. All things have gone within themselves like a glove that has been turned inside out, but the analogy fails because the 'going through' has been into an inner dimension that the mind cannot grasp.

It was in order to have some designation for the neutral plane between being and non-being, or between extensive and intensive being, that H.P.B. coined the word Be-ness, a word which must be taken to refer to the most abstract quality which inheres alike both in extensive being and intensive being. At any rate, whether the words will bear analytic scrutiny or not, we can only say that the non-being (or intensive being) of the Night is as 'real' as the being of the Day, but it is somehow negative.[1]

---

[1] There is a linguistic trap even here, for 'real' means the quality of a thing, 'thingness', and that is just what is not found in 'non-being'.

(8) *Alone, the one form of existence stretched boundless, infinite, causeless in dreamless sleep; and life pulsated unconscious in universal space, throughout that All-Presence which is sensed by the opened eye of the Dangma.*

The one Darkness alone Was, in a state symbolised as dreamless sleep. The analogy between the two states is also referred to in the Upanishads where we read: 'Like those who, unaware of the place, daily walk to and fro above a hidden treasure and find it not, so all these beings, though daily going to the world of *Brahman* (in deep sleep) yet find it not, being carried away by what is untrue (*i.e.* the latent tendencies towards the enjoyment of an external world).'[1]

The analogy, like all such, must not be pressed too far. Its usefulness consists in pointing out a state, familiar to all of us, in which the subject-object relationship is comparatively in abeyance. To any who might be inclined to urge that this state of dreamless sleep is a somewhat dull one, it is enough to remind him that few things are more welcome to us after a busy day. The average man is unable to remember anything of it owing to his lack of inner development; accustomed only to remember concrete images or happenings, he comes back from sleep with his memory a blank, since there were no such images to remember; the state itself is in fact an extremely blissful one.

In truth, neither the state of dreamless sleep nor its macro-cosmic analogue, the Darkness (*Parabrahman*) during *pralaya*,[2] are in the least empty states, but conditions of massive bliss[3] which, because of their unmanifested nature, cannot at all be compared with ordinary differentiated states of consciousness.

Finally, whether we accept it or not, the evidence of all those who have themselves experienced that state of being is that the condition in *pralaya* is not a blank nothingness but a

[1] *Chhāndogya Upanishad*, VIII. iii. 2.
[2] See note 3, p. 52.
[3] *Ghanānanda.*

plenum, so full, indeed, that all our fullest experiences are less than a gossamer web in comparison.

Life, we are told, pulsated unconscious in Universal Space, unconscious, that is, in any sense that we can give to the word consciousness. Universal Space is another of the symbols of the Darkness, and in Stanza III. 7 we shall come across it again under the variant of Dark Space. The Darkness is that 'Space' within which all is. All that exists, in manifestation no less than in dissolution (*pralaya*), is within that one Reality. It does not refer, of course, to the space of visual perception, nor even to those abstract but still overt spaces or space-times beloved by mathematicians, though these are symbolic derivatives of it. In fact it is not the space of space-time but the space of All-Presence; it is not space at all in our sense of the word, but that from which all arises, in which it exists, and into which it withdraws, the ever-invisible robes of the Eternal Parent of verse I.

In trying to think of this space the images that arise are all of the Matrix, for the Darkness is of too subtle a nature to be grasped by the mind. The most we can do is to point to that undifferentiated unity from which the Universal life or Root of consciousness, the Father, and the Receptacle or Matrix, the Mother, both take their rise.

Whatever we may say as philosophers, in practice it is almost impossible to avoid imagery derived from visual space in thinking about the Darkness. This is not only an inevitable but also a correct procedure, since a true symbol does not merely refer to the thing but is also a manifestation of it. In this it differs from arbitrary symbolism or mere allegory which, as Blake said, is the 'daughter of Fancy'. The danger lies both in forgetting that a given concrete symbol is a manifestation of several archetypal realities simultaneously, and in confusing the strands which lead back to the one of which we seek knowledge. In this particular instance visual space is a manifestation of, as well as a symbol of, Universal Space.

It is now time to turn our attention to the 'pulsation' which

continues even in *pralaya*. Again, the verbal description is not
to be taken as a philosophical statement and dismissed as
nonsense because it is illogical to say that pulsation, which
involves time and differentiation, could not exist in the timeless
and undifferentiated state of *pralaya*. We repeat that the words
are symbolic and refer to something that cannot be expressed
in any other way. Even the most 'exact' descriptions of our
scientists are but symbols, and to suppose that one has snip-
snapped reality because one has exposed contradictions in
verbal symbolism is a mistake to which a certain type of
philosopher is peculiarly liable.

The symbol in question reminds us vividly of the line in the
well known Creation Hymn of the Rig Veda: 'That One
Thing, breathless, breathed by Its own nature.'[1] There too we
get this same symbol of a rhythmic breathing or pulsating in
that which is breathless and pulse-less. We have already
referred to this eternal pulse, the archetype of all the rhythms
in the universe, as being something that does not stop even
in *pralaya*.

The one Reality is not a static absolute as conceived by some
philosophers. It is not a gigantic geometric figure laid up
somewhere in the heavens, or rather in the void. It is living
Being, and the pulsation of its life continues ceaselessly even
in, what might seem to us to be, the frozen sterility of the
Cosmic Night.

The pulsation is a rhythmic alternation of stress or tension
between the two poles which appear within the one Reality;
a pulsating relationship between Father and Mother, Subject
and Object, or Spirit and Matter. This polar division becomes
overt during the Cosmic Day, while during the Night the
two poles fuse together, sending the whole universe into
latency. Just as under verses 2 and 7 we saw that time and being
enter into their own hearts and, as it were, emerge in a nega-

---

[1] *Rig Veda*, X. 129. The whole hymn is worth studying as it shows a close similarity
to the thought of our Stanzas. A translation and comments have been given in *The
Yoga of the Bhagavad Gītā* (Appendix F) by Sri Krishna Prem.

tive form on the 'other side', so here we should note that the subject-object polarity does not cease during the Night but goes through itself and re-appears in a negative and, to us incomprehensible, intensive form.

Let us take the aid of an analogy from material in our own experience. We ordinarily recognise in ourselves three states of experiencing in waking, dreaming and deep sleep; and for most of us that is a sufficient analysis. But if we look more closely we find there are considerable variations, not only, for instance, in the degree of our wakefulness at different times, but also in the types of experience we associate with different periods of the day. As an objective example of the former one can point to graphs showing production efficiency and accident rates for different times of day in factories where the fatigue to which these graphs are related is closely connected with wakefulness. In the latter case we must look to the psychic qualities which characterise our experience of morning, mid-day, evening, and night; distinctions which are mostly to be described in terms of feeling. We distinguish between the expectant stillness of the dawn and the soft fading of the evening twilight; between the practicality that infuses morning labour, and the dull drudgery of the afternoon; we contrast the purposive material aims of daytime business with the relaxing atmosphere of evening enjoyments, and this again with the bracing vigour of early morning exercise. On another level too, those who practise meditation may find the hard material objectivity, that characterises the noon period, producing a correspondingly dulling effect on their spiritual aspirations. These are pulsations or rhythms which, whether we regard them as subjective or as objective in origin, lie quite outside the small circles of our personal integrations; it is seldom therefore that our self-absorption can completely blind us to their presence.

The polarity of our out-turned experience, then, varies both in quantity and in quality. The intensity of sleep is also not uniform, for we usually plunge deeply inwards, and then follow a gradual curve up to waking; for this reason we are seldom aware of the dream period as we pass from waking to sleeping and remember only those dreams that come to us on the gradual return from sleeping to waking.

From these variations of the subject–object polarity in ourselves we can get some idea of the sort of movements within the Cosmic Night and Day to which the Stanzas refer as the pulsations of life.

On the approach of sleep, the subject–object polarity for a moment collapses, making a belt of unconsciousness, the barrier past which memory is with difficulty carried. On the other side of this is the state of dream experience in which those parts of our personality with which we identify ourselves in waking life now re-appear as the objective contents of dreams, usually in symbolic form, tigers, kings and staircases. The 'subject' becomes the 'object' while the subject figure (oneself), tends to take on the passive role of negative polarity. In dream, much more than in waking, things 'happen to one'. This reversal of polarity accounts for the curious 'Alice-through-the-looking-glass' nature of dreams, and explains the traditional dictum 'dreams go by contraries'.

It will be well to note in passing that dreams only appear unreal after one wakes from them; and the argument that, were they real, one would awake to find oneself physically in the location of which one was dreaming, is a mere muddle-headed mixing of categories based on a bland assumption that physical waking experience is the criterion of reality of all experience whatsoever.

We may remain dreaming all night, especially if ill or if greatly mentally disturbed, but we usually pass on to deep sleep, crossing as we do so another, though less marked, barrier in consciousness consequent on another variation of polarity.

In sleep we leave all sense of self-identification with any psychic integration and enter a realm of entirely peaceful and inward concentration. Sleep itself passes to a maximum intensity and lightens again as we approach, and then repass, the barrier into dream on the return journey to waking.

If we watch ourselves with care, we find that on waking from sleep there is a short and not easily apprehensible period in which we are neither dreaming nor waking; a moment of transition in which we may, as it were, stand with a foot each side of a door-sill and pass from one state to the other, as, by a mere turning of the head, one's gaze may pass from one room to the other while one is not fully in either. This is the threshold of the waking state across which come the memories of dreams and other worlds (*i.e.* other states of consciousness), and which, by virtue of the strangeness—not devoid of danger—of its qualities, has thrown a magical atmosphere over all material thresholds that are its symbols.

Following the process of waking, we find ourselves pulled out of this drowsiness by an increasing self-identification, first with bodily sensations, and then—as the waking potential increases—with those mental and emotional movements which constitute the forces of out-turned activity.

Awake, our body and our personal characteristics were subjectively self-identified. In dream, those accretions to our being were half thrown off, objectified, though in some degree still retaining their self-reference, and felt to be projections of ourselves. They formed a private world, without the shared experience which is the criterion of objectivity, and without the full self-identification of waking. In sleep, we are neither self-identified subjectively with a psycho-physical integration, as in waking, nor mixed up in the half and half state of the dream, but, while there is still what we can only term experience, the two poles blend in a central, massively concentrated state in which, 'Verily, while he does not there see, he is verily seeing, though he does not see what is usually to be seen. For there is no cessation of a seer because of his imperishability. It is not however a second thing, other than himself and separate that he sees.'[1] During such experience there is seeing, but only on waking can one say 'I saw'.

[1] *Brihadāraṇyaka Upanishad*, IV, iii, 23.

Most men mistake this inner condition for complete emptiness. The memory of this state is not ordinarily accessible to them except as a rare sense of 'happy I slept'. There being no separation of polarities, there are no empirical ego-integrations to form attachments in that state, and therefore no strong pull to bring the memory of the state through the triply guarded doors between sleep and waking. We are, indeed, so accustomed to regard the experience of our waking integration as being the criterion of significance that other means of experience are treated as unimportant. Dreams occasionally thrust themselves on to our attention, but a great number of modern men like to pretend that they never dream at all.

The dream world is indeed a twilight realm, 'the misty mid-region of Weir', but the state of sleep is dark only to the ignorant. As long as man emphasises the importance of his waking integration, and thereby blinds his eyes by over-exposure to the dazzling sun of his egotism, he will remain unable to see anything but darkness in the inner worlds. The world of sleep is not dark, but is bright with the light of true knowledge to him who will but look, not with the outer eyes, it is true, but with the opened eye of *Dangma*, the inner eye of the seer. It is this that is referred to by such statements as 'What is night to the ordinary man is day to the seer', and Apuleius's 'I have seen the sun shining at midnight.' That this description of the states of dreaming and sleeping is factual may be verified by anyone who will give his time and attention to the study of his own nature.

The above evaluation of sleep is by no means intended to imply that we are considering the ordinary state of deep sleep to be in itself spiritually superior to our waking state when we are in full possession of our faculties. But our waking faculties are only a partial development of what is possible for the fully evolved man. If we can succeed in carrying our essential waking intelligence through dream into sleep, sleep is then no longer the dark and empty blankness we ordinarily think it to be.

Reverting to the primary pattern of our analogy, the sleep of the Cosmos, we can see how the cycle of man's sleeping, dreaming, waking, and return through dream to sleep, finds its parallels in the cycle of night, followed by twilight, day, twilight, and night; and in the year, in winter, spring, summer, autumn, and winter; and in each may be found parallels for any of the possible cyclic divisions we may prefer.

At the middle of the Cosmic Night or the winter solstice of the Year the subject-object polarity is annulled and all forms blend and dissolve, one within the other and all within the One. As the Day approaches, sleep gets lighter, the sky pales, the sun which has remained almost stationary in the solstitial region noticeably begins his northern course, and within the cosmic heart begin the first movements of the manifestation that is to be, like the first stirrings of the roots of plants in the darkness of the still wintry soil. Dream, twilight, and the period of the equinoxes represent the time of the manifestation of the subtle worlds which, with the full dawning of the day, will harden into materiality. The subject-object polarity gradually increases to its maximum at the midday or summer solstice, then falls away to the autumnal *pralaya*.

Each of these variations in the fundamental polarity finds its parallels in the types of human consciousness that are manifested at different times. But, even if we were to work out some of the cycles in detail, we should be no nearer to our goal. The important thing is to perceive the general pattern of cycles, and not to get lost in a welter of ultimately meaningless particulars, nor to waste time in elaborate calculations for which we have no adequate premises.

Because the cosmic cycles are not simple but infinitely complex, the degree of polarisation of the manifest universe, representing the stage of development, is not the same throughout its parts. For instance, in the Indian terminology, not every race is in the *Kali yuga*,[1] or any other *yuga,* simultaneously.

[1] Equivalent to the 'Iron Age' of the Greeks, the most materialistic of the cyclic periods.

At the same time, for instance, that European thought has
been held in the grip of the differentiating and analytic intellect,
having all the characteristics of the extreme objective polarity
of the summer solstice, we still find amongst primitive and
unsophisticated people, even in the same countries, the synthetic life of the instinct with its attendant, the lower psychism,
which is equinoctial in character. The latter, instinctive mode
of thought is extinguished by the burning sun of mid-summer
objectivity with its analytic intellect, and this in turn gives way
to the synthetic intuition which manifests the awakening
buddhi. At the autumnal equinox the *pralaya* occurs, and the
universe slides into the darkness of the Night as the polarity
is annulled. Time goes negative, being becomes non-being,
and the long strange Night-life of the universe commences.[1]
Slowly the negative polarity increases, and the inner Night
Worlds emerge, or rather immerge, until dream passes to
sleep, and at Midnight the maximum intension has been
reached in a strange, spiritual, non-dual and blissful union deep
within the impenetrable Darkness. After that mystic Midnight,
the inner subjective polarity lessens once more up the long
slope to the dawn of the Vernal Equinox, the manifestation of
a new Cosmos. Thus do the Cycles revolve, universe succeeding universe in infinite yet ever-new succession. Thus too is
solved the riddle of the Seven Eternities which puzzled us so
much when first we met them in verse 1.

The nature of the causation of the manifested Cosmos,
which we left half-discussed in the last verse, can now be stated
with greater completeness. The 'Causes of Existence' are the
two great Poles of the Darkness, but it is the sheer *life* of that
Reality which brings it about that there should be a constant
pulsation or rhythmic alternation of tension between those
Poles. This pulsation or Breath is also termed Motion, since

---

[1] Compare H.P.B.'s footnote 16 to *The Voice of the Silence* (1st edn., p. 62). 'Some
Sanskrit mystics locate seven planes of being, the seven spiritual *lokas* or worlds,
within the body of *Kāla Hamsa*, the Swan out of Time and Space, convertible into
the Swan *in* Time when it becomes *Brahmā* instead of *Brahma* (neuter).'

it is the root from which all motion comes.[1] We cannot do more than say that it is the very life and Heart's Blood of That which is the Root of all being. Because of it, nothing is ever in a static state of rest, but is forever changing and 'passing into its opposite'. Were the universe rooted in something dead and mechanical, it would no doubt be necessary to account for the origin of such a movement, but it surely needs no explanation that *living* being should thus be in a constant state of (metaphysical) motion, for such a self-movingness constitutes the very essence of life. All we need do is to guard ourselves against conceiving that Motion in a mechanical instead of in a psychic manner.

Forever and forever, that Life pulses within the heart of all that is. Its ageless, tireless rhythm is sometimes strong and sometimes faint as the cycles go through their appointed courses, but it never ceases altogether except at the two critical points of Dawn and Dusk when, for a moment, the polarity is annulled before changing into its opposite.[2]

During the Cycle of the Cosmic Day, and to a lesser extent during all its microcosmic epicyclic correspondences, the emphasis-value is more upon the Object or matter, while, during the Night, it lies upon the Subject, Spirit. When the intensity of the object-value reaches a certain critical point, the

---

[1] H.P.B. writes of the three great symbols of the Absolute—Abstract Space, Duration and Motion. The first of these is that which contains, the *Mūlaprakriti* aspect; the second, that which endures, the *Purusha* or unchanging Root of Consciousness, and the third, the Breath, pulsation or tension between the two, which results in power, energy, motion. See *S.D.* I, p. 43.

[2] It is because of this correspondence between our days and nights and those of the Cosmos that Indian tradition teaches that the periods of twilight at dawn and dusk are the most favourable times for practising yogic meditation. Apollonius of Tyana, too, gave the same teaching to his disciples, and it is by no means a fanciful one as hasty minds might conclude. Terrestrial twilights are manifestations of the same principle that causes the Cosmic ones, and consequently, if not counteracted by an artificial polarity produced by our ordinary ways of life, tend to produce in us a cessation of the subject-object relationship which is favourable for entry into the inner worlds.

It is also worth noting that 'the dead vast and middle of the night' is traditionally the hour of magic and ghostly phenomena, corresponding in this with the strange inner life of the mystic Cosmic Midnight.

point of Dawn, it first annuls and then overpowers the subject-value, so that the content of the one Reality bursts its banks and overflows—that is Creation.[1] When, after Midday, the Subject begins again to assert its predominance, the flooded waters ebb and, at the Evening Twilight, sink back once more into the Primal Source from which they flowed.

Such are the *Brāhmic* Days and Nights of which the Gita speaks: 'They who know them are the Knowers of Day and Night.'[2] This is the creative play of eternal Life. To use another, one of the most beautiful of Hindu symbols, it is the eternal love-play of Krishna and Radha, the dark God clothed in the flaming yellow mantle, the gold-complexioned Goddess wrapped in the dark blue robe; the Two who yet are One, the One who yet is Two.

(9) *But where was the Dangma when the Ālaya of the Universe was in Paramārtha and the great wheel was Anupādaka?*[3]

In the last verse we read that the One, the All-Presence, though never known is yet 'sensed' by the opened eye, the so-called third eye, of one who is a *Dangma* or perfected Seer. This third eye, symbolic representations of which are so often found on Hindu images, is the eye of wisdom or spiritual intuition, the eye that gives certain knowledge of the truth; one, because it transcends duality. It is not, of course, the subtle physical organ of ordinary psychic clairvoyance, it is not in fact an organ at all, but is more nearly described as a state of being.

Buddhist tradition differentiates carefully between these two modes of supernormal vision. It speaks of the *divya chakshu* or eye of the gods, which corresponds to psychic clairvoyance and gives visions of events distant in time or space. We read

[1] Compare Plotinus, V. ii. 1. 'The One is not a being but the source of Being which is its first offspring. The One is perfect, that is it has nothing, seeks nothing, needs nothing, but, as we may say, it overflows and this overflowing is creative.'

Enneads, Stephen Mackenna's translation.

[2] *Bhagavad Gītā*, VIII. 17.

[3] Sanskrit *Anupapādaka.*

F

also of *divyachakshur-avabhāsa,* illusory visions of purely subjective origin.[1] Contrasted with this is the power of seeing with the wisdom eye (*prajñā chakshu*).[2] This is not just a poetic metaphor for the holding of correct opinions, but a real faculty capable of revealing truths not hitherto perceived. While the 'eye of the gods', as Vasubandhu points out,[3] is only operative in the realms of form and is confined to visual representations, the 'wisdom eye', penetrating into the formless worlds, is able to reveal truth directly and without the intermediacy of forms. It is important to realise that the formless vision of the latter is quite as definite as the more sensuously vivid visions of the former. Whatever it loses in sensuous concreteness, it more than gains in consequence of its far greater range and comparative freedom from the danger of misinterpretation. The clairvoyant user of the 'divine eye' will see, for instance, the inter-relatedness of things in terms of concrete, though subtle, structures or entities, while the more deeply penetrating wisdom-eye perceives the formless realities of which those subtle entities, no less than the gross ones of the physical world, are but appearances or symbols. The perfect Seer or *Dangma* has command over both these modes of vision, being able to see forms when he chooses, while at the same time perceiving the inner significance which lies behind them. But, as verse 8 tells us, even the highest spiritual vision of the *Dangma* can only 'sense', never see, the All-presence, since the latter can never be an object for any consciousness, however sublime.

At this stage, however, we can only ask where was there a Seer to see or even 'sense' It? For the *Ālaya*[4] of the universe, the Eternal Parent or Matrix, was in *Paramārtha,*[5] the state of supreme Reality, and the Great Wheel of the manifested

---

[1] *Abhidharma Kosha,* V. 27.

[2] There are various terms used to express different shades or aspects of the same idea. e.g. *dharma chakshu* (eye of truth), *jñāna chakshu* (eye of knowledge).

[3] *Abhidharma Kosha,* VII. 54.

[4] A Buddhist term belonging to the *Yogāchāra* School. It signifies store or receptacle. Compare the remarks on the Platonic Receptacle under verse 1.

[5] *Paramārtha* is a term used by the *Mādhyamika* School (as well as by Hindus) and is equivalent to the *Parinishpanna* of the *Yogāchārins.* See verse 6 of this stanza.

Cosmos was without parents (*anupapādaka*), the two, who were to bring it forth. The question may be asked, but scarcely answered. The perfected Seers of the previous Day had all entered the Darkness with the universe in which they lived. The new universe was still unborn, its very Parents not having yet become manifest. Of those Seers of Yesterday we can say in the words of the Buddha: 'All manifestations of form, feeling, thought, will and consciousness, everything that might have served to denote the existence of the Enlightened One has passed into non-being—grubbed and stubbed, leaving only the bare cleared site where once a palm tree towered—a thing that once has been, and now can be no more. Profound, measureless, unfathomable is the Enlightened One as the mighty ocean.'[1] All we can say of a positive nature is that the Treasure of the Universe, the Jewels of perfected Seership and Wisdom, shine darkly in some deep unfathomed way within the strange and secret Body of the Night.

---

[1] *Majjhima Nikāya*, 72. Slightly altered from Lord Chalmers' translation.

STANZA TWO

Being the second of seven Stanzas from
The Book of Dzyan

1. *Where were the builders, the luminous sons of Manvantaric Dawn? . . . In the unknown darkness in their Ah-hi Paranishpanna. The producers of form (rūpa) from no-form (arūpa)—the root of the world—the Devamātri and Svabhāvat, rested in the bliss of non-being.*

2. *Where was silence? Where the ears to sense it? No, there was neither silence nor sound; naught save ceaseless eternal breath which knows itself not.*

3. *The hour had not yet struck; the ray had not yet flashed into the Germ; the Mātripadma had not yet swollen.*

4. *Her heart had not yet opened for the one ray to enter, thence to fall, as three into four, into the lap of Māyā.*

5. *The Seven were not yet born from the Web of Light. Darkness alone was Father-Mother, Svabhāvat; and Svabhāvat was in darkness.*

6. *These two are the Germ, and the Germ is one. The Universe was still concealed in the Divine Thought and the Divine Bosom. . . .*

LATENT POWER

In Stanza I the negations with which we have now become familiar were framed in a way to suggest a deepening withdrawal of all being into the night of non-being. Here, in Stanza II it is as if the darkest hour of the night had passed, and behind the negations we can sense the first stirrings of that which is to be.

The polarity is still the negative one of the Night, but the increasing emphasis value of the Object Pole is approaching the point where it will annul and overpower that of the Subject. There is still no manifest life or activity, but within the imperishable darkness a negative, dream-like activity begins to take place, and there, shining with a dark subjective light, is an image of the Cosmos that is to be. The insistent and increasing emphasis on the Two shows how the inner tension is increasing and will shortly reach the threshold state. The coming Dawn that is as yet below the horizon is being faintly felt.

(1) *Where were the builders, the luminous sons of Manvantaric Dawn? . . . In the unknown darkness in their Ah-hi Paranishpanna. The producers of form (rūpa) from no-form (arūpa)—the root of the world—the Devamātri and Svabhāvat, rested in the bliss of non-being.*

The power which builds the universe is, like everything else, rooted in the nature of its Source. The power of the Source is the life of the Source, its very nature as living Being. Nevertheless, when we are considering power in manifestation, there are several aspects from which we may do so.

In the first place we may consider the power as residing in the Matrix out of which come all the moving forms of the universe and, therefore, also all power. Like the earthly mother who is her symbol, she is the root of all creation in the sense of 'bringing forth' or emissive power.

But the power of the Mother is not independent. Unless she is fertilised by the Light of the Father, no creation takes place. Hence, it is also not incorrect to speak of power (in its fertilising sense) as rooted in the Father or transcendent Subject.

Even then, we have not said all. If the two Poles of the one

Reality remained isolated from each other, again no creation would take place; it thus becomes clear that the real source of power, potency, is the tension or interaction between the two, an interaction that, as we have seen, comes from the underlying Unity in which the Two are differentiated. It is this interaction which gives rise to the Seven levels of being; and the Builders referred to in this verse are the various differentiations of this creative power.

The particular aspect of power with which the verse is concerned is 'building' or the production of 'form' from 'no-form'. As we shall see in Stanza IV the term *arūpa*, formless, is used in a technical sense to mean the subtle or invisible universe and not the sheer transcendency of the Darkness. The Builders, then, are the effectuating powers of the creation who mediate between the formless (*arūpa*) or incorporeal universe of the Archetypes, (the Greek noëtic world of intelligibles, to be apprehended only by understanding, not by the senses) and the manifest or existent worlds of form (*rūpa*). They are thus intermediary powers or gods, neither of the unmanifest darkness, nor of the bright manifestation, but luminous gods of the dawn of creation. This is why the 'root of the world'—a rendering of *Mūla-prakriti*—is here called *Devamātri*, Mother of Gods.[1]

We can also approach the subject from another angle. The formative power in the universe is the power which we know as imagination. Fundamentally, the power of imagining is the same as the power of knowing. This may seem startling, for we are often apt to contrast knowing with mere imagining as fact with falsehood. This, however, is a superficial view. The act of imagining is just as much an act of knowing as is any perception of sense-data, but it is one which takes place on a subtler level than the physical. The data known by the imagination are real data, but they are the psychic data of the inner senses. 'Imagination,' said H.P.B., 'is the great tool of the occultist'; and the fact that ordinary men are able to make no

[1] Cf. Gaia, 'Mother of Gods and Men'.

effective use of this means of knowing is because, as with any other faculty that is insufficiently used and trained, their imagining power remains in a childish and practically useless state. The power is there, but it remains chaotic and undeveloped. Unable to be used as an instrument of knowing, for most people it is wasted in idle day-dreaming. The practical confusion which arises between knowing and imagining is really a confusion between knowing the data of the outer (physical) senses and knowing the data of the subtle or inner senses. Naturally, any confusion of the data of these two separate levels will give rise to considerable mistakes in practice.[1]

Many people fancy that the imagination is a perfectly arbitrary power which can be exercised just as we wish. Nothing could be further from the truth. We can no more imagine just what we wish to than we can perceive just what we wish to with our outer senses. Imaginative knowing is as definitely law-determined as is sense knowing, but the laws in question are those of subtler levels of being.[2]

In taking, as we did a few paragraphs further back, imagining as the type of the formative power, we were making a concession to the fact that it is in imagining that the creative nature of knowing is most obvious. The other forms of knowing are just as creative, but because imagining is the mode of knowing most associated with desire, its creative nature is more overt, since in desire is manifest the interaction, tension, or power aspect of Reality. Thus, though *knowing* is the wider of the two terms, we gain a more vivid realisation of the actual process if we say all knowing is imagining than if we reverse the equation and say all imagining is knowing.

We may sum up the above by saying that whatever modes

[1] Some exception to the above remarks should certainly be made in the case of the imaginative artist. Discussion of his use of the imagination would take us too far afield, but it would seem to be a different use from the one we are here considering, though one not without bearing on and points of contact with the problem.

[2] Compare Eliphas Levi: 'For the wise man to imagine is to see, ... but the imagination of the adept is diaphanous, whilst that of the crowd is opaque'. *Doctrine and Ritual of Transcendental Magic*, p. 61.

there may be of obtaining the material of mental content (sensing, intuiting, imagining) or of handling that content (thinking, feeling, acting) they all represent different modes of interaction between the two poles of Reality which are the powers that bring the universe into manifestation.[1]

The Builders, then, are the great powers of divine imagining, they who 'call spirits from the vasty deep'. The spirits they call forth are the Cosmic levels with all their varied content, while the vasty deep is the great Matrix. The Builders not only produce the levels, they become them, and each creatively builds or shapes the content on the form of his own being in much the same way as the ego-centre in a man shapes for himself the content of his experience into a whole. As the tension or interaction aspect of Reality they are luminous or conscious Powers becoming manifest at the very commencement of the Cosmic Day or *Manvantara*.[2] These 'morning stars' had not yet begun to 'sing together', for they were still latent in the Darkness of ultimate Being or *Parinishpanna*.[3]

We also learn from the phrase *Ah-hi Parinishpanna* that the Builders are identical with the *Ah-hi* (I. 8) or Divine Serpents of creative desire. We are thus enabled to understand why it was that the 'Serpent', by tempting Eve, who in this context is the Cosmic Mother, brought about the expulsion from the Garden of Eden, and why also that Serpent was identified with Lucifer, Son of the Morning. In Eden the serpent represented the urging to a knowledge of the pairs of opposites, exemplified as good and evil, without which no polar tension could arise.

The symbol of the serpent has always had a twofold significance. On the one hand it is the symbol of wisdom and of the

---

[1] Although our general view is not that of Berkeleian subjectivism, we are clearly not very far from his doctrine that *esse* is *percipi*. We should prefer to say that manifestation is knowing in any of its forms, and we may also note the similarity to the Vedantic *Drishti-srishti-vāda* or view that creation lies in seeing.

[2] The more usual and correct Sanskrit term for the Cosmic Day is *kalpa*, literally an imagining. A *manvantara*, according to *Manusmriti*, I. 79, is the period between two *Manus* of whom there are fourteen in one Cosmic Day.

[3] See Stanza, I. 6 for reference to this word.

Seers who possess it.[1] It was the *Nāgas* or wise Serpents who, according to tradition, taught the secret *Prajnā Pāramitā Sūtras* to Nāgārjuna, and also gave him some magical 'clay' for the *building* of sanctuaries.[2] On the other hand, equally well known is its use as a symbol of desire and evil. In the Biblical story of the brazen serpent which Moses raised upon a pole to cure the Israelites of the bite of the fiery serpents we get both aspects, since Christian tradition takes the former as the symbol of Christ. The analogous Chinese dragon likewise has two sides to its nature: on the one hand a wisdom-being, and on the other a monster of irresistible strength and wickedness.

As Builders whose nature is the divine imagining power, the Serpents are beings or rather powers of Wisdom. Moreover, as the tension of Desire, they are the Teachers, for it is the urges of desire that lead us (and the Cosmos) on to new adventures. It was as such that they were mainly worshipped in the archaic religions, the wise Serpents, sons of the Mother Earth.

It was after the passing of the Summer Solstice of greatest absorption in 'matter' that the Serpent, like everything else, passed into its opposite. As long as the Cosmos was pressing outwards to wider and wider manifestation the Serpent was the Teacher. With the passing of the critical point of the Solstice, however, a change sets in. That which was 'good' now becomes 'evil'. What were once the wise *Ah-hi* are now the tempting forces of Desire, the Buddhist *Trishna*, luring outwards onto the rocks of matter the selves that should now be setting sail towards the haven of spirit. Hence they are now 'evil', and Apollo, shining God of Light, slays and supersedes the Python, the Serpent son of the Mother Earth, him who for many ages had been the God from whom the Delphic Oracle derived its wisdom. The same theme is contained in the Christian myth in which Lucifer, son of the morning (really

---

[1] Names compounded with *Nāga* (serpent) were common among Buddhist teachers, e.g. *Nāgārjuna, Nāgabodhi, Nāgānanda, Nāgasena*. See also *Quetzal Coatl*, the 'plumed serpent' of the Aztecs; the snake which coils round the staff of Asklepios the Divine Healer; and the snakes on the caduceus of Hermes. Also see Stanza I. 3.

[2] See the *Chos-Bhyung* of *Bu-ston*, 110b, translated into English by Obermiller.

a Promethean figure bringing Light to men) becomes 'the devil' and is overcome by Christ.[1]

The Builders are at this stage still in the darkness of latency, since the two Poles between which they work, the Mother and the Father, are still undifferentiated. These two are here referred to as *Devamātri*, the Mother of the Gods, and *Svabhāvat*, literally 'becoming itself'. The latter is the subjective Pole of Being, the Father who, becoming Self, says 'I am', the transcendent Self of all that is. This Self or *Ātman* is also known as the *Shānta Ātman*, the calmly contemplating peaceful Seer.

These two are still in the bliss of unity within the Darkness. The Darkness is here called non-being to distinguish it from the no-form of the noëtic universe. Lacking the tension arising from the separation of the Two, there can be no manifestation of power; consequently no 'building', no production of form, can occur.

(2) *Where was silence? Where the ears to sense it? No, there was neither silence nor sound; naught save ceaseless eternal breath which knows itself not.*

Again the two Poles are mentioned, this time under the symbols of Silence and Sound; apt symbols for the Two, the Silent Sky watching in calm the Sounding Sea below. Mystics have often spoken (and still speak) of the great Sound (*shabda*) which reverberates and throbs through the blue space of dazzling light like a great engine of resistless power, like mighty breakers on a shoreless sea. In the *Tibetan Book of the Dead* we read: 'From the midst of that radiance, the natural Sound of Reality, reverberating like a thousand thunders simultaneously sounding, will come. That is the natural sound of thine own self. Be not daunted thereby, nor terrified, nor awed.'[2] This is the great creative Sound, the Word of Pthah, the name of God, in which is power to bring forth all the worlds. It occurs again

[1] See *The Yoga of the Bhagavad Gītā*, chapter 16.
[2] *Tibetan Book of the Dead*, edited and translated by Dr. Evans Wentz and Lama Dawa Samdup, p. 104.

in connection with the Great Vortex of Orphic cosmogony, and is symbolised by the Bell whose sound pervades all space and whose image is often found in the hand of Tibetan deities. All these are symbols of the one creative Mother, just as the silence of the desert and of lonely mountain peaks, the silence, too, of mystic contemplation in the cave of the heart, are symbols of the ever silent Spirit, watching in utter calm while all things change and pass.[1]

In the Rig Veda, *Vāch*, the creative Speech or Sound, 'the Queen, the gatherer-up of treasures' is represented as saying:

'Through me alone all eat the food that feeds them.
They know it not but yet they dwell beside me.
I rouse and order battle for the people and I have penetrated
    Earth and Heaven.
On the world's summit I bring forth the Father; my home
    is in the waters, in the ocean.
Thence I extend o'er all existing creations and touch even
    yonder heaven with my forehead.
I breathe a strong breath like the wind and tempest, the
    while I hold together all existence.'[2]

But just as there was no eye of *Dangma* to sense the All-Presence of the One, so there was no ear to hear the still unmanifest *mantras* of the Sound. Only the ceaseless 'breathing of the breathless one' went on in the Absolute Consciousness which, to us, is no consciousness at all. It knew Itself not, It was not self-conscious.

'Alone that one breathed calmly, self-supported,
    Other than it was none, nor aught above it.'[3]

---

[1] It may be mentioned that the pair, Silence and Sound, re-appear lower down the scale of being in the Upanishadic pair, *manas* and *vāch*, which latter is again re-symbolised as a cow with streaming udders, the cow of fertility. In the Hermetic works XIII. 1 and 2 Tat asks, 'I know not, Thrice Greatest One, from out what matter and what womb Man comes to birth, or of what seed,' and Hermes replies, 'Wisdom that understands in silence, and the True Good, the seed'. *Thrice Greatest Hermes*, (G. R. S. Mead).
[2] *Rig Veda*, X. 125, Griffiths.
[3] *ibid.*, X. 129.

(3) *The hour had not yet struck; the ray had not yet flashed into the Germ; the Mātripadma had not yet swollen.*

The approaching Hour of Dawn has not yet come. The universe is still a dream within the Darkness, and its secret Night life is as unattainable to our thought as is the inner fantasy world of the dreamer lying asleep at our side. The Object Pole has not yet gained sufficient emphasis-value to draw forth the creative Ray of psychic projection from the Spirit or transcendent Self (*Shānta Ātman*). During the Night, as we have seen, the polarity is reversed, so that the Spirit, 'gone feminine', received into itself the centripetal onset or rather inrush of Matter and utterly devoured it. At Midnight this mystic ebb ceased, and the tide of objectivity began to flow once more, entering the ambiguous state of dream; though not until the Dawn does the flow gain sufficient strength to carry it through the zero point and beyond the embrace of Spirit. Once through that zero point the objective Pole expands into the outwardness of the Day, becoming 'female' in its turn and drawing forth the fertilising Ray of the Spirit which is that Spirit's self-projection into the now centrifugal tide of objectivity.

That point however has not yet been passed, and the Ray has not yet flashed forth to impregnate with its glance the Mother Lotus (*Mātripadma*), nor has the latter 'swollen'[1] in preparation for the fertilisation.

Following the analogy of birth, the Germ is the ovum which will be fertilised by the male 'Ray', and it is within the Mother in the form of the potential Universal Mind. The symbol of the Mother *Lotus* derives its point, as H.P.B. explained, from the saying that seeds of the lotus plant, if opened, reveal a miniature lotus plant complete within them.[2] Note how closely packed with meaning are these ancient symbols. Simply to have referred to the Mother would seem to have been enough

---

[1] Cf. the term *ucchūnāvasthā*, the swollen state, as used in the Tantric system of *Shakti* about to create.

[2] S.D., I. 57.

but it would not have been so, since in this compound word *mātri-padma* is set forth the whole idea of the Universal Mind already existing in germ as a potentiality or possibility of manifestation within the Matrix, awaiting that which shall call it forth, as the lotus awaits the sun's rays to cause it to bloom. The nature of that potentiality is similar to the ego's complex structures which pass into latency during sleep, but emerge again on waking. In just such a way does the Universal Mind go into latency during the Cosmic Night.

(4) *Her heart had not yet opened for the one ray to enter, thence to fall, as three into four, into the lap of Māyā.*

Just as the Spirit or Father-Light is not yet ready to flash forth its great 'I am', so the Matrix or Root of Matter is not yet ready, not sufficiently differentiated from the 'sleeping' unity of the Night, to undertake its role of receptivity, of being 'That is'.

This verse also gives the first substantial list of the number symbols, for it anticipates that the one Ray will enter the heart of the Mother, thence to fall into the outer manifestation, the Lap of *Māyā* or Magic Play[1] 'as three into four'. The first, the Father, enters the second, the Mother, who gives birth to the third, the Son. But the third is, as we have seen, the Universal Mind which is a manifest principle endowed, as the off-spring of the Two, with its own creative life. It therefore proceeds to overflow into further manifestation. Its creative imagination, the gift of its Father, seizes possibilities, the endowment of its Mother, embodies them in images, the Magic Play, ensouls them with its life, and lo! it has fallen into the Lap of *Māyā*, and four lower levels come into being; the Three have fallen into the Four.

As this has not yet occurred we shall content ourselves with

[1] The root and earliest meaning of *Māyā* is a magic creation or display. Hence it came to have the derivative sense of illusion. It is really a process of creative imagination and corresponds to the *abūtaparikalpa* of the *Yogāchārins*. The latter word is rendered by Friedmann as 'constructive ideation' (see his translation of Sthirmati's *Madhyānta-vibhāga-tika*): literally this term can be rendered 'the imagination of that which was not'.

the statement that the process by which they come into being is one of continuous psychic projection. The Four are the modes of this projection and correspond to the four lower levels shown on the scheme set out under the next verse. The question of these modes will be taken up under Stanza III. 4.

At this stage there can be no Four or even Three, for the positive polarity of the Day has not yet come into being and the Mother has not yet become receptive; in the words of the verse, her heart is not yet open and so no fertilisation can take place.

It is to be noted how in every instance the Stanzas present the creative process as the mutual interplay of the two poles of Reality. Stress is not laid on one aspect of Being to the detriment of the other. The Matrix contributes just as much to the Cosmos as does the Father-Light. Important though the pole of Consciousness is as the source of Reason, Order and Limitation, it can effect nothing without, as it were, the willing co-operation of the 'Irrational' Mother with her living and fecund potentiality.

Neither is to be ethically preferred, for they are mutually responsible for all the powers and qualities deriving from their union. The ethical, or what amounts to the same thing, the purposeful aspect of the creation is to be sought not in one or other of the Poles but in the Will of the transcendental Source, the Ever-Darkness from which both Poles spring.

(5) *The Seven were not yet born from the Web of Light. Darkness alone was Father-Mother, Svabhāvat; and Svabhāvat was in darkness.*

The Seven are the Actors in the Play, the cosmic levels.

The Three
{
1 The Father-Light, Transcendental Self or Root of Self. (*Shānta Ātman*)

2 The Matrix, Transcendental Root of Objectivity or 'Matter'. (*Mūla-prakriti*)

3 Universal Mind or Self (*Mahat Ātman or Mahat-buddhi*)
}

The Four
{
4 Level of individuation; Higher or Pure Mind (*Shuddha Manas*)
5 Level of differentiation; Lower or Impure Mind. (*Ashuddha Manas*)
6 Formative level; Desire Nature. (*Kāma Bhāva*)
7 Elemental Nature; the Physical World. (*Sthūla Jagat*)
}

This arrangement differs somewhat from that given under Stanza I. 4. Here, the Ever-Darkness (*Parabrahman*) is left out because it is the all-containing Absolute and not a 'level', and the division is made, not between unmanifest and manifest, but between divine and human, or universal and individual.

It should be noted that numbers one and two represent the two eternal poles of the one Ultimate Being. Considered purely as such, they too are not levels, but opposite poles of the One. Nevertheless, in manifestation they become modes of experience and, as such, find their place in the enumeration.

But the Seven 'were not yet born' from the web of Light which is the web of interaction between the two Poles, the field of Power from which the whole Cosmos springs into being.

The wording of the verse becomes a little obscure here. The word *Svabhāvat*, the self-becoming, can be applied either to the Transcendental Self seen as the calm pole of the Father-Mother polarity, or to the self-becoming aspect of the Darkness in which the poles, though fused, are still implicitly present. Therefore the verse says 'Darkness alone was Father-Mother', the polar aspect; '(Darkness was also) *Svabhāvat*', the non-dual aspect of the Absolute as incipient becoming; 'and *Svabhāvat* was in darkness', the absolute darkness of non-becoming. What further can remain to be denied?

(6) *These two are the Germ, and the Germ is one. The Universe was still concealed in the Divine Thought and the Divine Bosom....*

These two, Father and Mother, are the Germ or seed of Life, for it is from the union of the two that the universe springs. They differentiate from the One Darkness of the

Self-Becoming and they unite again in the one body of their Son; but as yet the Germ of what will be the Son, the future universe, is still concealed in the Darkness. No manifestation has yet taken place; the Dawn has not yet come.

Here let us pause a moment and ask a question. What is this continual insistence on what has not yet happened, this 'damnable iteration', of what has not yet taken place? The Two are *not* yet manifest, the Ray has *not* yet flashed, the Son is *not* yet born, the Three have *not* yet fallen into the Four, the Seven are *not* yet born. 'Methinks the lady doth protest too much.' Are we not reminded of the unwilling duellist in the *Pickwick Papers* who reiterated to his friend 'Don't inform the neighbours, don't go and tell the police', when those were the very desires of his heart?

The reason is to be found in that subliminal increase in the tension of the Pulsation we have already referred to. It often happens that in those hidden regions of the psyche which are not integrated into the personal consciousness of our waking egos strange forces operate and tensions increase. Dimly we sense something stirring within us, psychic tension and discomfort perhaps, yet we are conscious of nothing definite. Gradually the tension increases as the threshold is approached. Then at last, sometimes with a startling suddenness, the conflicting forces within take form as an image or images of which we become conscious, sometimes even hallucinatorily conscious. Those images that we see in dream and reverie, or that the madman sees in actual hallucination, are the embodiments, the symbols, or the manifestations of the psychic processes which were in conflict in the darkness. They are the projections of those formless psychic states into the bright and shining world of outward manifestation.

So it is in the Darkness of the One. The rhythmic Breath is gradually bringing about an accumulation of energy. Each successive 'breath' increases the emphasis-value of the object pole, and this energy takes form in dream-like structures of Cosmic Desire. Yes, the structures of the Cosmic Seven *are* in being, though as yet that being is 'negative'. They are seven because, as we have already stated, those seven are the only ways in which the Two, and the unity-based tension as a Third, can interact. The reiteration that they are not yet manifest only conceals, as it did in the case of the unwilling duellist, the fact that they already 'are' in the dark Heart of Being, but have not yet gained sufficient energy to cross the zero-point and so to flash forth as an outer world of images or creations.[1]

Here, as always in such realms, words play us false. The Seven do not exist: they are not manifest. Yet, within the Darkness, the forces, tendencies, processes, archetypes, call them what you will—and perhaps the Sanskrit word *samskāra* is as good as any—are taking form (a formless form indeed!) and increasing in energy which will later burst forth as the outer images of Creation. These are what we shall come across in verse four of the next stanza as the 'inner Seven'.[2] They are 'concealed in the Divine Thought and the Divine Bosom', without existence and beyond knowledge, but even in this phrase we see the increasing approach to manifestation. Instead of being simply in the Darkness of the One they are in the Divine 'Thought', that inner Pole which will be the Father or Spirit, the origin of thought, and in the Divine Bosom, that which will be the Mother, the origin of Matter.[3]

The Darkness pulses with creative life: it quivers, as it were, with inner tension. Something must happen to resolve the strain. The Cosmic Dawn is near.

---

[1] One of the Sanskrit words to describe this creation is *kalpanā*, imagination, whence the Day of *Brahmā* or period of manifestation is known as a *kalpa*.

[2] The inner Seven are referred to by H.P.B. in *Transactions of the Blavatsky Lodge*, p. 106, as the 'planes of non-being'. Also in *The Voice of the Silence* (p. 5, 1st edn.) 'Three Halls . . . . will bring thee through three states into the fourth and thence into *the seven worlds*, the worlds of Rest Eternal'. See also the footnote on the italicised words.

[3] Some of the Tantric schools liken this state of undifferentiated duality to the two halves of a grain of gram within the surrounding integument.

G

STANZA THREE

Being the third of seven Stanzas from
The Book of Dzyan

1. *The last vibration of the seventh eternity thrills through infinitude. The Mother swells, expanding from within without, like the bud of a lotus.*

2. *The Vibration sweeps along, touching with its swift wing the whole universe and the germ that dwelleth in darkness, the darkness that breathes over the slumbering waters of life.*

3. *Darkness radiates light, and light drops one solitary ray into the mother-deep. The ray shoots through the virgin egg; the ray causes the eternal egg to thrill and drop the non-eternal germ, which condenses into the world-egg.*

4. *Then the three fall into the four. The radiant essence becomes seven inside, seven outside. The luminous egg, which in itself is three, curdles and spreads in milk-white curds throughout the depths of mother, the root that grows in the depths of the ocean of life.*

5. *The root remains, the light remains, the curds remain, and still Oeaohoo is one.*

6. *The root of life was in every drop of the ocean of immortality, and the ocean was radiant light, which was fire and heat and motion. Darkness vanished and was no more; it disappeared in its own essence, the body of fire and water, or father and mother.*

7. *Behold, O Lanoo! The radiant child of the two, the unparalleled refulgent glory: Bright Space, Son of Dark Space which emerges from the depths of the great dark waters. It is Oeaohoo the younger, the . . . (whom thou knowest now as Kwan-Shai-Yin— Comment). He shines forth as the Sun; he is the blazing Divine Dragon of Wisdom; The One is Four and Four takes to itself Three and the Union produces the Sapta, in whom are the seven which become the Tridasa, the hosts and the multitudes. Behold him lifting the veil and unfurling it from east to west. He shuts out the above and leaves the below to be seen as the great illusion. He marks the places for the shining ones and turns the upper into a shoreless sea of fire, and the one manifested into the great waters.*

8. *Where was the germ and where was now darkness? Where is the spirit of the flame that burns in thy lamp, O Lanoo? The germ is that and that is light, the white brilliant son of the dark hidden father.*

9. *Light is cold flame, and flame is fire, and fire produces heat, which yields water: the water of life in the great mother.*

10. *Father-Mother spin a web whose upper end is fastened to Spirit, the light of the one Darkness, and the lower one to its shadowy end, Matter; and this web is the universe spun out of the two substances made in one, which is Svabhāvat.*

11. *It expands when the breath of fire is upon it, it contracts when the breath of the Mother touches it. Then the sons dissociate and scatter, to return into their Mother's bosom at the end of the 'great day' and re-become one with her. When it is cooling, it becomes radiant, its sons expand and contract through their own selves and hearts; they embrace infinitude.*

12. *Then Svabhāvat sends Fohat to harden the Atoms. Each is a part of the web. Reflecting the 'Self-Existent Lord', like a mirror, each becomes in turn a world.*

THE BIRTH OF MIND

The inner pressure that was steadily increasing in the previous stanzas here bursts out into manifestation. Darkness radiates light.

The unmanifest principles of being separate from their state of primal fusion and give birth to the manifest glory of Universal Mind, the flame of living consciousness that burns in the core of all existent being.

(1) *The last vibration of the seventh eternity thrills through infinitude. The Mother swells, expanding from within without, like the bud of a lotus.*

The moment of the Cosmic Dawn has come, bringing with it that sense of the lifting of the sky from the earth in which the ancients saw the separating of the primal pair, Shiva and Devi, Ouranos and Gaia, the paternal night sky and the maternal earth, after they had united in the darkness of the night. Within that Darkness, whose content the preceding two stanzas have striven by their negations to describe, a separation takes place;[1] the two poles of being are distinguishable, neither fused by the uniting in-tension of the night, nor yet torn apart by the objective extension of full day. One pole is the calm seer, and the other pole is the other half of his being, complementary to him in her latent movement, power and passion. These two poles give rise to a field of relationship in which objective content can be discerned; and in this field the patterns of the Divine Archetypes, previously hidden in latency, will make their first appearance.

The in-turned subjectivity of the night has not yet become the out-turned dual consciousness of full objectivity, but it is in an intermediate state of changing polarities symbolised as dream; and, as in human dreaming, the images of what has been mix inextricably with images of what is to be, the one foreshadowing the other in preparation for the creation of worlds *yathāpūrvam*, as they were before.

[1] This is what Jacob Boehme terms a diremption or forcible separation.

It is as if the poles were only apart in imagination, but not in reality; as if the parents of the universe were dreaming under the influence of the increasing tension towards separation, and, until they can shake off the still surrounding darkness of their own sleep, they will not be really aware of the dawn that is stealing on them.

Nevertheless, all that is happening is not 'merely' imaginary. Under the increasing pull of the tension that is forcing them apart against their mutual and fundamental attraction, 'the Mother swells'. The pressure of latent inner content yearns to be exteriorised—a content which will come to manifestation in the body of the Son—just as the lotus bud expands to escape the pressure in its heart.

This swelling, which is part of the inherent life cycle of the Mother, may be compared with the preliminary changes which take place in the uterus and prepare it for fertilisation. It is the arousing of the unfertilised Mother, the opening of her 'heart' (II. 4) to the fertilising 'Ray'.

The seven Eternities that we met in the first verse of the Stanzas have come to an end; their vibrations are the beatings of the cosmic heart, and with the last vibration a thrill goes through the darkness, marking the awakening of movement within that which is still utterly calm. This thrill is the *Ānanda-Lahari* or wave of bliss, the ripple of the Waters of Creation. From one point of view we might say that this thrill is the last increment of energy which surcharges and causes to quiver all the Divine Archetypes hidden within the Darkness; but such a description would be inadequate, for the energy is not something separate from the Archetypes but is their very being. It would be truer to say that the Archetypal structures in the Darkness have come so close together that their increased energy can no longer be borne. No further increase can take place; what will happen now?

What do we do ourselves when psychic structures in our hearts come into such close relationship or conflict that they manifest an energy too great for us to bear? We project them 'outside' ourselves in images. When passion grows resistless in our hearts we body it forth in images of beautiful women that dance before our mental eyes. So with hunger or the surging waves of anger; when they grow intense, images of tempting dishes or of hateful enemies lure the energy outside and draw us from ourselves. The images spring from our hearts, glow with our life, the life they have drawn from us. We have projected them 'outside' ourselves, and now we lose ourselves in their pursuit. The world? They are the world; there is no other. All that we see around us is the tissue of our dreams. The world is psychic through and through. We have constructed it and filled it with our life, and now we rush forth to battle or to pleasure. Like Cuchulain, bewitched upon the Irish shore, we battle with the waves. The magic web we wove has wrapped us round, and we go forth, forgetting all, questing for Trojan Helen, seeking food, slaying our hateful foes.

Thus it is with the Cosmic Heart. The tension has become so great that it can no longer be contained but must burst forth. The Divine Archetypes are therefore projected to draw the psychic Life-energy after them. No more can they be contained within the Darkness, and so they burst forth as Images or Creations, seeming, because of their objectivity, to be 'outside' the One, though in truth nothing is outside It, for there is naught but It anywhere. All are within the One, and all life is Its own Life—there is no other. This must be borne in mind, for in future we shall speak of the creation as outside the One, since it would be too cumbersome always to be qualifying our words. But the 'outside' is only in seeming. The Image or Creation has acquired sufficient energy to proclaim its independence, or to put it in another way, its energy can only be borne if it is projected into the independence of externality. It lives in and for itself, forgetting the One whose Life it draws upon. This is *called* being outside the One. Did not the Pythagorean Monad after creation retire once more into the darkness? Moreover, we shall see this same process taking place again and again on the different levels of the

universe as the wave of creation descends further and further
into the Day.

The use of hunger, anger, and what-not, to illustrate the
process of world projection does not mean that the world
process is to be regarded as a fit of cosmic spleen. It is true that
just such an illustration as we have given occurs in the form of
the three symbolic figures of Desire, Hatred and Stupidity that
are found at the hub of Buddhist pictures of the Wheel of Life,
and that such illustrations would be welcomed by the 'cosmic
blunder' type of philosophy (that of Schopenhauer, for example). But images of truth and beauty can also be and are
projected, so that we can as well consider the universe a
cosmic poem, as a cosmic battle (*Bhagavad Gītā*), a cosmic
symphony, as a cosmic meal (*Upanishads*), a cosmic dance
(*Natarāja Shiva*) and as a cosmic pilgrimage.

All such descriptions are attempts at evaluation, with which
we are not at the moment concerned. We have therefore
chosen as illustration those psychic contents the projection of
which is apt to be most vivid. Actually the whole content of
the universe, however we may evaluate it with our sets of
categories, is a projected content; and the energy that projects
it is the one energy that the Buddhists call 'Thirst' (*Trishna*),
the Rig Veda 'Desire' (*Kāma*),[1] and Heracleitus 'Ever-Living
Fire'. 'This world order, the same for all beings, neither any of the
Gods hath made nor any man; but it always was, is, and shall be,
ever-living Fire, kindled in measure and quenched in measure.'

(2) *The Vibration sweeps along, touching with its swift wing the
whole universe and the germ that dwelleth in darkness, the darkness
that breathes over the slumbering waters of life.*

The last vibration of the preceding seven eternities is the
first of the next, and its thrill sweeps through the whole of
being, rippling the waters of life and touching 'the germ that
dwelleth in darkness'.

---

[1] *Rig Veda*, X. 129: 'Thereafter rose Desire in the beginning, Desire, the primal seed
and germ of Mind.'

The verse reminds us that the Darkness is not dead or inert, for it 'breathes over the slumbering waters of life'. The Germ which dwells within it is thus its power to manifest its self-nature; it is the dormant seed which will awaken to active growth when nurtured by the warmth and moisture of the cosmic Spring.

Let us not be misled by the concrete nature of the symbols. The Germ is not a 'thing', for no thing exists in the Darkness. It is the abstract potentiality in Non-Being of expressing itself in Being. It is this potentiality which is imaged as being stirred into activity by those incomprehensible rhythmic changes which characterise all life—the beating wings of the Swan of Time (*Kāla-Hamsa*).

Not even abstract symbols, however, can compass the awe-inspiring darkness of the Cosmic Night. Within that unified Being there is no explicit duality by which the presence of light, as the opposite term to darkness, may be inferred. We are creatures of duality, and the symbols we have at our disposal are necessarily limited to the realm of created things. What words can adequately express the being of that 'from which the mind turns back together with the power of speech'? Only when within that darkness the first stirrings of duality suggest themselves, and one term of the darkness is perceived to be the darkness of the 'sea', can we infer the coming of the light; and then, like all watchers for the dawn, we discover the first light more by our awareness of what we can see of objects than by our perception of the light itself.

The Darkness breathes over the slumbering Waters—and we become aware of an above and a below; directions have emerged from an entirely unorganised and undimensioned space. Our thoughts leap ahead of the verse and we find the third term already pressing to be recognised as the space between sky and sea, the lateral space of the horizon over which the coming of the sun is anticipated. The whole scene is poignant with the promise of a new birth, just as the swelling of the lotus bud of the Mother foretells both the light and warmth of the environment in which it will open and the colour of its inner nature which will be its response to the light. Such is the pressure of our thoughts and such too is the pressure within the darkness of the Dawn, urging to the fulfilment of the relationship which we can depict as the now inevitable unrolling of the series of numbers from the two to the infinity.

The Darkness breathes over the slumbering Waters, and we are reminded of the verse in Genesis, 'And Darkness was upon the face of the Deep'.[1] In the Hermetic Corpus the same theme occurs: 'There was darkness in the deep and water without form and there was a subtle breath, intelligent, which permeated the things in Chaos with divine power. Then when all was yet undistinguished and unwrought there was shed forth holy light and the elements came into being'.[2] Again, in the famous Vedic Creation hymn included in the Hindu *sandhya* ritual, Darkness and waters are the symbols of the primal pair: 'From That arose the primal darkness; from That arose the waters of the ocean'.[3] In the Zohar, Darkness is called the strongest fire of the many different coloured (*i.e.* manifest) fires—the Heracleitean Fire in its condition of ultimate un-knowability—and the same text speaks of a nucleus, which is the 'germ' of our verse, that is of no colour at all. This absence of colour is found in the Upanishads: 'The One who himself without colour, by the manifold application of his power distributes many colours in his hidden purposes'.[4] These citations have been included, not because they make the position very much clearer for the average reader, who may perhaps find them altogether too full of 'darkness', but because they show the universality of the doctrine which the Stanzas are setting forth.

(3) *Darkness radiates light, and light drops one solitary ray into the mother-deep. The ray shoots through the virgin egg; the ray*

---

[1] Cf. *Transactions of the Blavatsky Lodge*, p. 35.
[2] *Hermetic Corpus*, III. 1b (Walter Scott)
[3] *Rig Veda*, X. 190. 1. *Tato rātrya jāyata tataḥ samudro arṇavaḥ.*
[4] *Śvetāśvatara Upanishad*, IV. 1.

causes the eternal egg to thrill and drop the non-eternal germ, which condenses into the world-egg.

In the last verse we became aware of an Above and a Below. A separation has taken place, though there can be no absolute separation, for the two are always one being, held together by the unity of their transcendent Source. Certain aspects of the Unity are accentuated and made to appear as parts, just as we may variously colour the segments of a circle without affecting its wholeness. The breathing Darkness is one aspect of the whole and the waters that slumber is the other, the maternal aspect, the Eternal Parent that, in the first stanza, had slumbered for seven eternities.

Between these two a tension is generated, for their essential unity demands that they shall be reunited. The same tension which caused the swelling of the Mother produces the concentration of energy which is the Father, and 'Darkness radiates Light'.

The flash of the fecundating ray of light marks the moment when the tension between the two poles of being suddenly reverses its direction. The remnants of the in-tension of the Night lag behind the reversing tendencies that are already apparent in the twilight (like the magnetic hysteresis in an iron bar) and are overcome by the rapidly mounting extensive forces of the Day. This sudden collapse of the opposing force gives rise to the initial spark that leaps the gap between subject and object, as lightning leaps from sky to earth, while the accompanying thunder voices the First Logos, the Om, the source of all sound and all order.

Before the ray leaps, at the very moment of their reversal of polarity, the whole infinity of power, the tension between the light and the dark principles within the Darkness, and all the content of the ideal[1] structures of the twilight are, as it were,

---

[1] These inner structures are only termed 'ideal' for want of a better term, and to emphasise that they bear *the same sort of relation* to the manifested structures of the universe that our own inner ideal world bears to the world of outer perception. The word is symbolic and must by no means be taken as equating them with what we know as ideas.

concentrated in the zero point of the dawn. They are in the state which Hindu thought terms *ghanibhūta* or concentrated and we are also reminded of what the Kashmir Shaiva school refers to as the *Bindu* or point-like state of *Shakti* ready to create. The whole content of Reality has become infinitely condensed, has disappeared into the zero point between positive and negative being. It is 'nowhere',[1] but with the vanishing of both extension and intension its energy has become infinite, the unthinkably great energy that will maintain the universe in movement, yet being but 'one portion of itself'.[2]

The disappearance of all content at the zero point of Dawn releases this immense energy, an energy which may be said, not so much to fill space, as to create or even to be Space.[3] It is this that in its final stages is now referred to as nuclear energy; energy locked up in material forms.

This initial flashing forth of energy is on a level far above that of physical nature; but it is the type that foreshadows the way in which each subsequent level of being will separate from the one above it, from the Absolute Darkness down to this physical world; between each level lies a similar neutral point. Some sort of analogy may be found in the approach to each other of the ends (of dissimilar polarity) of bar magnets. When they touch, the tension between them increases to a maximum, but the field depending on their being apart disappears. The tracing back of the degradation of energy, as described by the so-called second law of Thermo-dynamics, has led to the similar concept of the whole physical universe collected at a given time in the past into a single point of infinite energy.

The dropping of the ray is the Father's fertilising act that shoots through the virgin egg; yet, besides this, the ray is the Father himself whose quickening presence within the Eternal Egg causes it to thrill with the first tremors of independent life,

[1] Compare the vanishing of the hyperbola at the co-ordinates O.O discussed in Stanza I. 2, p. 455
[2] *Bhagavad Gītā*, X. 42.
[3] 'Space' does not here mean merely the space of visual perception but the psychic 'spaces' of the various higher levels as well.

the freedom which is the very nature of the Father. The two poles of the Darkness re-unite, not now in the massively fused condition of the Cosmic Night, but as complementary aspects of being in manifestation. It was in this act that the ancients saw the death of the Father, the widowing of the Mother, and the birth of the Son who is his own Father. This graded transition from the Dark Father to the Father-Light and then to the Son sometimes gives rise to difficulties in distinguishing between them.

There are similar difficulties in distinguishing between Mother and Daughter. At quite what point do the Waters of the Matrix become the Waters of manifestation? When does the unmanifest Mother pole of the Darkness become the Daughter or feminine aspect of Universal Mind? If the effulgency of the 'Son' is not distinguished from the effulgency of the 'Father', then either the Father lusts after his Daughter, as in the Hindu myth of *Prajāpati*, or, with similar implications, the Son castrates his Father at the instigation of the Mother, as in the Greek myth of Ouranos and Kronos.

The light of consciousness is always the Father-Light, and the content of consciousness is always the Matrix, but there are various degrees in the line of descent from unmanifest principles to manifest worlds. These are symbolised as varying types of relationship between the different generations of the Cosmic family. To apply the yardstick of conventional morality to the relationships of cosmic principles is as silly as it would be to apply it to animals or to chemical reactions. Nevertheless, even conventional morals reflect truths. We are dealing with living, growing principles, and when a 'daughter' grows old enough to become attractive to her 'father' it is high time she was pushed out to start the next generation. But a living process is always on the move and its stages are not easily classified. We must not, as elders always do, express surprise at the way children outgrow the clothes we have made for them.

There are, as it were, three generations of cosmic levels. The first is the Father-Mother duality. The second is the Universal Mind, the Son-Daughter, and the third is the latter's child, the outer universe of form. These three generations are stages i n the creative process towards manifestation and correspond to the three acts of the Ray distinguished by the verse. The Ray drops into the Mother-deep. The Ray shoots through the Virgin Egg. The Ray causes the Eternal Egg to thrill and drop the non-eternal germ.

These three acts are the modifications of the one outbreath of the Darkness. They are three creative Logoi (utterances),[1] outpourings, or waves of life. They correspond to the threefold divisions of the OM into A, U, M, or the threefold division of OEAOHOO into the Oi-Ha-Hou (IV. 4). Each moment of the one creative breath may be said either to partake of, or to bring into being, the qualities of one of the three upper cosmic principles, Father, Mother, and Son. Each act of the male Ray also corresponds to distinct modes of its feminine counterpart, the different forms of 'egg'.

Of the first cause, the dynamism of the three Logoi, and so of the whole universe, little more need be or can be said than what Jacob Boehme wrote, that a Will 'arises in the nothing to introduce the nothing into something, that the will might find, feel, and behold itself . . . and its seeking is a desire, and its finding is the essence of the desire wherein the will finds itself.'[2]

The first act of the creative Will, the First Logos 'BE' (more strictly 'BECOME'), transforms non-being into being. It is the first explosion of energy, the effulgent Ray that drops into the mother-deep. It unites the Selfhood of the Father-Light with the Being of the Matrix and results in the divine Self-affirmation 'I AM', with its objective complement 'THAT IS'.

We must not allow the symbols to mislead us into thinking of the 'Ray' as a beam of light. Its solitariness lies in its unitary and uncompounded nature and not in dimensional form. It is

---

[1] Cf. the three *Vyāhriti* or utterances which precede the repetition of the *Gāyatri* mantra, the *bharga* of which represents just this creative power.

[2] *Signatura Rerum*, Jacob Boehme, II. 8 & 9.

'essentially' single and alone; it cannot mix with anything, nor can it lose its identity. It is the oneness of the Father complementing the multiplicity of the Mother. Later, under Stanza IV. 5 we shall meet it again as the 'effulgency of light', for it is the effulgency of consciousness, the creative outpouring which pervades and enlivens the infinite space of potentiality which is the 'mother-deep'.

The singleness of the Ray has a limiting effect on the infinite potentialities of the Matrix. It is the root of rational order and demarcation so that its presence within the Matrix is what defines and limits the extent of the creation. Virgin before she is pierced, she thrills to the awakening within her of the union of knower and known by the third term of knowing. Subjectivity and Objectivity are lifeless terms without relationship; 'the light of a whole life dies when love is done'. The divine Eros has thrust them apart in order to bring them together again in integral self-knowledge. These two are the Fire and Water of our stanza, complementary yet antagonistic elements. They both attract and repel each other, for the love that relates them manifests as a battle as well as a uniting.

The Egg thus refers to the fertilised Mother within whose infinite possibility the presence of the Ray delimits an enclosed area of operation or 'egg'. It is in fact the maternal or content aspect of Universal Mind; the 'Mother' has become the 'Daughter'. But the formation of the egg is not only due to the action of the Ray. The direct outbreathing of the Father, bringing things into being and urging the universe to manifestation, is contained or held back by the Mother, for in her desire to be known she winds herself about the Light, devours it and combines with it, refusing to let it descend. This is why the Matrix is both the womb of birth and the womb of death, because forms can only be separated from her by the constant pressure of life, a pressure which bursts out in waves or pulsations each time the increasing flow of energy overcomes the 'reluctance' of the womb to let it go. Then, when the life flow withdraws or lessens, the form born of the creative wave falls back again into non-being. This is the divine aspect of Death, the process of change or transformation which breaks up forms in order that they may be replaced by new ones; it is the source of all progress, the basis of all hope.

The restriction of the outflowing energy produces an increase of inner pressure. It may be likened to the increase in psychic pressure or 'tension' produced in a man when he restricts the outflow of his energies. This increase of potential is equivalent to the energy of the Second Logos, the second stage of the outflow.

The limitation of the area of operation effects the realisation of the unmanifest concept of unity. 'I AM' is now expressed as 'I AM ONE'. This 'One' demands its complement in multiplicity and the Second Logos 'MAY I BE MANY' is, as it were, a corollary to the affirmation of unity; it is an immediate consequence.

On the objective side, the infinite potentiality of the Matrix has been exchanged for the limitation of number. 'THAT IS' has been exchanged for 'THEY ARE'. The Ray causes the Eternal Egg to thrill, the breath of life ripples the undifferentiated waters of the Mother, and the surface is covered with a myriad facets in each of which the Sun of consciousness is reflected.

This Sun of Divine Mind is universal in that its subjectivity is diffused throughout its being. There is no emphasis of attention on some particular aspects of its contents and not on others; but there is a simultaneity of ideal or archetypal images, known variously as gods or angels by the different religious traditions. With the increased energy of the Second Logos the facets or points of reflected light are caused to shine more brightly and the subjective pole is carried into identification with them. The movement is akin to what happens in ourselves when we are urged by forces arising from the inner darkness of our psyches to move from a detached contemplation of intellectual images to the act of choice by which we become identified with a particular view. The difference between the universal and the individual is that the former can support all the viewpoints simultaneously.[1]

There is only one transcendent Subject, yet all these individualised points of reflected Light feel themselves to partake of that subjectivity. Divine Mind's affirmatory utterance 'I AM' is therefore exchanged for 'WE ARE', for each point is now aware of its location in relation to the others, just as our choice of one particular viewpoint defines our position with regard to the viewpoints we reject. The points are individualised, but still held together by the unity of Mind. Not until they are urged by another increment of energy, the Third Logos, will Mind turn outwards dissociating the points and projecting its ideal content into an external world of productive movement. Each point of subjective awareness must assert its 'I am separate', and each project that sense of separateness on to its environment, so that they are all separated from each other and separated from the content of their experience. Thus, the non-eternal Germ drops out.

The non-eternal Germ is the living nucleus of self-related consciousness which, rooted in the waters of the Matrix, will become the temporal universe. It is the seed of living awareness rooted in every differentiated point within the potentiality of form. It lives with the life of both its parents, of the very Darkness itself. Because it lives it grows, and through its growth potentiality is developed into actuality. It is the growing point of the evolutionary movement which gives rise to all progressive movement, to man's flesh, to his brain tissue, to his need to produce artifacts, and finally to the urge to transcend his corporeal limitations. But all this is a process in time, and, like all process, has a beginning and an ending.

It is this process of growth, this transition from potentiality to actuality, from subtle to gross, that constitutes the condensation of the Eternal Egg into the World Egg through the action of the non-eternal root of life or Germ.

The Timeless Darkness has breathed out into metaphysical

[1] Cf. *Bhagavad Gītā*, IX. 5 where Krishna describes himself in his highest manifestation as 'the support of beings, yet not rooted in beings, my Self their bringer forth'.

space its 'Breath' or 'Sound' which is the expression of its self-nature. Our habits of thinking and the linear medium in which we express our thoughts will force a temporal interpretation on our words and make those things which are prior and posterior in eternal values appear to be antecedent and subsequent temporal events. Nevertheless, paradoxical though it may seem, the out-breathing of the Darkness is not in time, not in the time we know as a psychic experience. It is as if the universe that is to be, is breathed out as an extended line of limited possibility—the limitation that unity imposes upon infinity. It is neither in Timelessness nor in Time but in the simultaneity of Eternity, an Eternity in which no event has a 'when', it is 'always' and 'now'. In the darkness of non-existence there cannot be one occasion when the universe is created and another occasion in which it is withdrawn, for the creation and the withdrawal are simultaneous in the eternal present. This is so because Time as a psychic experience demands the presence of an experiencing subject fundamentally related to the content of its experience. Universal Mind is the first experiencing Subject of the Cosmos, the flame of integrated consciousness and being which knows the present moment. Prior to this nothing exists, neither time nor motion nor objective phenomena; nothing is manifest, it has no experiential reference.

It is necessary to stress that when we say existence is dependent upon an experiencing subject, we do not mean a human observer. Every integration of energy, every atom or 'event' occurring in the field of manifest being is organised around an experiencing nucleus. Its intelligence may be minimal, but awareness of existence shines in the atoms of every grade of manifestation.

Divine Mind is thus the Subject which experiences simultaneously the total being of the universe existing in time. It is not a mere aggregate of the total individualised points of conscious being, but the all-pervasive light with which these points shine. This Universal Mind or Son of the Divine parents is

H

'eternal' in the sense that it lasts throughout the 'Seven Eternities' of the Cosmic Day. It is not eternal in the sense of the timeless duration of the Darkness but eternal in infinitely extended time. It is an integration of conscious modes, but no integration, no aggregate can be timeless; the Eternal Egg therefore bears within it the seed of non-eternity, the events which take place in time. Divine Mind is the Eternal Egg of our verse, and the points are the individualisations in and through which the 'non-eternal' Germ grows and condenses into the World-Egg.

The Universal Mind in itself remains unchanged during all the cyclic changes of the manifest worlds which it brings to existence. Within it lies the ever-present simultaneity of all the forms that we experience here as an ordered procession of events. Yet these events are also 'within' Divine Mind. They exist within it, and the time in which we experience them is its time. When at the end of the long ages of manifestation the creative Will of the Darkness withdraws into itself, then the Father-Mother polarity collapses, the tension which brought Mind into manifestation disappears, and the bright out-looking consciousness retires into the Darkness from which it came forth.

It is this experiencing Subject or Person of the universe which, like so many Kings, Gods and Hunter-heroes of myth, rushes through the chaotic jungles of outer space in pursuit of the Virgin Daughter of the great Mother. For it is in pursuit of the realisation of the unmanifest bliss of the darkness that the divine hunter (Orion=Rudra-Shiva=*Kāla Purusha*) speeds along the lineal track of the Breath, the track of Eros Protogonos, the 'first-born' love relationship between the Father and the Mother of all things.

And so that flaming being rushes ever onwards along the immaterial line of eternal possibility. Its flame is the present moment and its movement is Time. Its fuel is potential being and its ash the accomplished past—a trail of unchanging patterns in memory. Before it lies limited possibility, neither absolutely determined nor absolutely free, a determined track within whose unformed potentiality lies the opportunity for change and growth, an opportunity which must be seized here and now in the moment of present experience if we, the bearers of the brightest sparks of Mind, are to give expression to the freedom which is man's birthright.

And what of the Goddess? Satī dies in the fire and is reborn as Pārvatī to re-become the wife of Shiva, as it were in the next generation. Chased by Minos the Cretan Britomartis leaps from the cliff and is caught in the nets of fishermen—the world net in the sea of existence. The Maiden (*kore*) is carried off to the underworld. These myths have as many meanings as they have versions, but in this context they refer to the outrush of divine desire, seeking, but never achieving, fulfilment in out-turned experience. The modesty of reluctant goddesses is only a symbolic way of showing that the attractive thing, in search of which the whole universe is running, can never be caught in Time. It clothes itself in form; we catch the form but not the thing, and even the form Time takes away from us. Always the thing itself eludes us, and must elude us so long as we search for it in externality, for it is indeed through us and in us that the divine Hunter continues his endless chase. His prey has plunged into the sea of existence and he too has leapt after it, entered it, and united with it. And now he and the projected image have become one; his eyes look out from her form. The *Purusha* in the pupil of the eye has become one with its blackness, the lover has become one with his black-eyed gazelle. The 'Father' has lusted after his 'Daughter' and the 'Son' has committed incest with his 'Mother'. The Son sees, not now with the light of his own vision, but with the borrowed light of the sun. The very act of incestuous union with the maternal source of form has 'blinded' the Wisdom Eye that needed no other light than its own.

Thus consciousness has descended a further stage in the generations of the cosmic family. Like a praying mantis, the female has devoured the male and the World Mother gives birth to a multitude of eggs in each of which the consciousness of the one Father is shining. He can go no further, for he is locked in the form he was pursuing. Yet he still seems to see that form beyond him in externality, for the form which now surrounds each individualised point in the light still seems to be the desired object. Each sees the attraction of the prey or the threat of the hunter in the other. They meet, but cannot blend. There can be no further generation downwards, and life must now flow along the horizontal path of Time.

(4) *Then the three fall into the four. The radiant essence becomes seven inside, seven outside. The luminous egg, which in itself is three, curdles and spreads in milk-white curds throughout the depths of mother, the root that grows in the depths of the ocean of life.*

The Ray drops, the Germ drops, and the Three fall. Spirit descends into Matter. From time immemorial, man, crawling at the bottom of his airy environment, has felt the gravitational pull of the earth to represent the bonds of materiality. The Mother, clutching her children to her nourishing bosom, restrains them against the demands of the free Spirit, the Father, who calls his offspring to the greater freedom of manhood through the initiatory rites of the second birth.

To picture the struggle for spiritual ascent as a struggle against the pull of gravity is permissible; and it is this symbolic truth that helps to throw a glamour of magic fascination over stories of yogis who float above the ground during their meditations. Such stories are not necessarily untrue in factual detail, but they are usually over-valued, for they imply, not spiritual ascendency over physical ties, but only a development of 'mediumistic' psychic powers. The physical body is of the same order as the earth to which it is held by gravity. The Spirit is of a different order altogether; it is not held by any physical force, but by the idea of physicality with which it has associated itself. It is this same psychic content which, projected into the world, drives men into the search for freedom in such activities as flying or space travel where the restricted movements of space-time are accepted in exchange for the ultimate freedom of the Spirit.

Again, the whole idea of outwardness and inwardness contains a snare for the unwary student of the inner life. We start by assuming that outwardness is synonymous with outside the body, until we realise that, though we look through the sense organs from 'within', even the inside of the body is 'outward' to us; nor is there any outlet to be found in any of the other physical directions. In speech we have to use these terms, but they are symbolical of directions that take us into a different order of being. The point is perhaps a rather obvious one, but it is amazing how often, though we may have an intellectual appreciation of the difference, we do in fact confuse spatial with spiritual directions.

Fundamentally these confusions of thought derive from our uncertain loyalties. Is our allegiance to the Transcendent Spirit —'my race is of heaven alone'—or to the material reality— 'I am a child of earth'? In our path towards wholeness we often find ourselves challenged by symbols which reflect this uncertainty by demanding a reconciliation between threeness and fourness, the three representing the Spiritual and the four the Material aspects of the psyche.

Yet perhaps these uncertainties in ourselves reflect deeper questions on which we have not yet touched. If the division in loyalty was between two terms of a simple duality, 'Spirit' and 'Matter', then the choice between the two should not be so very difficult, but the experience of all who have faced the problem is that it is one of extreme difficulty. As we are now perhaps in a position to understand, if our concern is with finding the true nature of our own being, we must discover not merely the duality between our conscious selves and the psycho-physical structures with which they are identified, but also the duality within our very selfhood which makes us experiencing subjects as opposed to mere moments in the all-pervasive light.

For this reason it is inadequate to describe our essential being only in terms of the stainless unattached consciousness of the Father. The path to wholeness must be expressed in terms of the whole, and this includes both Father and Mother and also their relationship; Being, Consciousness and Bliss (*Sat, Chit, Ānanda*). The Mother has therefore to be found not merely as a deceitful illusion but as the real source of that desired object in whose pursuit consciousness has been led out into identification with form. She is not only the devouring beast of the dark jungles of space, the Lion of Durga, the Bear of Artemis, she who devours the light, but she is also Sophia and Prajñā, the divine Wisdom, the content aspect of the Darkness, that which is known. She is the beloved who wraps herself around her lover; but here the lover sleeps, sleeps with his eyes open, and so sees only his beloved's illusory form and not herself. We are the sleepers in the cave, and, could we but wake, we would find ourselves already in her embrace.

It is this aspect of the inner life which has found expression in the tradition that the great Advaita Vedāntin, Śankarāchārya, for all his world transcending knowledge, did not attain liberation until he had composed his famous hymns in praise of the Mother-Goddess, Annapūrnā.

This double aspect of the duality underlying phenomena appears in the later verses of the stanza as a quaternity of powers between which the web of the universe is woven.

The 'Three' of the verse are the three transcendent terms, Source, Father and Mother, integrated as an experiencing Self in Universal Mind, the Person of the Universe, the Knower who both knows and has knowledge. This trinity of conscious modes, acting and interacting in unison, constitutes the principle of individualised consciousness, the core of all experiencing beings and the type of the self-related awareness that is ours. 'The enjoyer, the object of enjoyment, and the universal Actuator, . . . This is the threefold Brahma.'[1]

At this stage, however, and in Universal Mind itself as a principle, there is no clear demarcation between universal

[1] *Śvetāśvatara Upanishad*, I. 12.

consciousness and universal content. The creative urge demands that the content, which is ultimately the content of the ever unmanifest Darkness, shall be clarified and made distinct by the process of projection into externality. It will appear to be external to or over-against the triune integration of Mind.

The characteristic modes in which the content can be projected are governed by the principles which are already explicitly standing behind the manifestation. These are four: Father, Mother, their relationship, and now the Son himself, the bright image of the Darkness. These determine the four major modes in which inner content is objectified.

The unmanifest Father-Mother duality now appears as a manifest duality between the mental triad and the projected content; the former becoming predominantly subjective and the latter, the field of objective phenomena. From the relationship between the pair springs manifest power.

The four modes of objectivity may be roughly classified as follows: From predominance of the Father-pole arises individuality, the separateness of the elements which appear in the objective field. From predominance of the Mother arises differentiation between the elements and also their multiplicity. The Father-Mother relationship appears as the inter-relatedness of all phenomena, the so-called causal nexus between them. And from the Son's independent being arises the sense of the external reality of phenomena.

This radiant, because manifest, essence of all sentience and all life now becomes 'Seven inside, Seven outside' from the interplay of its three modes of subjectively related awareness and four modes of projected objectivity of content. The inner seven are the worlds or levels of the divine Archetypes, the living imaginal principles which precede the outer seven or worlds of form. Wherever we turn, by whatever faculty of sense we experience the manifest world, or by whatever function of our psychic being we handle that experience, our whole 'inner' and 'outer' environment is made up of the interplay of the Three and the Four.

Fourness now becomes synonymous with outwardness and manifestation, what we know as the outer worlds of objective reality or sensible form. There are direct correspondences detween these four characteristic modes of objectivity and the four lower cosmic levels: the levels of individuation and differentiation, the formative level of desire-motivated relationship, and the physical level of (relatively) shared continuity of objective reference.

On the human scale these also correspond to the Individual Self or Higher Mind, the Personal Self or Sense Mind, the plastic or formative being sometimes referred to as the Desire nature and sometimes as the Astral body, and the Physical body or vehicle of sensation.

The Four are aspects or modes of outlook of Universal Mind which now looks out squarely through the windows of the Four-square Heavenly Jerusalem, producing a sense of direction and organisation in what was disorganised and random space. Whereas prior to this there was only an above and a below, there is now also an inside and an outside to the square container. 'That which is below is like unto that which is above' says the Emerald Tablet, and Solomon Trismosin[1] echoes 'All that is without thee also is within'.

These are the four major modes in which what is 'inner' and unmanifest can be projected as 'outer' and manifest; and in fact four gateways through which flow the organising forces of the creative Mind. They are the modes of the four-faced *Brahmā*, the Creator, who by meditation on what is within discovers the patterns of what is to be created without. '*Svayambhu* the Self-existent one', says the *Kaṭhopanishad*, 'pierced the openings outward, therefore one looks outward.'[2]

These four are at the same time both inner determinant patterns and the outer projections of those patterns. Within is the in-turned consciousness and its total content, the 'seven inside'. Without is the out-turned consciousness and its

---

[1] Putative author of the Alchemical text, *Splendor Solis*.
[2] *Kaṭhopanishad*, IV. 1.

projected content, the 'seven outside'. The Three have fallen
into the Four, and the Radiant Essence has become patterned
'without' in accordance with the determinants 'within'. It is
as if fourteen, not only seven, levels had come into being, but
the outer seven with all their apparent solidity are in fact but
projected images of their inner archetypes. No matter how
'real' outer objects appear to be, nor how significant seems the
waking experience, they are as unreal as shadows when contrasted with the real being of Universal Mind. Nor does that
inner content disappear when the universe awakes to its four-
faced outwardness and the content is projected, any more than
the contents of our dreams and the determining factors of our
psyches disappear when we are awake. Our inner life may be
forgotten under the pressure of out-turned activity, but it is
never very far away, for we return to it each night and in
every drowsy moment; fantasy and imagination are its cousins,
and the motivations of our every action arise in part or in whole
from these inner states of the psyche, states of whose being we
are seldom aware.

The non-eternal germ of the previous verse has been
dropped, the egg is laid, but not until verse seven does the
sun rise or the solar cock break the shell. The cosmic dream
continues, and just as in our dreams forms are plastic and can
emerge and become distinct from a matrix of thoughts, so the
embryonic universe is in a plastic gestatory state. Through this
state the inner pressure of life and the patterning of thought
find their common actualisation in manifestation, and thereby
undirected power is enformed within the limiting structures
of ideas.

Within the square are generated the inner motivations of
the cosmic Son as he engages in his day's activities. These
inner thoughts are the archetypes of all future creation, and
from these (seven) types of divine thought derive the (seven)
levels of manifest being.

Before we can go any further we must try to gain some idea
of the nature of the Universal Mind, for it is on that nature

that the whole manifested universe depends. Known in some traditions as *anima mundi*, the Soul of the World, it is the radiant, over-arching Sky, within whose embrace are sun, moon and stars, as well as this lower earth with all the clouds that hide the heavenly luminaries from our vision. So great and wonderful is its nature that many have taken it to be the supreme God, and, in proportion as we are able to gain some understanding of it, so are we able to understand all that is 'above' as well as all that is 'below' its radiant being.

In the Rig Veda it is symbolised as *Varuna*, and we read how it is the might of *Varuna* which 'sustains erect the Tree's stem in the baseless region, the Tree whose root is high above and whose rays stream ever downward.'[1] He, the 'Dweller at the source of the River of life, surrounded by his Seven Sisters'[2] supports 'the three earths and the three heavens'[3] and lets 'the great Cask, opening downward, flow through the heaven and earth and air's mid region',[4] a phrase which refers not primarily to the fall of rain from the sky as supposed by some scholars, but to that projection, that overflowing into outwardness, that constitutes the fall of the Three into the Four. *Varuna* it is who, having 'encompassed the Night' (*i.e.* having absorbed its energies within himself) 'established the Morns with magic art',[5] the *māyā* or illusion-projecting art of which he is the master and, having 'wrapped these regions as a robe',[6] himself firm-seated, 'rules the Seven as King'.

We may symbolise this Universal Mind, this Great Self, as a great sphere of Light, holding within itself as its content the archetypal images of all the worlds to be, images which float in that Light as jellyfish within a sea. Its great characteristic is its unitary nature. The sphere of Light, referred to in old symbols as the *Brahmāṇḍa* or Brāhmic Egg, is, as it were,

---

[1] *Rig Veda*, I. 24. 7.
[2] *Rig Veda*, VIII. 41. 2.
[3] *ibid.*, VII. 87. 5.
[4] *ibid.*, V. 85. 3.
[5] *ibid.*, VIII. 41. 3.
[6] *ibid.*, VIII. 41. 7 & 9.

conscious all over at once; and each of its archetypal images, though ideally distinct from others, yet pervades the whole. Description is impossible, though it was attempted in the eleventh chapter of the *Bhagavad Gītā* in mythological symbols, and in philosophical ones by Plotinus.

'Let us then form a mental image of this Cosmos with each of its parts remaining what it is, and yet interpenetrating one another, imagining them all together into one as much as we possibly can . . . in fine, as though all things could be seen in it. Let there, then, be in the soul some semblance of a sphere of Light (transparent), having all things in it whether moving or still. . . .

'And holding this sphere in the mind, conceive in thyself another sphere, removing from it all idea of mass; take from it also the idea of space and the phantom of matter in thy mind; and do not try to imagine another sphere merely less in bulk (*i.e.* more attenuated) than the former.

'Then invoking God who hath made that true sphere of which thou holdest the phantom in thy mind, pray that He may come. And may he come with his own cosmos,[1] with all the gods (the Divine Powers) therein. He being one and all, and each one all, united into one, yet different in their powers, and yet, in that one (power) of multitude all one, . . . (and) they are all together, yet each again apart in some kind of unextended state, possessing no form perceptible to sense. . . . Nay, so vast is that divine world order that even its "parts" are infinite.'[2]

Many people are apt to think that the emergence of a universe is an event similar to the growth of a nebula of stars seen through a powerful telescope, and that a cosmogony is a similarly objective account; but, whether we speak of the emergence of worlds or the emergence of men, the knowledge of their being is to be found within our own being and nowhere else at all.

[1] The Universal Mind.
[2] Plotinus, V. vii. 9. on the Intellectual Beauty. G. R. S. Mead's translation in *Thrice Greatest Hermes.*

We must not expect a definitive intellectual clarity in any treatment of these ultimately paradoxical problems. There are places, in any cosmogony or in any system of philosophy, no matter how precisely it is argued, where all the awkward little pieces of the puzzle gather into a tangle and refuse to be smoothed over for the gratification of our orderly minds. Often enough this tangle has gathered in the blind spot of the expositor, and waits to be pointed out by a critic whose own blind spot happens not to coincide. The important thing is to recognise that there is a mystery, and that these Stanzas are but a pointer to its existence. The commentary is an attempt to colour the same pointer in other and more familiar hues, but neither Stanzas nor commentary make pretence of being a logically unimpeachable whole.

This verse and the following one contain matter over which just such a tangle has occurred and formed the subject of an age-old controversy between the two schools of *Vedānta*, the *Viśishṭādvaita* or Differentiated Non-duality, and the *Advaita*, Non-duality. The former teaches what is technically known as *pariṇāmavāda*, the view that the universe is created by a series of real changes such as that which occurs when milk is turned into curds; while the latter holds the doctrine of *vivartavāda*, namely, that no real change takes place in creation, but an illusory projection which leaves the original Reality unchanged. The famous illustration given for the latter process is that of a rope being mistaken for a snake. The importance of the point lies in the fact that, were the phenomenal universe a 'reality', something brought into being by a real change in its generating cause, it would not be possible for it to be transcended by knowledge. On the other hand, when it is recognised that the various phenomenal levels of being are but psychic projections, the way is open for a transcending of those levels by a knowledge which shall see them, not as they seem, but *yathābhūtam*, as they really are.

People familiar with this controversy will be apt to suppose the use of the symbol of the curds to imply that the Stanzas favour Rāmanuja's *pariṇāmavāda,* but this is not so. Both Śaṅkarāchārya and Rāmanuja based their systems of thought on Hindu religious doctrine (*Śāstra*); the Stanzas, however, are telling us of a path whose beginning may be in religious doctrines, but to travel on which we must leave all orthodox vehicles behind. This is what neither of the two great Vedāntins would do. Rāmanuja's literal-minded interpretations of *Śāstra* have the effect of weighing down his thought with the dead weight of over-evaluation of the sanctity of Hindu tradition; while Śaṅkarāchārya, free though he was with his 'interpretations' (*Lakshaṇāvritti*), for which he was accused of twisting traditional doctrines to suit his own purposes, was nevertheless wedded to the concept of the authority of 're-vealed' doctrines.

As in most long-standing controversies, the two sides represent different aspects of one truth confused by the inevitable distortions of interpretation. Rāmanuja's 'real' changes and Śaṅkarāchārya's 'illusion' are not in fact as much opposed ideas as they may seem. The derivatives of an absolute reality partake of the reality of their source, but because of the nature of the psychic mechanisms of experiencing we are deluded into taking the derivative for the original.

The changes that occur when the 'Three fall into the Four' are quite real, the milk has curdled, but we must not now allow our thought to be limited by the illustration and think that, because curds cannot ordinarily be turned back into milk, neither can the manifest universe cease to exist. This is why the later verses of the stanza change this metaphor and speak of a woven web which is the universe. When the warp is withdrawn the web collapses; and the web is the screen that intercepts and reflects the projected light of consciousness. So long as the web is there, there is a real world, or the illusion of a real world; it matters very little what we call it. But when the web, the structure of the macrocosmic levels compounded of Father and Matrix, is withdrawn into the *pralaya* of the Darkness, then the light of consciousness streams out unchecked and unreflected, so that there can be neither the focalised dwelling points of *Jīvas* nor the self-reflecting consciousness of Universal Mind (*Iśvara*). So long, however, as the primal division of the Absolute into Father-Light and Matrix is maintained, then no individual element of consciousness (the *Jīva*) can as such transcend that 'change'.

The *vivartavāda's* simile of the rope mistaken for a snake also has its limitations as an illustration; for one thing, unless there was a snake somewhere the rope could not be mistaken for it. The root meaning of *vivarta* (from *vritti*) takes us neither to change nor to illusion, but to an unrolling;[1] an unrolling that we shall meet in verse seven when the bright consciousness of Universal Mind is pictured as unfurling the Veil of Light, and leaving the 'Below to be seen as the Great Illusion'. The creative act that makes manifest the inner content of Mind is indeed an unrolling of the levels; a three-dimensional screen is flung up between the undifferentiated light and the sea of unrealised possibilities. The appearances we see are the differentiations of the One Light clothed in the web woven of subject and object. Both Light and Web are ultimately He, One without a second.

So long, however, as the unmanifest Divine polarity is maintained, the dependent reality of the universe may be transcended, but it can never be annulled, for it is maintained by the Divine Will. Thus in all human endeavour there is a limitation which the Stanzas term the 'ring called "Pass Not" ' (V. 6), and there are such binding rings of limitation on every level of being. Man cannot, for instance, absolutely transcend the limitation of his physical body at will; on occasion he may be able to reach states in which the beatific vision is opened to him (trance, *samādhi*), but he must return to ordinary consciousness and continue to inhabit his body until the collapse of that structure releases him. At the close of the Buddha's life he is reported to have said, 'Just as a worn out cart, Ānanda, can be kept going with the help of thongs, so,

---

[1] Unrolled is the root meaning of explicit.

methinks the body of the Tathāgata, can be kept going only by bandaging it up. It is only, Ānanda, when the Tathāgata, by ceasing to attend to any outward thing, becomes plunged by the cessation of any separate sensation in that concentration of heart which is concerned with no material object, it is only then that the body of the Tathāgata is at ease.'[1]

Beyond the limitations of the physical body and the soul's vehicles on every sub-level of the universe there are again the limiting structures of other finite systems and indeed of the universe itself: the lesser rings are held within the greater. The final 'Ring' which holds the Cosmic order in being is the polar duality between Father-Light and Matrix, between pure consciousness and potential form. This duality is in itself transcendant to any individualised integration, there is therefore no meaning in speaking of its being transcended, only of its resolution in the course of the entirely trans-individual (and trans-temporal) cosmic process. Though it is undoubtedly possible for the man of spiritual achievement to separate the essential consciousness from the individualised structure that was 'his' individuality, so that it remains what it always is, the unstained all-pervasive Father-Light, yet nothing and no one then remains which can in any sense proceed to transcend that duality, nor does any separate thing remain to be liberated. That which was ever free remains itself: all human individuality is gone; the lamp is broken; light remains the Light.

We must be careful not to misunderstand the word illusion or illusory which is so often bandied about in discussion of this problem. To say that the phenomenal universe is an illusion is not to say that it is nothing at all, like, to use the old Sanskrit illustrations, the horns of a hare or the son of a barren woman. It is illusory because it is not what it seems to be, namely, an external reality standing in its own right, but, as a process of psychic projection, it has its definite status and it only disappears with the withdrawal of the projection.

The often made comparison of the universe with a dream is

[1] *Mahā Parinibbāna Sutta* (Dialogues of the Buddha).

valid enough if the true nature of dream experience is understood, and, indeed, it is for this reason that *The Voice of the Silence* refers to the Dream State as the Hall of Learning. If, on the other hand, a dream is taken, as it is so often by shallow minds, to be a mere chaotic nothing, a meaningless réchauffé of images arising from disordered bodily functions, then in that case the analogy is misleading. The fault, however, lies with those who hold so trivial and inadequate a view, and not with the Seers who first used the analogy on the basis of their profound knowledge of the nature of dream life. The dream, says Sigmund Freud, is the royal road into the unconscious; we may not accept all Freud's views, but this is certain, namely that in the dream life is hidden the key to many mysteries. Only he who has understood the nature of dream is able to comprehend properly the nature of waking life; and he who has mastered his dreams has mastered many secrets of life and death.

The luminous Egg is itself Three, the triune integration of Mind. It is 'luminous' but not yet radiant, not fully manifest.

And now this non-eternal germ of manifest consciousness spreads throughout the waters of life and they 'curdle'. The singleness of the Ray, uniting with the multiplicity of the Waters, gives rise neither to a single lump, nor to an infinitely extended homogeneous continuum, but to a finite though 'countless' multitude of conscious individuals, or rather the rooted seeds or nuclei of what will become individuals, from atoms to stars, from amoebae to men. These are the milk-white 'Curds' which spread throughout the depths of the now delimited ocean of Life. And this is the 'condensation' of the eternal Egg into the World-Egg.

Singleness and multiplicity have united. The Curds are a mass of separate individuals, numerous by virtue of the Mother's multiplicity and separate by virtue of the Father's singleness which delimits each one. Yet all are bound together into a whole by the universality of the Divine Consciousness from which they have sprung and in which they are held.

This state of things gives one the impression of a mass of precisely similar individuals, a theme which is bound up with our ideas of divine justice, for ought not we all to have been given an equal start? But differentiation has already been implanted in the field of manifest being. The Radiant Essence has become 'Seven inside, Seven outside' from the very fact of its becoming manifest. The unmanifest plenum of the Darkness, the infinite potentiality of the Mother, the all-inclusive range of the Father-Light of consciousness, how can these manifest in a monotony of sameness? No, if we accuse the living creative Will of injustice because of inequalities of human opportunity, then the yardstick by which we measure justice is being applied to inappropriate materials. Men are unjust in so far as they exploit the inequalities in other men to their personal advantage. But is it injustice that some of the 'curds' should be implanted with qualities which will later go towards making a clod of earth, others a cow, and yet others the body of a man? And is it injustice that the vast range of differences in which divinity expresses its nature through the medium of its human vehicle should also call for different sorts of vehicle with different aptitudes? And is it unjust that the inconceivably difficult task of bringing the 'luminous' consciousness of the early creation to incandescence in the mind of man should be beset with dangers at every point? Let us be more realistic. Differentiation is not only essential to life, in a sense it *is* life. 'A sower went forth to sow. And when he sowed, some seeds fell by the wayside, some upon stony places, and some among thorns. But others fell into good ground and brought forth fruit.'[1] And it is after telling this parable, illustrative of the inherent inequalities of life, that Jesus of Nazareth is reported to have enunciated the stern law of the Cosmos, 'Whosoever hath, to him shall be given, and he shall have more abundance, but whosoever hath not, from him shall be taken away even that which he hath.' What constitutes 'having' and 'not having' is, however, a matter to be taken up elsewhere.

[1] Gospel of St. Matthew, XIII, abbreviated.

I

These 'curds', then, by whatever name we call them, are the ultimate 'bricks' of the universe, conscious bricks which will build and be built into the numerous grades of being that go to make up the manifest worlds. Like the stones of Thebes obeying the music of Amphion's lyre, they will move themselves into position in accord with the cosmic harmony. They are the basis of 'matter', the only 'matter' in the universe, yet a 'matter' that will be composed of empatterned organisations of energy around these individualised points in or of consciousness. How the energy arises and the manner of its organisation is taken up in the later stanzas, in particular in Stanza VI.

Thus the milk-white curds spread or diffuse themselves throughout the depths of Mother, of the great outward-turnedness of the Matrix which is the universal background of all manifestation. In this Mother, fertilised or illumined by the Ray of the Father, the embryonic universe takes root and 'grows in the Ocean of Life', out of whose maternal depths it draws its life energy.

We are reminded of the ocean of 'whey' which surrounds *Krauncha Dvīpa*[1] in the so much misunderstood symbolic geography of the *Purāṇas*; and also of a beautiful image in the *Ahirbudhnya Samhita* which describes the Universe during the Cosmic Day as being like a sky sprinkled all over with cirrus clouds, while during the Night it resembles a sky without a single cloud, or a waveless ocean.[2]

As for the 'Seven inside, Seven outside', like the Platonic Ideas, which, as Whitehead puts it, ingress or, so to say, ensoul even the humblest forms of daily life, they, the sevenfold differentiation of Order within the Universal Mind, impress their qualities on the 'Curds' throughout the levels of the

---

[1] *Krauncha Dvīpa* corresponds to the level of the Universal Mind. The whole set of concentric 'continents' separated by fantastic 'oceans' is in fact (at least from one point of view) a symbol of the cosmos with its various levels of experience. Careful study of the different 'oceans' will give a key to the correspondences.

[2] *Ahirbudhnya Samhita*, IX. 16. 14. 38, quoted by Schrader in his *Introduction to the Pāñcarātra*, p. 29.

manifested Cosmos. Whether we think we perceive a clod
of earth, a tree, a chair, a man, or even a thought, it is in reality
the divine archetypal images of the Universal Mind that we
are in fact perceiving or misperceiving. We have called them
archetypal images, but they are really images only in relation
to the formlessness of the Mother. From our point of view
perhaps it would be better to call them Archetypal Imaginal
Principles, for they are not so much actual images as formative
principles which give rise by ingression into the Curds to
images lower down the ladder of being. They are the realities
to which, symbolically, all images refer, but in themselves they
are beyond all that we know as form. As the Upanishads say,
'by the soul must they be seen.'[1]

What we think of as 'matter' is fundamentally that which is
external to or over-against us. So long as we view this externality as having real independent existence we are unable to
reconcile the incompatability between the psychic nature of
the experiencer and the physical nature of experience content,
for we do not admit of a polar relationship existing between
dissimilar categories. The dichotomy is resolved when we see
that the manifest content of experience arises from the interaction of the two unmanifest poles of being and is, as it were, a
fragmentation of the total and unmanifest self-nature of the
One Darkness.

The content aspect of the One Darkness is made to appear
external in order to become manifest or explicit. The appearance
is illusory in the sense that the modes of consciousness compel
us to sense the external worlds as if they were composed of real
distinct existants, whereas their existence as objective content
is entirely dependent on the maintenance of the cosmic
subject-object polarity. Because of the universality of consciousness, we, as individualised experiencing subjects, share
the same objective content both with each other and with
those low-grade centres of living awareness around which the
elements of chemistry and their constructs are organised.

[1] *Manasaivānudrashtavyam.*

'Matter' is thus the content aspect of experience. We can describe experience either in terms of Consciousness, or in terms of Being, or as the interaction of the two. But whatever terms we use we have to remind ourselves that no definitive terminology is possible. We have to stretch beyond the limitations of words and see that the components of experience are poles, modalities, aspects, or divisions of one and only one ultimate reality.

We need to get away from our customary feeling that we are essentially separate experiencing subjects in a world of real physical objects to which we are somehow related by a mechanical process of sensing. The three components of experience, the Knower (subjective awareness), the Known (objective content), and the process of Knowing (the function relating subject and object), originate as those modes in consciousness to which we here refer as the Father or root of subjectivity, the Mother or root of objectivity, and their relationship which is the derivative of their previous state of fusion in the Darkness. Out of the union of these separate and unmanifest principles is born the Son, Universal Mind, in whom the three are joined in an inseparable trinity, 'the luminous Egg which in itself is Three'. The transcendant triad give birth to themselves in the body of their son, and with his birth the Darkness vanishes (III. 6) and Māyā (illusion) is born (II. 4).

Because he contains within himself the qualities of both his parents, because he both emits and receives the energy of creation, the Son was symbolised in some traditions as an androgynous figure such as the Indian Ardhanāriśvara, half God, half Goddess (Shiva and Pārvatī), or, as in Egypt, as brother and sister twins (Isis and Osiris).

When the two poles of being separate within the One Darkness, the relationship which springs up between them may be thought of as a uni-directional flow from Father to Mother, from Projector to Receptrix. The Father, as the ultimate pole of subjectivity, is not receptive to his own Light; to him the

Matrix is therefore dark, for he projects into it, but can receive nothing from it. The birth of the Son is the birth of the triune integration of Mind, an integration of the three components of experience, through which it becomes possible for the Knower to become receptive to the relating energy and so have knowledge of that which it seeks to know.

In this triune Mind, energy projected by the Father component is now received by the Mother component and related 'within' Mind in a process of knowing. The perceiving pole of consciousness is integrally united with the content pole. The energy springing from the relationship of the two poles of the ultimate Darkness is now modified so that it has to return upon itself and be received by the Mind from which it flowed out. This 'returning' of the energy of relationship makes the content appear to be external to Mind and therefore manifest. For this reason the Son is said to be the first manifest level or principle, the manifest Son of unmanifest Parents. The field of the Matrix which was dark now appears to be bright.

Our sensing is a derivative of this process, for we have knowledge of the external world by virtue of our being receptive to modulations of energy striking upon our sense organs from 'without'. Our inner life of imagination is an even closer parallel, for in this the energy from which the images spring and the light with which they shine has its source in ourselves.

The Space, or field of consciousness, into which the energy is projected and in which content becomes objectified is the Space of the Matrix. As Being she stands behind all phenomena, giving to them whatever substantial reality they seem to possess. She is the darkness against which light forms become apparent by virtue of contrast, the depth and breadth in which three dimensional form takes shape, the field of discrimination between unity and plurality, the basis of all differentiation. This space is 'the lap of Māyā' (II. 4), the space in which inner content is made to stand forth as if it possessed independent reality.

(5) *The root remains, the light remains, the curds remain, and still Oeaohoo is one.*

The embryonic universe is rooted in the Ocean of Life, the living womb of the Mother. Within the Ocean is shining the creative effulgence, the Light of the Darkness. The unmanifest Waters of the Mother have themselves 'curdled' and become the Ocean of existence. Yet 'Oeaohoo', the One Darkness, remains one and undivided. It cannot be divided, it cannot suffer change. It is non-being and non-existence, yet it is the ground from which all consciousness and all form take their rise. 'In the beginning was the Word, and the Word was with God, and the Word was God.'[1]

The 'word' Oeaohoo is not in itself any particular word or name. It represents the totality of the vowel sounds, and in many of the ancient languages the equivalents of such 'names' can be found. In the *Pistis Sophia*,[2] for instance, we find reference to the mystery of the seven vowels and their nine and forty powers; these being the seven Greek vowels which often appeared on Gnostic gems either in connection with a serpent or a crowned lion. We also read of the seven thunders in the Apocalypse of St. John which are a variant of the same idea. The key to the meaning is to be found in Indian occult phonetics (*mantraśāstra*) in which the (fourteen) vowels of the Sanskrit alphabet are considered to be the *shaktis* or powers of the consonants, since without them the latter cannot be pronounced. The consonants are thus purely formative, while the vowels represent the fundamental power of utterance, the heart or essence of the creative Word.

The 'seven vowelled'[3] word Oeaohoo thus represents the fundamental creative power or Sound, the One Breath whose modifications appear in the next stanza as 'the reawakened energies' (IV. 3). As one syllable, Oeaohoo is the totality of dormant powers within the Darkness. As a trinity, it represents

[1] Gospel of St. John, I. 1.
[2] Translated by G. R. S. Mead.
[3] S. D., I. 68. (Oeaohoo . . . these seven vowels, which may be pronounced as *one*, three, or even seven syllables by adding an "e" after the letter "o".'

the power aspect of the three creative outpourings (Logoi), the Oi-Ha-Hou (IV. 4). As a septenary, it is the differentiated totality of the Son, Universal Mind, or 'Oeaohoo the Younger' (III. 7). Similar ideas are attached to the Om, which can be taken as composed of one, three or seven elements.[1] Within Mind these vowels or powers of expression (Cf. Plato's Sirens) are joined to the articulate consonantal powers of limitation (the 'Numbers' of IV. 5), thus dividing the inarticulate outflow into distinct and significant parts and forming structure patterns or archetypal images. These latter are then breathed out or 'voiced' by the 'first seven breaths of the Dragon of Wisdom' (V. 1) as the active forms of speech of the Divine Man, the 'names' which were taught to Adam,[2] and which 'condense' into or are written as substantives or 'writings' (IV. 6). These 'writings' are the physical forms which we are apt to regard as things-in-their-own-right, but which are in fact only vortical integrations of active energy capable of being construed as substantives—like the gerundive forms of verbs. The forms of Nature are thus to be seen as exteriorised representations of Sophia, the Divine Wisdom.

The question will perhaps be asked whether these vowels or other sounds have actual power vested in them, or whether they are merely symbols? The answer is that nothing in the universe has power by its own nature alone. All the phenomena of the universe are symbols, yet none of them are *merely* symbols. The power which seems to reside in any of the elements which make up the world is ultimately the Power of the One Reality, and proximately the Power of those archetypal principles of which the concrete forms of our experience are but expressions. The power of an archetype manifests through each and all of its symbolic expressions; but for that power to be seriously effective in consciousness, the symbols must be consciously

---

[1] As a single syllable the Om represents the *Parabrahman* (see *Bhagavad Gītā*, VIII. 13). The threefold analysis A, U, M, is given in the *Māndukya Upanishad*, and the sevenfold, which is too technical to quote, is discussed in *The Garland of Letters* by Sir John Woodroffe; see the chapter on 'The Causal Shaktis of the *Praṇava*', pp. 188–9.

[2] *Qu'rān*, II. 31.

linked up to their archetypes. The electric current generated in a ring of copper wire by waving a magnet over it is negligible in practice; it needs delicate instruments in order to be detected, yet the tremendous currents which supply a city with light and heat are generated by an application of just that principle. Between the experiments of Faraday and the modern dynamo lay years of devoted and intensive research, and it is related of Faraday that when asked what was the use of his experiments he replied, 'What is the use of a baby?'

If anyone thinks he is going to produce phenomenal results by the pronunciation of *Om* or Oeaohoo, and that to do so he only needs to know the 'correct' pronunciation, he is certain to be disappointed. The Power of the One *is* manifest in vowels, but, for it to achieve any practical results, it is necessary to have a will of a high order and knowledge of the sort that is not found in books. As stated by Eliphas Levi, 'the secrets of the great work have a triple meaning; they are religious, philosophical, and natural'; that is to say they have meanings on the planes of the soul, mind and body, respectively. 'All masters of science recognise that it is impossible to achieve material results until we have found all the analogies of the universal medicine and the philosophic stone in the two superior degrees . . . the science is true only for those who accept and understand the philosophy and religion, and its processes are successful only for the adept who has attained sovereign volition.'[1]

The tremendous importance attached to the knowledge of names in ancient religious and magical literature often proves a stumbling-block to the appreciation of the true worth of such works. Neither people nor objects ordinarily appear to respond to their names in any way that would inspire one with confidence in the claims put forward for the potency of 'name', even when pronounced solemnly with the full ritual and regalia of magic. There are still secret societies who, with great pomp and ceremony, convey to their initiates some series of sounds and

[1] *Doctrine and Ritual of Transcendental Magic*, pp. 264-5.

call it the Ineffable Name, but with as little effect as 'Jack Robinson', save only that the latter has more meaning. 'Abracadabra' and 'Hajabarala' are all garbled versions of such words and like 'hocus-pocus' and 'mumbo-jumbo' have come to represent meaningless nonsense. All this is not, however, due to any fault on the part of those who orginally wrote in praise of the power of names. The fault lies in the attitude of mind which recognises nothing but material causation, and therefore denies the possibility of there being any means of producing effects other than those derivable from our waking experience in this order of being. A subtle world is assumed to be unreal just because it is subtle, and the falsity of this assumption will become apparent if we apply a similar statement to the physical world, namely, that the real physical (gross) world is real because it is physical.

It is not difficult to find evidence for the ingress of subtle powers into this world, but it is rare to find anyone who can demonstrate them at will. To do so one must be able to enter the area of the subtle world with his will unimpaired so that he is, as it were, in the world of dreams yet not dreaming. In this state the dream material that takes its form from the imagining faculty is plastic to his will, and there, if he can remember and pronounce 'words of power', they will be effective. It is in this realm that the possession of a name gives power over a person, or over a personified power, and it is to attain to this state of the waking experience of dream that so many religious and magical practices are directed, for only when he is *awake*, on whatsoever level of being, is man able to exercise his innate freedom of spirit; in all other states he is bound to the circle of necessity. It seems to those who die that they are called by name to whatever sort of judgment their religious background has conditioned them for. Those who answer to their names are compelled to go, such is the power of name; only those who have detached themselves from personal association with all names and all forms are free from compulsion.

In itself the Darkness is necessarily nameless, for the Source of all things cannot be encompassed by its derivatives. Like the hundredth name of Allah or the ultimate secret of the Tetragrammaton, the Ineffable Name is never spoken because it cannot be. Yet, as Dionysius says, 'Conscious of this the Sacred Writers celebrate It by every Name while yet they call it Nameless'.[1]

It is a human characteristic to feel that our knowledge of anything is incomplete until we can put a name to it, whether that 'thing' is an object of sense, a person, an idea or a divine attribute. Naming things brings our thoughts to a focus; clarity of thought demands clarity of definition. As with the human mind, so with Divine Mind: the universally diffused inner content has to be made clear. This is the naming of the animals in paradise by Adam[2] the Divine Man from whom 'emanated the . . . Sacred Animals' (IV. 3), those symbolic animals of the zodiac which represent the unchanging patterns of the Archetypes.

In the outflow of creation the archetypal ideas must first be clarified or 'named' before the ectypes can be effected. Similarly when we look upwards to view Divinity, before we can attempt to pierce the screen of His attributes we must first clarify our understanding and see beneath the chaotic movements of events the eternal patterns of the cosmic harmony which are His Names.

(6) *The root of life was in every drop of the ocean of immortality, and the ocean was radiant light, which was fire and heat and motion. Darkness vanished and was no more; it disappeared in its own essence, the body of fire and water, or father and mother.*

This stanza makes use of the symbol of water in a number of different contexts, each with its qualifying adjectives; slumbering waters, the Mother-Deep, the Ocean of Life, the Ocean of Immortality. They are always the same Maternal waters, though they are spoken of as having different qualities.

[1] *The Divine Names*, I. 5.
[2] *Genesis*, II. 19 and 20.

Underlying these distinctions we have to feel the presence of the feminine quality of maternity running through them all in rather the same way that we can perceive the maternity that is present in a physical mother, whether she be human, cat, dog, cow, or tigress.

Just as a man emerging from slumber perceives his surroundings, but is yet overhung by the black cloud of sleep, so the Cosmos, awakening to manifestation, is still overclouded by the Darkness from which it is emerging. But now the waters of the Matrix, the amniotic waters of the womb, are radiant with the light of existent consciousness, the light of manifestation. Those waters which formerly reflected only the overhanging darkness are now alive with the immortal life of the Father; they have become the Ocean of Immortality, and in every drop of the Ocean the now embryonic Germ has taken root.

From the union of opposites, the union of Fire and Water, of Father and Mother, arises motion, and the Waters have responded with rippling movements to the leaping flames of Fire. The primary poles of Being which have been differentiated from the Darkness are again united in the act of Knowing, for motion and action are inherent qualities of their Son.

Darkness now vanishes as does the darkness of sleep to a man fully awakened. The Darkness of Non-being becomes Essence, that which is. This is the radiant 'body' of the Son whose birth is described in the next verse, a diaphanous ocean of Fire and Water. The dark and massive fused experience is gone, not to return till the next Cosmic Night.

> 'Ye will not find him who produced these creatures
> Another thing hath risen up amongst you'[1]

In saying that it has vanished, the verse means, of course, vanished from the point of view of manifestation. Its Life-energy streams forth through its now manifested Poles, linking them to each other perpetually in the subject-object

[1] *Rig Veda*, X. 82. 7.

relationship, and thus providing the motive power of the newly manifested Cosmos. Though it has disappeared as Darkness, it is always present as the power which links the Two and is thus recognisable by us as the ever mysterious and unanalysable 'knowing' which links together the knower and the known, the 'acting' which joins the actor and the acted on.

In themselves knower and known are now too outward turned, too full of energy to be able to see what is 'behind' them. The Darkness is forgotten, and if we ever turn our eyes to scrutinise too closely the mysterious bond which 'knowing' constitutes, we find it vanishes elusively beneath our gaze, leaving us with only the two poles, knower and known. Yet, when we turn away our eyes, knowing is back again, the most obvious thing in the world to the many, and yet for philosophers a very riddle of the Sphinx.

We can never have direct cognisance of the Darkness; its presence can therefore only be inferred by human reason. To those who find it difficult to transcend the rational intellect a doubt always remains whether the light form of the Divine Being, He who Is, does or does not retire into the darkness of Non-Being.

(7) *Behold, O Lanoo! The radiant child of the two, the unparalleled refulgent glory: Bright Space, Son of Dark Space which emerges from the depths of the great dark waters. It is Oeaohoo the younger, the . . .* (whom thou knowest now as Kwan-Shai-Yin.—Comment). *He shines forth as the Sun; he is the blazing Divine Dragon of Wisdom. The One is Four and Four takes to itself Three and the Union produces the Sapta, in whom are the seven which become the Tridasa, the hosts and the multitudes. Behold him lifting the veil and unfurling it from east to west. He shuts out the above and leaves the below to be seen as the great illusion. He marks the places for the shining ones and turns the upper into a shoreless sea of fire, and the one manifested into the great waters.*

With this verse we come to the most dramatic point of the whole creation, namely the flashing forth into full and conscious manifestation of the Universal Mind; for this it is, the Radiant (*i.e.* energetic) child of the Two, whose unparalleled glory the disciple is asked to contemplate. This is the birth of that which the Greeks called Cosmos, or the adorned one, and worshipped as a God. This is the Shining Wonder, a mere glimpse of which has made such seers as have been fortunate enough to attain this vision drunk with the wine of utter God intoxication. 'If the splendour of a thousand suns were to blaze out together in the sky, that might resemble the glory of that mighty Self.'[1]

Blazing with unimaginable Light, a Light that does not dazzle; vibrant with Power, yet calmly peaceful as the eyes of Buddha; strong with the male, life-giving splendour of the sun, yet soft with the cool magic of the moon; the strength of man and yet the grace of woman: such is this Universal Mind, the wondrous Child of the Eternal Parents. All strength, all beauty and all truth have their abode within its light. Its symbol is the shining vault of heaven, containing sun, moon, and stars, all linked in interpenetrative harmony. The content of this Mind is a living content; the gleaming Archetypal Images are a hierarchy of living spiritual powers, each with its being mingled with that of all the rest, for, above all, this is a plane of harmonious unity, the music of the spheres. It is here that, in the Biblical phrase, the morning stars sing together. The very thought of it fills the heart with the sound of flutes, with the thunder of drums and of great waters, with the soughing of the wind among the pine trees, with the song of birds in the spring, and with the whispering of the Lover in the ear of the Beloved. Here is that Beauty which throbs in works of poetry or art; here also that which shines austerely in the sciences.

But what is the use of piling up images and symbols, for none

---

[1] *Bhagavad Gītā*, XI. 12. Cf. Also *Praśnopanishad*, I. 8:
> '(him) Who has all forms, the golden one, all knowing
> The final goal, the only light, heat giving
> The thousand-rayed, the hundredfold revolving,
> Yon sun arises as the life of creatures.'

can do justice to the wonder of that Mind. Let us then repeat the words of Plotinus and have done.

'For There everything is transparent, nothing dark, nothing resistant; every being is lucid to every other, in breadth and depth; light runs through light. And each of them contains all within itself, and at the same time sees all in every other, so that everywhere there is all, all is in all, and each is all, and infinite the glory. Each of them is great; the small is great; the sun, There is all the stars, and every star again is all the stars and sun. While some one manner of being is dominant in each, all are mirrored in every other.'[1]

The Universal Mind is referred to in this verse under three symbols. First it is Bright Space, son of Dark Space. Dark Space we have already met, the one great Darkness which contains all that is; just as those dark regions of our psyche that lie beyond the magic circle of the personal ego contain all the countless myriads of memory images which have been forgotten by us. The Universal Mind, on the other hand, resembles that brightly lit magic circle within which those memories we successfully evoke, or which force themselves upon us, display themselves to our gaze.

Bright Space is said to be the son of Dark Space because its two actual parents are but the two poles of that Darkness, and the great Dark Waters from which it emerges are, of course, the Mother, who is also *Aditi*, mother of the *Ādityas*, the luminous gods or bright Spaces.

Secondly it is referred to as Oeaohoo the Younger. Oeaohoo the Elder was the One Darkness, the one all-embracing creative Unity; and in the Universal Mind we have the manifest image of that Dark One. Both alike are living creative unities, but the younger is limited instead of unlimited, and is brightly conscious instead of dark with that absolute consciousness which to us is unconsciousness. It is a bright Sun which covers

[1] Plotinus, V. viii. 4. (Mackenna).

up a dark Sun at its back, the Golden Vessel with which 'the face of the Real is covered over'.[1]

In terming it Oeaohoo the Younger it is also intended to assimilate it to the Elder Darkness in respect of its containing within itself the Seven great Powers, the levels of the Cosmos. It is in this connection, too, that it is termed the Blazing Dragon of Wisdom, for, being as it is a bright image of the Dark One, knowledge of it gives knowledge of That which in itself is beyond all knowledge. Here the reader may refer to what has already been said about serpents and dragons. It is this Mind that is the Divine Teacher, omniscient and all-pervading, dwelling in the hearts of all and yet embracing all. It is the Son of which Jesus said that none could go to the Father save through the Son.[2] In it reside all the Divine Teachers (who are one), and from it all Truth comes; all true Knowledge being but participation in its Wisdom. It is for this reason that the Rig Veda says 'Varuna (the Universal Mind) placed Vaśishṭha in the vessel (cf. the Egyptian boat of Ra) and deftly with his might made him a Seer.'[3] In this Mind the Divine Wisdom in its fullness exists, and always has existed, and it is because Mind is the prior and basis of all further manifestation that the world has never been and can never be without the Wisdom. He who can read them aright knows that the symbols of all religions (as opposed to their intel-lectualised doctrines) are all equivalent and that they refer to this body of primordial Wisdom. This Wisdom, which is reflected even in the myths of the most primitive peoples, is utterly universal, because it antedates the manifestations not only of this but of all the worlds within the universe. The Knowledge thus precedes the ignorance. From that Widsom we have all come, and though we have turned our backs on it awhile to seek adventure on the seas of ignorance, yet it is ever there as the basis of all we know. Eternally it acts upon us

[1] *Iśa Upanishad*, 15.
[2] *Gospel of St. John*, XIV. 6.
[3] *Rig Veda*, VII. 88. 4.

as an unseen gravitational field which checks all our wander-
ings, compensating unerringly the unbalance of our one-sided
strivings, and ensuring that, when the adventure is accomplished and we complete our circumnavigation of the triple
worlds of form, it will be to that Wisdom that we shall return.
Indeed we have never left it save in dream, and he who can
awake from dream even now will find himself possessor of all
Knowledge, fully Awakened, Buddha, teacher of gods and
men.

Up to this point the stanza has been dealing with the descent
of the Spirit into Matter, but in this verse the Son 'emerges
from the depths' in much the same way that our bright
consciousness seems to rise up out of the depths of our psychic
background, out of the darkness of the 'unconscioussed'. In
the following list of numbers the One which is Four is therefore
the material aspect of the Darkness, the dark un-self-conscious
ocean of life. From this viewpoint it is not the Three which
falls into the Four (III. 4) but the Four which 'takes to itself
Three'. The change of view is significant, for it shows us the
other half of the picture, the desire of the Matrix to be known.
The great Mind of the universe thus has its 'material' or
content aspect. It is not pure consciousness, but the combination of the triune subjective awareness and the four determining qualities of the Matrix which must be present before any
content can exist as a knowable object in spatial dimension,
even though that 'space' be only the mental space of divine
imaginals.

This Four is the sacred Quaternary which plays so important
a part in the symbolism of all religions. Among many other
things it is the Tetraktys of the Pythagoreans, the four-faced
Brahmā of the Hindus, the four-square Heavenly Jerusalem of
the Christians. It is also the four-lettered Tetragrammaton of
the Kabbalists, knowledge of which, according to Rabbinical
legend, gave Jesus his power of working miracles. Dr. C. G.
Jung, the psychologist, has come across it in his researches into
the symbols of the dream consciousness and, recognising its

religious significance, says that it stands for 'a sort of creative background, a life-producing sun in the depths of the unconscious mind', and that it represents 'the God within'. He also regards it as a symbol of the principle of balance within the psyche, which it certainly is for reasons which we have seen a few paragraphs back.[1]

The union of the Four and the Three constitutes the *Sapta* or Seven, the Seven levels or worlds of being 'in whom are the Seven', the inner Seven or Divine Archetypes. Those inner Seven have somewhat the same relationship to their outer counterparts as the soul has to the body. They are their fundamental motive power, their principle of life and movement, their inner being, in a word, their soul. Therefore they are said to 'become the *Tridaśa*' or Thirty, a standard round number for the well known thirty-three gods of the vedic tradition.[2] These Gods are the creative Powers of the Cosmos and they manifest to us in the elemental powers of nature which are their earliest snd most appropriate symbols; symbols apt to be confused with the ever-living Powers which are at once the referents of the symbols and the real basis of their overt manifestations.[3]

The Inner Seven, then, or Divine Archetypes, become by differentiation the Thirty (or Thirty-three) creative Powers working on all the levels, and by still further differentiation, the 'Hosts' or archetypal inner Powers and the 'Multitudes', their concrete outer embodiments. We may note here how

---

[1] *Psychology and Religion* by C. G. Jung. 'Unconscioussed' is perhaps closer to the meaning of the word used by Sigmund Freud in this context and rendered by English translators as 'unconscious'.

[2] The names and allocations of these thirty-three gods are unnecessary for our purposes; they had perhaps become confused even in Vedic times. We may however refer to *Rig Veda*, I. 139. 10 & 11 which speaks of Eleven Gods whose home is in Heaven, Eleven who dwell on Earth and Eleven who live in the Waters. In other words the Thirty-three represent the living creative Powers of all the Three Worlds. The word *tridaśa* (3 × 10) is an accepted round number for these Thirty-three: see Monier Williams' *Sanskrit Dictionary*.

[3] D. H. Lawrence once said that he refused to believe the Sun was a fizzing ball of gas. His intuitive judgment was perfectly right, though he would perhaps have found it hard to give reasons for it.

K

Hindu tradition also expands its list of the Thirty-three gods, saying that the final number is Thirty-three crores.[1]

We have still to ask why this enumeration should have been given just here. It is to indicate that the whole set of principles, inner as well as outer, is represented in the Universal Mind, the blazing Dragon of Wisdom, knowing which, one knows all. This Mind is said to contain even the principles higher than itself, because it is composed of the very stuff of its two parent principles, while the One Darkness is manifest in the unity which links them together. That the Inner Seven should also be reflected in it follows from the fact that they become explicit in the very modes of that unity, for they are the archetypal patterns that guide all manifestation. It is important always to remember that these various principles are not contained in each other in the manner of one of those sets of Chinese boxes, one within the other, but that the principles themselves all coexist in a living unity from which, however classified for our convenience, they emerge as independent levels only by a process of abstraction or differential emphasis.

We are next asked to behold the Mind lifting the Veil and unfurling it from East to West; lifting, as a banner is lifted and unfurled for display, which is here the display of manifestation.[2] This Veil, the Abyss of the Kabbala, is that which separates the manifested cosmos from the unmanifest principles beyond, namely the utterly unmanifest One and the, to us, unmanifest Parents. It is the firmament which divided the waters which were above from the waters which were beneath;[3] the veil of appearances which bright consciousness interposes between itself and the dark background out of which it arises. It is unfurled from the East, the Gateway of

---

[1] A crore is equal to ten million.
[2] As the *Peplos* or Veil of Athene was raised aloft and carried through the streets at the Panathenaic festival, spread like a sail on the mast of a ship. Compare the thought of this line with the Psalms of David, 104. 2: 'Who coverest thyself with light as with a garment Who stretchest out the heavens like a curtain.'
[3] Genesis, I. 7.

the Day, the Universal Mind, to the West, the Sunset Gate which leads to the Death Kingdoms, the world of the senses. Thus the whole gamut of manifested levels, from the highest to the lowest, is isolated from its background and emerges as a finite Cosmos. The Above, or unmanifest principles, are 'shut out', while the Below, or manifest principles, are left as the Great Illusion, the magic play or *Māyā*.

He, the Mind, is said to mark the places for the Shining Ones; that is to say, by means of the shaping Power derived from the Father he organises his content into the Hierarchy of Divine creative Powers, the 'thirty' Gods[1] that we have already referred to. Symbolically these Shining Ones are the stars, fixed unalterably in the heavens, wheeling forever round the Pole in the majestic cycles of the Cosmic Harmony. It is failure to understand this that has led to accusations of astrolatry against the ancients. It should, however, be realised that the instructed among those ancients worshipped neither sun, nor moon, nor stars, nor yet those mountains, rivers, rain clouds, fire and what-not, that are all that many people can see behind the gods.

These Shining Ones are what Plato and Plotinus termed the Eternal or Divine Ideas, and Hermes Trismegistus, the Powers. From one point of view they are the hierarchies of gods, while a philosopher might term them Imaginal Archetypes.[2] Whatever name we give to them it must be remembered that they are living spiritual Powers; they are both shining with Light and creative because of the Life-energy with which they are charged.

Lastly, we read that Oeaohoo the younger turned the Upper into a shoreless Sea of Fire, and the One Manifested into the Great Waters. Those who have won the vision of this Mind know well that shoreless Sea of flaming Light and those turbulent Waters. All that is 'above' the Universal Mind (*i.e.* all that is unmanifested) appears simply as an impenetrable

[1] *Devas* or shining ones.
[2] *e.g.* E. D. Fawcett's 'Imaginals'.

wall of Light, while the One Manifested (*i.e.* Mind itself)
becomes the great ocean of manifested existence.

In these two, the Sea of Fire and the Sea of Water, we can
recognise the two Poles of the One Darkness as they manifest
in the Universal Mind. Note, however, that although, in the
One, they were side by side, they are now above and below,
the Fire of Spirit 'above' and the Waters of Matter 'below'.
We shall have to return to this topic later; here it will be
sufficient to state that all such mystic directions are of course
symbolic.

Before leaving this verse it may be of interest to quote an
Orphic account of the manifestation of the Universal Mind
that has been preserved in the *Clementine Homilies*.[1]

'Both fourfold Matter (the Root of Matter or *Mūla-
prakriti*) being ensouled and the whole Infinitude being as
though it were a Depth, flowing perpetually and indis-
tinguishably moving (compare the gently flowing interchange or *sadriśapariṇāma* that takes place in the *guṇas* in the
pre-cosmic stage according to the *Sāṅkhya*), and over and
over again pouring forth countless imperfect mixtures (the
infinite potentialities of the Mother), now of one kind and
now of another, and thereby dissolving them again owing
to its lack of order, and engulfing so that it could not be
bound together to serve for the generation of a living creature—it happened that the infinite Sea itself, being driven
round by its own peculiar nature, flowed with a natural
motion in an orderly fashion from out of itself into itself, as
it were a vortex, and blended its essences, and thus involun-
tarily the most developed part of all of them, that which was
most serviceable for the generation of a living creature,
flowed, as it were in a funnel, down the middle of the
universe, and was carried to the bottom by means of the
vortex that swept up everything and drew after it the

[1] The translation is that of G. R. S. Mead and may be found in his *Thrice Greatest
Hermes*, vol. I, p. 389. The passages in brackets have been added by the present
writers.

surrounding Spirit (the Light of the Father), and so gathering itself together as it were into the most productive form of all, it constituted a discrete state of things.

'For just as a bubble is made in water, so a sphere-like hollow form gathered itself together from all sides (compare the 'sphere' mentioned by Plotinus a few pages back).

'Thereupon, itself being impregnated in itself, carried up by the Divine Spirit that had taken it to itself as consort, it thrust forth its head into the Light (became conscious)—this, the greatest thing perchance that has ever been conceived (the Hindu *Mahat,* the Great One), as though it were out of the Infinite Deep's universe a work of art had been conceived and brought to birth, an ensouled work in form like unto the circumference of eggs (the *Brāhmic* Egg), in speed like to the swiftness of a wing (compare with this the winged sphere of Egyptian symbolism and the 'winged wheels' of Stanza V. 5. Also compare *Iśopanishad,* 4; 'Unmoving the One is swifter than the mind, the Gods (*devas*) reached not It, speeding on before.').'

(8) *Where was the germ and where was now darkness? Where is the spirit of the flame that burns in thy lamp, O Lanoo? The germ is that and that is light, the white brilliant son of the dark hidden father.*

Having described the birth of the Radiant Child in the last verse, the stanza takes us back to the matter of verse 6 and asks: Where is now the Darkness? A similar question was asked in the Vedas:

'That which is earlier than this Earth and Heaven, before the Asuras and the Gods had being—
What was the Germ primaeval which the Waters received where all the Gods were seen together?
The Waters, they received that Germ primaeval wherein all the Gods were gathered all together.

It rested, set upon the Unborn's navel, that One wherein
abide all things existing.
Ye will not find him who produced these creatures.
Another Thing hath risen up among you.'[1]

These words of the Vedic seer, the meaning of which should
be quite clear to him who has followed the Stanzas thus far,
can serve as a commentary on the present verse which commences by asking where, in the face of that Mighty Being that
has just been described, that 'Infant who at his birth devours
his Parents'[2] where is now the Germ from which it sprang;[3]
and where the Darkness in which it had dwelt? To this question
of the disciple the Teacher answers by another; where is the
living Spirit of the Flame of consciousness that burns in thy
Lamp or heart?

The answer to the one question is the answer to the other.
The Germ, the potentiality of manifest and living consciousness
within the Darkness, has become the radiant glory of Divine
Mind. This is the white, brilliant Son of the Darkness, for the
Father in this context is not to be understood as the abstract
polar principle of subjectivity but as the ultimate Source.

On the other hand, the flame of consciousness that burns in
our hearts is the Flame which shines so brilliantly within the
Universal Mind, the one consciousness that shines in all
beings, the 'Light that lighteth every man that cometh into
the world'.[4]

For that is where it is to be found. Neither this nor any other
cosmogony can provide an entirely comprehensible description of the emergence of this sphere of waking experience from
the unmanifest source of Being. There lies a mystery whose
solution cannot be expressed in words; indeed, it cannot be
objectified at all, for it is the mystery of the subject-object

---

[1] *Rig Veda*, X. 82. 5–7.
[2] *Rig Veda*, X. 79. 4.
[3] See Stanza III. 2.
[4] *St. John*, I. 9. Compare what H.P.B. has to say on the symbol of the Swan, *hamsa*
and its anagram *so'ham*. S.D., I. 78 *et seq.*

relationship which is the root of all knowing whatsoever. The outward press towards differentiation within the unitary being culminates in the foci of experience that we know as the self-assertive individualities of men. The solution to the mystery of Being is then to be found within or at the root of our own beings, within our own hearts. Every individual can find for himself the solution to the mystery, but he cannot convey that solution to others; he can only point out the way that he himself has travelled, and affirm the reality of his knowledge. He factually knows the truth, for his own being is that truth; any expression of that truth here, however, is necessarily in terms of this present state with all its inherent falsities.

To understand this, the disciple must meditate upon it in his own heart. All consciousness being one, what is true of the consciousness which manifests or burns in his own heart will be true of that which burns in the great Universal Mind, the Heart of the Cosmos.

'Sages who searched with their heart's thought discovered The Existent's kinship in the Non-existent.'[1]

This verse explains how it is that by knowing the blazing Dragon of Wisdom, the One Darkness is also known; or that, as Jesus put it, 'he who hath seen the Son hath seen the Father';[2] and it teaches the disciple how, by searching in his own heart's core, he may come to learn for himself 'the Existent's kinship in the Non-existent', to know in very truth That which transcends all knowledge.

There are two directions in which the ancestry of man may be traced; one along the line of his physical parentage, the other along that of his spiritual being—that inner being by virtue of whose presence he is Man. The first we may call his manifest ancestry, and the second his unmanifest, shut off from our normal vision by the bright light of out-turned consciousness, just as the Above is shut off by the Shoreless

[1] *Rig Veda*, X. 129. 4.
[2] *Gospel of St. John*, XIV. 9.

Sea of Fire in the previous verse. Between the two extremes of man's body and his Spirit lies an area of physical, emotional and mental characteristics whose source may be traced in either direction. For all such characteristics we can find precedents both in terms of physical ancestry and in terms of patterns impressed on the individual psyche by the garnered experience of previous lives (*samskāra*). One line of Hindu thought envisages the Universal Mind as similarly finding within itself the pattern of things 'as they were before'.

Although, then, the veil has been drawn behind it, and the bright consciousness of Universal Mind is, as it were, turned away from the unmanifest parents, those powers which brought Mind into being are still there, and we have now to find in manifestation existent representations of those unmanifest beings. This divine birth has not, however, the discrete material objectivity of human birth and so we do not find the parents as separate beings, but as modes of Universal Mind.

(9) *Light is cold flame, and flame is fire, and fire produces heat, which yields water: the water of life in the great mother.*

The Great Mother is the Matrix herself, and the 'Water of Life' in the Great Mother is the area of manifestation marked out by the One Ray of Light. In verse 2 the Waters of Life slumbered under the Darkness, and here the Water of Life is in the Great Mother. Just as there was a lack of distinction between Father and Son, so there is here between the Mother as a transcendent principle of potentiality and as the demarcated field of existence. The content aspect of experience is always in some sense the Great Mother.

At the end of verse 7, the Son, the 'White Brilliant Son of the Dark Hidden Father' (III. 1), turns the One Manifested into the Great Waters, those same Waters which in verse 6 were called the Ocean of Immortality, the Ocean of 'Radiant Light which was Fire and Heat and Motion'. This verse now summarises the successive stages by which the diffusion of the Light of Consciousness throughout the Space of the Matrix produces the field of manifest energies in which the ideal intellectual patterns of the Logos can be clothed in form.

The Ray of the Father-Light is the cold, detached Flame of the Divine Reason. But this cold Flame is rushing out in the effort to unite with its opposite pole, the Matrix; and its uniting is a Fire, a Fire in which the energy of the light is absorbed so that it now manifests on a lower scale as Heat, the Heat of Desire.

This Heat is the living energy which swirls around each individualised point in Mind, linking the whole into an impressionable sea of existence, the Waters of Life. It is into this fluid Matrix that Mind projects the patterns of its imaginings.

These stages correspond with the levels of manifestation: the Light of Universal Mind, the individualised Flames ('the Flame that burns in thy Lamp', verse 8), the Fire of the lower or sense mind which unites consciousness to content, the Heat of Desire which seems to draw out consciousness into ever greater identification with its content, and the Watery expanse of flowing energy which, as it cools under the 'Breath of the Mother' (III. 11), condenses into the World Egg (III. 3).

Thus the fiery consciousness burns in the heart of the Waters of existence—a fervent mating of opposites which leaves the atom in a state of tension and man's soul in unrest.

(10) *Father-Mother spin a web whose upper end is fastened to Spirit, the light of the one Darkness, and the lower one to its shadowy end, Matter; and this web is the universe spun out of the two substances made in one, which is Svabhāvat.*

Our study of the previous verses has shown us that the web-like universe in which we live cannot be considered as a simple duality between the spiritual and the material aspects of being. This verse describes Spirit as the 'light of the One Darkness', and verse 8 told us that light is the 'white brilliant Son' or Universal Mind, the Subject of the universe. This 'Spirit' is then the light of integral consciousness shining in every point within universal Space. And Space is the dark field of objectivity without whose contrasting shade nothing could become manifest: it is the field of differentiated content, just as the Matrix was the field of undifferentiated content, for each point in space is now a duality of individualised consciousness and individualised content.

Thus we see that these two poles are no longer the unstained light of the Father and the undifferentiated potentiality of the Matrix. They are the two principal modes of manifest being about which we have been speaking in the preceding verses: the subjective triad of conscious modes, 'Spirit', and the quaternity of modes of objective content, 'Matter', the Three and the Four. This is the warp of the web.

Across the warp, the hyphenated or linked Father-Mother duality weaves the inter-relating woof in the form of externalised connections between each and every point. Each point has become a seemingly independent subject, related through its private field of content or 'body' to the 'bodies' of all the other points. There are therefore two directions in which the content of the spatial field or web of the universe is linked into a unity; a 'vertical' direction, representing the universal simultaneity of divine Mind and its total content, and a 'horizontal' direction, representing the inter-linking of all phenomena through forces acting in the manifest field, such as electro-magnetic attractions or emotional affinities. The former linkage is in eternity, the latter in time.

Thus we get the ancient symbol of the cross within the circle ⊕ which shows how the interplay of the Father ⊙ with the Mother ⊖ give rise to the Son ⊕ with its four poles instead of the original two. This allocation of directions also gives rise to the usual psychological feeling that Spirit is 'above', Matter is 'below', while Subject and Object are, as it were, on one level with us.

As should be clear, however, this quarternity is a development of the original Father-Mother duality. Nothing new has entered the system, and the fourfold universe is fundamentally spun out of the two substances, Father and Mother, 'made in

one', the One self-becoming power of the Darkness. 'He on
whom the sky, the earth, and the atmosphere are woven . . .
Him alone know as the one Self.'[1]

'*Svabhāvat*' is not merely a name to which we can ascribe
arbitrary meanings, nor is it a technical term describing a
special stage of the creation. It can be translated as 'the self-
becoming', a term that is as fitly applicable to the whole unity
of Being as it is to certain of its parts. The verse says 'This web
is the universe. . . . which is *Svabhāvat*.' Just as the Source
is the dark self-becoming, so is the Son the same self-becoming
now manifest in bright self-consciousness. We could term the
latter *Svabhāvat* the Younger. These two, the unmanifest
Father and the manifest Son, are the 'Two forms of Brahma;
the formed and the formless, the mortal and the immortal,
the moving and the stationary, the actual and the yon'.[2]

It may also be noted that this fourfold manifestation of what
are essentially only two Poles is responsible for the archetypal
principle of rotation. This principle is symbolised by the
swastika, itself the symbol of the quaternary, with its two
forms 卐 and 卍 standing for the outgoing and the incoming
modes known in Sanskrit as *pravritti* and *nivritti*. With rotation
time comes into being, as it must with the manifest Brahma.
'There are assuredly two forms of Brahma; Time and the
Timeless.'[3]

(11) *It expands when the breath of fire is upon it, it contracts
when the breath of the Mother touches it. Then the sons dissociate
and scatter, to return into their Mother's bosom at the end of the
'great day' and re-become one with her. When it is cooling, it
becomes radiant, its sons expand and contract through their own
selves and hearts; they embrace infinitude.*

The Web expands under the breath of the Father as manifest
in consciousness of subjectivity; but contracts under the touch
of the Mother as manifest in objectivity or form. This we can

---

[1] *Mundaka Upanishad*, II. 2. 5.
[2] *Brihadāraṇyaka Upanishad*, II. 3. 1.
[3] *Maitrī Upanishad*, VI. 15.

see in our own experience: in consciousness the universe expands into that wonderful vista, the great 'spread-outness' that extends in space till it is lost in the antinomies of infinity. The greater the range of our consciousness, the wider and vaster becomes the universe. On the other hand, from the standpoint of 'matter', man shrinks into the compass of a six-foot machine, and even humanity as a whole becomes what someone described as a mere minor crustal phenomenon. Our field of consciousness expands when we subjectively identify ourselves with it through our desires, thus causing the smallest part to seem immeasurably important, and contracts when we objectify the parts and make the whole seem separate from ourselves.

We may say that the expansion is the projective power of consciousness, joyously sallying forth into the universe of things, entering, knowing, and making them its own. The universe is *its* universe, existing as its content; it is the Lord of all it surveys.

As opposed to this joyful, conquering, expansion there is the other movement, the contractive touch of the Mother. When this movement is dominant the emphasis is shifted from consciousness to things which, like a ring of sullen enemies, crowd in on man proclaiming their utter independence of consciousness. The universe is dead, dead lumps of matter, matter which is the mistress of everything; consciousness is nothing but an epi-phenomenon. Nearer and nearer creep the things, invading even the body of man, consciousness withdrawing before them till it is allowed only to flicker dubiously, a point within the heart, and even from that stronghold its foes (*e.g.* Behaviourism) seek to expel it.

But this analysis is inadequate as it stands. It reflects the ordinary duality between Spirit and Matter: the feeling that we must choose between one or the other, that the materialistic view of the universe cannot be reconciled with the spiritual. Yet these two movements, the expansive and the contractive, are necessary to each other, and it is by their reconciliation in a universe of alternating modes that a relatively stable manifestation of worlds in living movement is achieved.

The expansive breath aspires to know everything, to achieve everything; but the contractive breath of the Mother, the cold touch of reality, sets a limit to these aspirations, for they have to be contained within the now limited possibilities of the Web. The unlimited Lord of the universe is contained within the circle of fate, that moving cycle of events which both provides and restricts the field of opportunity in which the Divine finds its manifest Self-expression.

Whatever we have to achieve in this world is not limited by the range of consciousness, but by our physical and mental capacities, our environmental conditions, and finally by our life span. Yet, if it were not for these material considerations, our aspirations would achieve nothing. The restrictions of form are as essential to the universe as is the expansive urge to transcend them.

Thus the rhythm of the universe proceeds, a rhythm that is ultimately based on the Great Breath. Night alternates with day, sleeping with waking, introversion with extroversion, and, in the world of thought, periods of soaring idealism with periods of narrow materialism. Such, on all levels, is the life-breath of the Cosmos.

The expansions and contractions that are the living movement of the universal Web continue to manifest in the individual minds that are the selves and the hearts of every point in the web; the selves being the conscious or male poles, and the hearts the feeling or feminine centres. Thus the great duality is continued; the single bright son of the dark parents is in himself all the sons, and each son contains both parents within himself.

With the outbursting of the third Logos, the Sons assert their independence of the universality of divine Mind. The outflowing energy dissociates them from their source and they scatter far and wide into outwardness, borne onwards by the ever advancing tides of Light. Each point within that Light becomes a focus through which the Light streams forth again upon the forms. Projecting itself into those forms it seizes them and issues forth afresh in strivings towards other forms which it again seeks to grasp and master.

Then begins the great withdrawal or *Nivritti*. The Light withdraws, saying of each form, gross or subtle, 'this is not me nor mine'. This is the macrocosmic parallel to the path of discrimination as taught by the Sānkhya, the discrimination of *Purusha* from *Prakriti*, or of Spirit from Matter. The individualised forms to which the Mother has given birth return again to Her Bosom at the end of the Cosmic Day, thus re-becoming what they were before, potentialities hidden in the darkness.

In the foregoing description we have taken the Son as the unitary Divine Mind or Subject of the universe, and the plurality of Sons as the individualised points within its spatial content. There is, however, another way of looking at this dissociation of the Sons.

The Son, Universal Mind, is conscious of his own unity, so that sense of separateness is first felt in him, although he is in himself entire and lacking in nothing, The separateness is simply the sense of being individual, independent of the darkness of his mother's womb; it is the Upanishadic 'I am One' (*Eko 'ham*) which calls forth the 'May I be many' (*Bahu Syām*). In fact he has never emerged from the womb; he is unborn, for there is no spatial womb, only that in which he is and from the darkness of which he has 'emerged' by virtue of the light of Bright Space which is himself. He is Self-Born (*Svayambhu*).

He looks out into Space, but in whichever direction he 'looks' he sees only himself, for there is only himself to see and to be seen. But because he is individual he sees himself as an individual, and because there are now many directions, he sees himself as many individuals and becomes plurality. He has objectified his own separateness and each of his selves 'contains all within itself, and at the same time sees all in every other'. Thus they 'embrace infinitude'.

In the first description the points or Sons, to which the later stanzas refer as 'sparks', are the nuclei of forms belonging to one universe. But is there only one universe? It is hard to believe that this universe in which we live is the only possible expression of the Self-Becoming Divinity. We have therefore included this second description as being suggestive of another sort of dissociation of the Sons giving rise to a number of separate self-contained universes. The unity of *the* Son of the Divine Parents is an essential, metaphysical unity, a transcendent principle of unity of which there cannot be more than one. But this does not mean that there cannot be a multiplicity of such unities, Sons, in manifestation. The spatial extent of our universe can no doubt be defined in terms of the boundary from which visible light returns, but the fact that this sets a limit to our physical sense perceptions by no means renders it meaningless to suggest the possibility of there being other such self-contained systems. We are not ostriches that we should deny existence to what we cannot see.

These Sons, too, scatter to the ten directions. Each is the whole level and each is a separate image. With their own light they dispel the darkness. At the end of the 'Great Day', when Subject and Object again merge and only the consciousness of the Dark remains, these Sons, too, will no longer shine with the light of self-conscious knowing but will re-become one with that dark Mother who, like the earth, absorbs the forms of her children back into her own being.

The radiance of the cooling universe is the radiance of increasing self-consciousness as the two poles of being become more and more deeply identified with each other. This is what gives rise both to the peculiar importance of the physical level and to the common feeling that the reality of the physical is not lightly to be exchanged for, what appears to be, the lesser certainty of more subtle levels of being. The web-like field of consciousness cools and the plasticity of the upper levels gives way to the harder and more set forms of the colder materiality.

While the universe is 'cooling', that is, while the expansive process of creation is in progress,[1] it becomes 'radiant'. The psychic energy of the expansion charges, as it were, each form it meets, so that that form radiates the Light in two modes: back towards its source, thus being 'perceived' as object by that source, and forward to become itself a secondary source of light or subject.

An illustration from the field of science may help the reader to grasp this point more easily. If a source of light is placed at the centre of a number of concentric glass globes, part of the light given out from the centre is reflected back to the centre from the inner surface of each globe and part of it passes out through the glass wall and goes out of the globe to serve as a source of light to the next outer globe. This phenomenon is repeated at the two surfaces of each successive globe. The diagram illustrates the point.

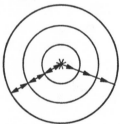

The first or backward radiation is responsible for the fact that consciousness perceives the contents of any given level, mental or physical. The second or forward radiation transforms the object of one level, into the subject of the next, and so carries the manifestation of the universe outwards and downwards. In this way the forms perceived by the higher mind become themselves, by their forward radiation, the lower mind; and so on until we reach the gross physical forms, so inert or *tāmasic* that no further forward radiation is possible but only the backward one of perception.

Thus has the outer limit of the universe been reached. The

[1] Note that even in the material world of objects the process of expansion lowers the temperature, while compression produces heat.

waves of energy have reached the furthest edge of the cosmos, beyond which is utter nothingness, and now roll back upon themselves, returning to the Source from which they came. As Plotinus said, pure matter is pure negation or nothingness. So far we have been dealing with what may be termed the radial expansion of the Universe along the spirit-matter dimension of the Web. This process results in the formation of a number of levels like the coats of an onion—though this, of course, is a crude and in some ways misleading analogy.

In addition to this we are told that each Son or point in the Web expands and contracts in itself, which produces, as it were, a horizontal expansion within each level. This is best seen on the level or our ordinary experience, the content of which expands in all directions, though still indubitably on the same level, till, as the verse says, it 'embraces infinitude' in the remotest solitudes of space beyond the furthest stars. On the other hand, in sleep, death, or introversion, the world contracts and vanishes into nothing. Such horizontal expansion and contractions should be considered as taking place, *mutatis mutandis*, on all the other levels as well, each plane extending into a created infinity in which the Soul can wander, almost for ever, and then again contracting to its central point as the Soul's boat goes up the Stream of Life towards its Source.

(12) *Then Svabhāvat sends Fohat to harden the Atoms. Each is a part of the web. Reflecting the 'Self-Existent Lord', like a mirror, each becomes in turn a world.*

This verse introduces us to the term *Fohat*, a word unknown to ordinary scholarship it seems, but which H.P.B. defines[1] as 'the active (male) potency of the *Shakti* (female reproductive power) in nature'. Elsewhere she says that it is closely connec- to with the One Life, that it is the unity of all cosmic energies, the prototype of Eros, the bridge which links the opposite poles of Subject and Object, Spirit and Matter. Also she quotes from somewhere that it is 'sprung from the Brain of the

[1] *Theosophical Glossary.*

L

Father and the Bosom of the Mother' and states that its Vedic name was *Apām-napāt*, the swiftly-speeding, golden Son of the Waters.[1]

Fohat is in fact that aspect of the One Darkness which appears as Power or Energy. Its essence is the creative impulse from that Darkness, the 'Be, and it was' of the Qu'rān. It is manifested primarily as the bond which unites Subject and Object on all planes from the highest to the lowest. As such it represents the unity of the One Darkness linking the duality of its poles. For the same reason also we can understand its being said to be the prototype of Eros, for it manifests in that striving of the subject towards the object which is the characteristic of all desire. 'Sprung from the Brain of the Father and the Bosom of the Mother' is an apt phrasing of what we tried to explain in connection with verse 9 of this stanza when speaking of the Heat which yields the Water of Life in the passive fecundity of the Great Mother. Thus we come back to H.P.B.'s definition of it as the 'active (male) potency in the female reproductive power'. In any case it is the Divine and Fiery creative power and is particularly manifest on the plane of the One Life. Its assimilation to electricity comes from its nature as a link between the two poles between which it functions as attraction or repulsion. Its purest (in the sense of most unmixed) manifestation is on the level of the desire nature on which plane the force of attraction or repulsion works unchecked. A western version is probably to be found in the Orphic '*Phanes*'.

It may be asked in what way *Fohat* differs from the creative power which has just previously been described as operative in all the expansions which have taken place and which caused the Sons to 'dissociate and scatter'. The answer is that it is not different; the Power in the cosmos is one power, the living, creative power of the One Darkness; there is no other power, though, from our point of view, it may conveniently be taken as centred, like everything else, in the Universal Mind.

[1] Those who wish to pursue the matter further are referred to the *S. D.* in which there are hundreds of references from which we have cited a few of the most relevant.

It is now necessary to say a word or two about 'Atoms'. The word is perhaps slightly misleading as it suggests a connection with the atoms of chemistry, whereas no such connection is here intended. As H.P.B. pointed out, to the ancient Initiates atoms signified Souls[1] or, as we might put it, spiritual units, and particularly the point-like individual Egos or *Jīvas*.[2] At this stage, however, we are not concerned with *Jīvas* but with larger units, namely the levels, which are also spiritual units as is shown by the use of the Sanskrit term *aṇu*, atom, as a title of *Brahmā*, the symbol of the Universal Mind.

As the degree of self-consciousness increases, so the sense of separateness intensifies, and each image of Universal Mind becomes more clearly defined, with harder outlines. This process is similar to the hardening a man's psyche undergoes as he learns to replace the loose thinking of adolescence by the clear perceptions of ordered thought, and again, when a man checks his thought from wandering, his psychic field at once becomes 'harder', more definite and more charged with internal energy. Thus, Fohat 'hardens' the 'atoms', the *aṇu*, the fine points in space that are the locations of Him, who is 'Smaller than the small, greater than the great',[3] in other words, *Brahmā*, the same Universal Mind seen in another aspect. The atoms are the points of view, the points from which mind looks out on objective being.

That *Svabhāvat sends* Fohat implies that the act is now in self-consciousness, whereas previous to the emergence of mind there was no separate integration that could perform deliberate action. Now, that gathering of himself together which is the hardening of the atoms seems to him to be achieved by his own will, although, from an impersonal point of view, what is happening obeys the utterly determined patterns that have emerged from the primal darkness 'as they were before'. Neither free-will nor determinism are in themselves absolute

[1] S.D., I. 567. H.P.B. also said of the analogous term Monad 'that it may apply equally to the vastest Solar system or the tiniest atom'.

[2] Literally: lives or living beings.

[3] *Kaṭhopanishad*, II. 20.

values; both are manifest terms, a pair that have arisen from a common unmanifest ancestor. The personal aspect of the Divine Being manifests the principle of free-will in the response he gives to a personal approach, with all the close intimacy of the most dearly loved; others who have not made themselves intimate with him sometimes see this and out of blind jealousy deny the existence of a God, for they call the love of God to his intimates a partiality and an injustice, and they say God cannot be unjust. Let such people, then, see all things as determined and cease from egotistical effort. If they will deny to others the privileges of intimacy that spring from a personal love—can love be impersonal?—let them deny to themselves both love and fear, and, rising above all human passions, find within themselves That of which they are a determined part.

Each point is a part of the web, for the web is space, and the points are points in space; though we are not yet speaking of the three-dimensional space (*ākāsha*) of physical experience. Each point reflects the 'Self-existent Lord', the Father who is the source of their being and whose unmanifest light they now make manifest. Each point is the image of the Father mirrored in the myriad ripples of the waters of Life. Each point becomes a world, a sphere of experience in itself.

Reflecting thus the unity of the Father, each point—however much its light may be diffused and scattered in the forms and content—is yet a unity, a world, for it is held together by the unity of that which contemplates it.[1] It is for this reason that the world of physics is a unity, complete in itself, and needing, from a purely physical point of view, nothing beyond or outside itself in order to explain itself. As long as we are content to apply the categories of physics, nothing in the physical world will ever lead us to suspect the existence of anything beyond that world. All is one complete and inter-

---

[1] It is of interest to note that the Sanskrit word *loka*, a region or world, derives from the verb *lok*, to see, to look. This is also connected with the root *ruc*, to shine, be radiant.

locking whole, and attempts to find 'God' lurking in crevices are misguided and certain to fail. On the other hand it is becoming increasingly evident that the categories of physics are quite inadequate for giving an account of life as a whole and that, as Eddington has pointed out, their seeming self-sufficiency arises from what he terms the device of circular definition or, as we might say, from the fact that they never trade with other circles of categories, but live exclusively by taking in each other's washing.

STANZA FOUR

Being the fourth of seven Stanzas from
The Book of Dzyan

1. *Listen, ye Sons of the Earth, to your instructors, the Sons of the Fire. Learn, there is neither first nor last; for all is One Number, issued from No-Number.*

2. *Learn what we, who descend from the Primordial Seven, we who are born from the Primordial Flame, have learnt from our Fathers . . .*

3. *From the effulgency of light—the ray of the ever-darkness— sprang in space the re-awakened Energies; the one from the egg, the six and the five; (then) the three, the one, the four, the one, the five—the twice seven, the sum total. And these are: the essences, the flames, the elements, the builders, the numbers, the arūpa, the rūpa, and the force of Divine Man, the Sum Total. And from the Divine Man emanated the forms, the sparks, the sacred animals, and the messengers of the sacred fathers within the holy four.*

4. *This was the army of the voice—the divine mother of the seven. The sparks of the seven are subject to and the servants of, the first, the second, the third, the fourth, the fifth, the sixth, and the seventh of the seven. These 'sparks' are called spheres, triangles, cubes, lines and modellers; for thus stands the Eternal Nidāna—the Oi-Ha-Hou (the permutation of Oeaohoo).*

5. *(The Oi-Ha-Hou) which is:*
Darkness, the Boundless or the No-Number, Ādi-Nidāna Svabhāvat: the $\bigcirc$:

I. The Ādi Sanat, the Number, for he is One.

II. The Voice of the Lord Svabhāvat, the Numbers, for he is One and Nine.

III. The 'Formless Square'.

And these three enclosed within the ○ are the sacred four, and the ten are the Arūpa Universe. Then come the 'Sons', the seven Fighters, the One, the eighth left out, and his Breath which is the Light-Maker (Bhāskara).

6. Then the Second Seven, who are the Lipika, produced by the Three. The rejected Son is One, the Son-Suns are countless.

THE CAUSAL HIERARCHY

The preceding stanza described the birth of the Universal Mind and gave a summary of the further stages of creation. In this stanza, the central one of seven, we are introduced both to the many energies which derive from the transcendent Principles and to the causal powers which organise those energies into the hierarchy of being. The inner aspects precede and have lordship over the outer and manifest aspects.

Before the entirely unmanifest content of the Ever-Darkness can be brought out into the full objectivity of the material universe it must first be brought to manifestation in Mind as ideas or divine imaginals. Like Brahmā the demiurge, 'he imaged them forth as in the previous time'.[1]

The contents of the Macrocosmic Mind emerge from the darkness of non-existence in much the same way that, in the microcosm, the patterns governing the projection of man's psychic energy into the world of things are held in the darkness of the psyche and emerge or are actualised through his creative activity.

Our treatment of the levels of the universe may sometimes be confusing; but the alternatives either of an over-simplification, with its consequence of appearing to put forward an

[1] *Yathāpūrvam akalpayat.* From the famous Cosmogonic Hymn, *Rig Veda* X. 190. 3.

unsubtle attitude towards an essentially subtle mystery, or of setting out a vastly complex hierarchy of powers, such as those of the Gnostic systems, hierarchies in which the correspondences of the levels are apt to be lost, would appear to involve equal if not greater disadvantages. The subject is a difficult one and any attempt to make it seem either simple or mechanistic would be irresponsibly misleading.

Just as the unmanifest content of the Darkness can only become explicitly known when differentiated and spread out in space-time, so all cosmogonies have to treat the 'levels' of the universe as if they too were spatially separate, whereas in fact they are simultaneously present. We are at this moment living in the creative process and every level of being is in us and around us.

(1) *Listen, ye Sons of the Earth, to your instructors, the Sons of the Fire. Learn, there is neither first nor last; for all is One Number, issued from No-Number.*[1]

Subsequent stanzas frequently take us over the ladder of the emerging levels as if to stress the importance of this aspect of their message. No matter how many levels and multitudes of manifest forms may be described, 'All is One Number, issued from No-Number.' There is no first nor last, no up nor down, no lower and no higher, for all is the One Existence which issues from the Non-Existence. Learn what you can, they say, of the relative truths,[2] the divisions of the universe, inner and outer, upper and lower, the Way of Manifestation and the Way of Withdrawal, the hierarchies of Creative Powers and the ancestry of man. Learn what you can of all this, but remember that beyond it is the ultimate truth (*paramārthika satya*), the Void (*Shūnyatā*) of the Buddhists, the 'Fullness' of the Vedāntic Brahma, the Divine Darkness of Christian mystics,

[1] On *S.D.* I. 30, this verse is punctuated as follows:
    'All is one: number issued from no-number', but in the body of the work the punctuation is as given above.
[2] The *samvritti satya* of Nāgārjuna's *Mādhyamika* school, the *paratantra* of the Yogā-chārins.

the *Ain Soph* of the Kabbala, the unnumbered Mystic Fool of the Tarot Trumps. Know that, and remember that all the rest, the glamorous 'ten-thousand things' are but the shining Images (*deva*)[1] in which is bodied forth the Magic Play. All was one, all is one, and all will forever be one. Even that oneness is only one in contrast to the manyness of the world, for in itself it is neither one nor many but just *Shūnyatā*, the mystic zero or no-number which the Vedānta carefully terms not 'unity' but *a-dvaita*, 'not two'. It is One Number in contrast only to the many numbers: in itself it is No-Number. It was from this point of view that Nāgārjuna wrote that 'there is no difference between *Nirvāṇa* and *Samsāra* (the world of change). That which is the Ultimate Limit of *Nirvāṇa* is also the Ultimate Limit of *Samsāra*. Between the two there is not even the subtlest difference'.[2]

There are those who speak impatiently of this *Shūnya-vāda* saying that, even if it be true, it can be of little use to us who seek practical knowledge of the Path and can well leave the metaphysical nature of the Goal to look after itself. But such an attitude is a mistaken one. All, whether manifest or unmanifest, is in fact one Reality. It is this transcendent knowledge that enables those great beings, best known by their Buddhist title of *Bodhisattva*, to avoid the two conditions which are all that some teachings offer, namely that of sorrow and bondage amidst the manifested plurality, or that of freedom and bliss in the unmanifest unity. By virtue of this secret and sublime Wisdom, they are enabled to remain poised upon the very edge of manifested being, dwelling within the bliss of Unity, yet seeing with unforgetting eyes the myriad sorrows of men, and helping with compassionate, god-like hands those sorrows where such help is sought and earned.

Moreover, even for us who seek but to set our feet upon the lower rungs of the Ladder, this truth is one which we should

---

[1] *Devas* literally means the shining ones, the 'planetary' and 'elemental' Powers who shine, but with the one Paternal Light.
[2] *Mādhyamika Kārika*, XXV. 19 and 20.

try to understand and bear in mind. If we do not, the universe with all its Levels and Powers becomes a collection of separate things standing in their own right; things of which neither the coming into being nor the vanishing from being can ever be understood. If this is not kept in mind, all that is said about the cosmic structure becomes a system of mechanistic mythology, more showy perhaps, but fundamentally as unenlightened as that of materialism.

The inner teaching has frequently suffered from this mistake. Its symbols have been taken literally, and the inner life of the spirit, the treading of the Path to Freedom, has been cramped and weighed down by vast and elaborate mental constructions which, taken in and for themselves, press down upon the heart and check the spirit's soaring flight. Ground between cycles of an endless past and of an endless future, entangled in a maze of 'Rounds' and 'Races', rooted on 'Planes' and 'Paths', too often the heart of the disciple is crushed and he forgets that the Eternal Peace is round him and within him here and now. If he but use the Wisdom Eye within his soul, even now, the whirling cycles shrink to a point and cease; Time and Levels vanish and only the bliss of Unity remains, for Now, not in some dim past or dimmer future, 'all is One Number, issued from No-Number'. It is for this reason that the Sons of the Fire preface all that they have to say about cosmic structure with the enunciation of this fundamental truth.

The Sons of Fire are not, at least not primarily, great beings who, in some privileged way, have command of truth and impart it authoritatively to men, backed by applauding thunder. The Sons of Fire are the teachings themselves. They exist in the very structure of the Universal Mind, which, as we already know, is bounded 'above' by the Sea of Fire. That which is 'written'[1] in the Universal Mind is true just because it *is* the

---

[1] Brahmā is the author of the Hindu Veda and his consort Sarasvatī is the goddess of learning; together they represent the knowledge and creativity of the *Mahat* or Universal Mind. In this sense Brahmā *is* the Veda and in this (divine) *Veda* all knowledge is 'written', as it is, too, in the uncreated Qu'rān of the Sūfi mystic, laid up in the eternal heavens, though, as Rumi says, 'not in Arabic'.

Universal Mind, the Consciousness which embraces the *whole* of the manifested cosmos. All that happens in this or any other world happens within that universal consciousness, and he who can gain access to its 'pages' wins omniscience.

But how can we gain such access? Is it not like saying that he who can become God will share God's knowledge? No, it is not in the least like that. If the Universal Mind were something 'up there', something far away in unapproachable god-like remoteness, it would no doubt be true that its knowledge could be of little avail to us 'down here'. But it is not so. The Universal Mind is not at all away 'up there': it is here and now. Neither beyond the starry skies nor yet on far mystic planes of being must that Universal Mind be sought, but in ourselves. We are motes of dust dancing within its Light which surrounds us everywhere. More, it pervades us through and through. We are but moments of that Light: it is our very Self. Inside and outside we are nothing but that Light; even our outer structure is the impress of its thought, and it is for this reason that, in actual truth, man is the measure of all things and contains within himself—even within his physical body—all the wonders of the universe.

We think of ourselves as composed of modifications of matter with or without the addition of what we vaguely term a mind, a mind which, we are inclined to think, is destroyed with the death of the body of which it is perhaps an epiphenomenon. It is for this reason that we are the Sons of Earth and that our so-called knowledge is of the earth earthy. For this we have no one to blame but ourselves. Whatever theories we may champion in our philosophical lecture rooms, in practice we persist in identifying ourselves with our physical bodies. 'I am a child of Earth and Starry Heaven', said the Orphic Initiate, 'but my Race is of Heaven alone.' These physical bodies and the material environment in which they move are but the dull surface crust upon the gleaming sea of molten metal; within our very selves is the great Sea of Light.

The sort of thinking that makes us Sons of Earth can be

seen in the way we unquestioningly identify our own good
with the good of the body, whether our 'own' or the projection of our possessiveness on to the body of our family or our
race, and also in the way we seek merely material solutions
to all social and political problems. It is the sort of thinking that
measures the standard of living by the number of flush closets
or motor cars to the square mile, thus confusing technical
progress with well-being. It confounds literacy with education,
and pleasurable sensations with happiness, sees adherence to a
code of moral behaviour as spirituality, substitutes a dry study
of systems of thought for inner knowledge, and replaces
sentiment by sentimentality.

Too few of us have learned to recognise the voices of the
Sons of Fire within ourselves for it to be possible to find
examples of their manifestations in the realm of common
thought. The inner teacher resides, as the Kundalini system of
yoga has it, in the 'centre between the eyes', balanced between
the pairs of opposites. He knows that not till men have drunk
their fill of joy and suffering and it has gone bitter in their
bellies will they turn to him for solace and listen to his teaching.
He knows that all below him is multiple, that the unity and
equality of man is not to be found anywhere in the levels of
multiplicity but only in the transcendent unity of Universal
Mind, and that those who attempt to realise such ideal states
in the outer world are but chasing shadows. He knows that the
way to him, like the way of ordinary birth and death, has of
necessity to be travelled alone, and that there are only a few at
any time who even wish to attempt it. He knows that the
world's great organised bodies of exoteric religion have without exception become symbiotic to social order or political
interests, and have lost the ferment of the spirit. His teaching is
no mere differentiation between the relatively good and bad,
those 'mere minor matters of morality'[1] whose standards are
subservient both to private interests and to their summation
in public welfare, but a teaching 'more subtle than the thous-

[1] The Buddha.

andth part of a hair' that, once grasped, will lead a man to the
source of his own being, the Fount of all the being in the
worlds.

It is therefore within ourselves that we must seek the Truth.
Withdrawing our consciousness from the outer crust of
material forms, we must attend to the living Truths of which
those forms are but the crystallised pattern. Nor, though
difficult because of our inveterate outward-looking habit, is
this in any way impossible for us here and now. True, the
process will take a long time, many lives even, before it can
thoroughly be mastered and brought to perfection, but, once
the Path is sincerely entered upon, progress is steady and sure.
It cannot be too strongly emphasised that now, at this very
moment and for our very selves, the Divine Wisdom is
available. Within us, yes us, the Sons of Fire are now sounding
forth their wisdom, born of the parent Flame. Not in remote
Himālayan caverns and to exceptional souls alone, but here in
the caves of our own hearts the Truth *is being taught*: it is we
who do not listen, and then fill earth and sky with clamour,
wailing like peevish children for our supposedly forlorn state,
abandoned in the darkness of ignorance. 'Listen, ye Sons of the
Earth, to your instructors the Sons of the Fire' who are within
and around you everywhere.

(2) *Learn what we, who descend from the Primordial Seven, we
who are born from the Primordial Flame, have learnt from our
Fathers.* . . .

Whence comes the stainless knowledge of the Sons of Fire,
and what is the guarantee of its truth? The answer to these
questions is the same whether we consider the Sons of Fire as
those great Beings already referred to as the holders of the
Secret Wisdom, or in the equally if not—to us at least—still
more important sense of those gleaming facets of eternal truth
that form a starry heaven within ourselves.[1] Those stars of
truth, though ever shining in that inner sky, are hidden from

[1] The *chidākāsha* of Hindu philosophy.

our eyes by the bright daylight veil of ordinary consciousness. But just as from the bottom of a deep well the stars of heaven can be seen, even in daytime, so, by withdrawal of the consciousness from the dazzle of outer forms, those inner stars can be seen by the soul even now, without the need of waiting for the Night of trance or death. Such ability to contemplate the inner heavens in the daylight of waking life is one of the essential characteristics of the true yogi. Like the Chaldean magi, his gaze is ever fixed upon the starry Sons of Fire, and his outer actions but re-produce in this world the intricate and wonderful harmonies of the majestic writing that shines in the heavens of the Soul.

But whence comes this writing, whence its title to be called the truth? It is the truth because it is the archetypal pattern of the manifest universe to which the latter must inevitably conform. It is born from the Primordial Flame, the Light of the transcendent witnessing consciousness. It is infallible because it is the imprint of the Primordial or Inner Seven, those ultimate Archetypes of the universe, which form, as it were, the Norm or plan of the whole cosmos. Nowhere and at no time can anything take place except as a manifestation of some facet of those Inner Seven. Their transcendental harmony is at once the source and master of all that happens in the outer universe.

A fragment of occult commentary quoted by H.P.B.[1] likens the inner seven to 'the embrasures of that black impenetrable fortress', the Absolute, and the Outer Seven to 'the light of Eternity escaping therefrom', and it is only through those seven embrasures that the universe can be shot forth or projected from the Darkness. To vary the metaphor: the inner Seven are reflected in the calm mirror of the passionless Witnessing Consciousness and then projected outwards upon the heaven of the Universal Mind, there to become the shining Sons of Fire, the windows of the palace of the Cosmos through which alone can come all light that is within it. It is for this

[1] S.D., II. 33.

reason that the knowledge they impart is a true and certain knowledge, one possessing an *a priori* character and governing all below.

It is for this reason also that the number seven plays such an important part in ancient cosmogonies, for it represents the Cosmos, the order and harmony underlying the chaotic appearances of the universe. From the One Darkness have come the Two Parents, and from these three fundamental moments of Reality have sprung all the myriads of patterns and sub-patterns that form the worlds of our experience. These are the 'Seven', the possible number of combinations of the 'Three'. From the three moments spring the Inner Seven, and from that Seven arises the 'sevenfold' nature of all manifestation. And perhaps those who perceive a fundamental sevenfold rhythm in all things are not such fools as has been sometimes thought.

The Inner Seven, then, are the Fathers or seven moments of the primordial Flame, and their sons are the Sons of the Fire, the seven or more aspects of those moments in manifestation. We may term them the unmanifest and the manifest archetypes. These Sons of Fire, sprung from the Light that Lights all worlds, share in the wisdom of their Fathers (the Inner Seven) which is incorporate within that Light. Knowing that Light, they know the universe which that same Light reveals or manifests from out of the Darkness. They are not the inanimate stages of an entirely material evolution, but conscious powers, manifesting in their different modalities what, in the human world, are known to astrologers as planetary types —a term that can as well be used to describe the type of a man's thought as it can his bodily type, and also to describe the quality of a plant or a metal. Seen as powers of forthgoing creation, they are the seven Rishis of India, progenitors of the race, Lords of Being, Lords of the levels, those whom Buddhist tradition terms *Bodhisattva Mahāsattva* (Wisdom Beings, Great Beings). On the return path they appear as the forms of those great and liberated beings who dwell in the upper boundary of the manifested cosmos. To these latter, their fathers are those who preceded them on the path and have now gone Beyond. They are their fathers in the sense that a disciple is the spiritual son of his guru from whom he inherits, not physical form, but wisdom.[1] One of the meanings of *Tathāgata*, a title of the Buddha, is 'he who follows in the footsteps of his predecessors'; and it is told of the Buddha that when his royal father reproved him for begging his food he replied that it was the custom of his race—that race which is referred to here as the Sons of Fire. The fruit of the seed that the guru places in the disciple at initiation is the upward birth into that race, and the seed is the seed of knowledge. Having received that seed the disciple himself must cultivate the plant of Knowledge.

The final guarantee of all truth is in its birth within ourselves. We have got so used to accepting it on external 'authority' of some sort, that it is not easy for us to adjust ourselves to the idea that no authority whatever, whether of sacred scripture or whether of men, can guarantee truth, but that it reveals itself in all its infallibility within the pure consciousness. Hence, if we would learn wisdom, we must seek it not primarily in books or teachers but in our hearts; we must strive to regard ourselves no longer as Sons of Earth, but to assimilate ourselves as far as may be to the glorious Sons of Fire who know the Truth because they are the Spirit in which it dwells.

(3) *From the effulgency of light—the ray of the ever-darkness— sprang in space the re-awakened Energies; the one from the egg, the six and the five; (then) the three, the one, the four, the one, the five —the twice seven, the sum total. And these are: the essences, the flames, the elements, the builders, the numbers, the arūpa, the rūpa and the force of[2] Divine Man, the Sum Total. And from the Divine*

[1] Compare the words of the Buddha to his disciples when, addressing them as his sons, he urged them to consider themselves Sons of the Truth (*dharma*), not sons of his body.

[2] 'Or' in the main body of *The Secret Doctrine* (I. 89); 'of' in *Transactions of the Blavatsky Lodge*.

Man emanated the forms, the sparks, the sacred animals, and the messengers of the sacred fathers within the holy four.

Anyone unaccustomed to writings of this sort might feel that the symbolism of the Stanzas had degenerated into an arbitrary numerological code, fit only for those already acquainted with the technical language of occultism. In fact their meaning may be read by anyone who has grasped the general principles on which we have been working. Numbers play an important part in the universal ideographic language of the psyche and have therefore found their way into many religious and philosophical texts. For instance, the word *Sānkhya*, meaning Numeral, is the name given to one of the oldest systems of Hindu philosophy on account of its characteristic enumeration of principles in which consciousness is reflected. The *Yoga* philosophy is similar in form. Again, much astrological and Kabbalistic numerology was introduced into the books of the Old Testament following the Babylonian Captivity of the Jews—a fact of which few professing Christians are aware.

The methods used to reveal the meanings of words and numbers by such systems as the Kabbala would be sheer jugglery if applied to the figures of a modern scientific exposition, but they are not at all so when used to explain ancient texts which deliberately used numbers in that very manner. Just as colours have many meanings for the psyche other than those used by scientific spectrum analysis, so the meanings of numbers are not exhausted by those used in mathematics; and these other meanings are just as 'legitimate' in their own sphere. Any analytical psychologist will confirm that what they term 'the unconscious' uses numbers in very similar ways to the ones used here.

In Stanza III. 3, we read 'Darkness radiates Light, and Light drops one solitary Ray into the Waters, into the Mother Deep'. This was the first outburst of effulgent consciousness from which the whole universe has sprung, the One Number of this stanza from which all subsequent Numbers arise. This

M

Logos, this principle of order, rushes out into the Chaos, the undifferentiated Matrix. Its outpouring is the dynamic energy from which all energies are derived and into which they are ultimately reduced.

> 'Unmoving, the One is swifter than the Mind.
> The powers cannot reach It, speeding on before.
> Past others running, This goes standing.
> This being present, Mātarisvan (he who grows in
> the Mother) generates action.'[1]

The Upanishadic paradox must be allowed to stand, for the pure light of consciousness is unmoving, yet it is the source of all movement. The Father-Light shines in the Son, Universal Mind, it shines in the minds of men, and it shines in every particle of matter. It is in them and they are in It. If we look at the world in one way, we see the varied forms of being dancing in Its Light, and if we look at it the other way, we see the divine Light standing in the forms. It is this paradox which makes it so difficult for us to understand ourselves; to reach certainty we have first to decide whether Man is essentially his bodily form, or the pure light of consciousness, or a special blend of both.

This is also the Light which in Stanza III. 8 is called the source of 'the flame that burns in thy lamp', and it is by following that creative Ray back to its source that we can even now know our essential being. The Light is both the creator of the diverse universe and the Eternal Wisdom through knowledge of which we return from diversity to unity. 'The Light of the One Master, the one undying light of Spirit, shoots its effulgent beams on the disciple from the very first. Its rays thread through the thick dark clouds of matter.'[2]

We are not ordinarily single, rather we are constellations of diverse modes of a psycho-physical process. We are one sort of man towards our parents, another to our wives, a third to

---

[1] *Iśa Upanishad*, 4.
[2] *The Voice of the Silence.*

our children, a fourth at work, a fifth in the club, and as many more sorts as we have friends and activities. Which of all these is the Man?

The structure-pattern of our birth is not rigid, for within its limitations we find the opportunity for purposive growth. The man who has become mature only in his profession has undoubtedly grown, but he has grown lop-sidedly, and so long as we allow ourselves to rush out after external achievements, we shall remain in a state of unbalance. To achieve a balance, to become Man and not just a menagerie of men, women, children and animals caged in a single body, we have to find the one central Light of consciousness, the effulgent Ray, whose essential unity cannot be altered by the diversity of the parts in which it shines. This is that One, whose unity is intrinsic, who is essentially the 'One without a second'.

In the last stanza we saw how the unitary Light combined with the potential multiplicity of the Matrix to enclose or delimit the Space of manifestation. It is within that Space that the one dynamism of the first Logos becomes the many energies of the second Logos, the many which arise from the interrelation of unity and multiplicity.

The re-awakening of the energies takes us back to the theme of Stanza I. 1, where the Eternal Parent had 'slumbered once again'. This concept of a recurrent universal cycle, which is by no means confined to Hinduism, does not arise merely as an extrapolation from the seasonal and psychological cycles of our experience here. That these lesser cycles are symbolic expressions of the greater living and dying which brings this and other universes into being and withdraws them again from being is affirmed by those 'Sons of Fire' who have transcended their corporeal limitations.

The difficulty lies not so much in accepting the idea of a cyclic creation and withdrawal as in understanding what it can mean, because time comes into being with the manifest universe and disappears with its withdrawal. After the withdrawal there is no time scale in which there can be any 'before' and 'after'. We tend to extrapolate from our awareness of the temporal process into a past which never existed, for, if we follow the time of this universe backwards, we paradoxically meet its origins not in infinitely extended time but in the same eternity in which our present stands and into which our future extends. In eternity the 'horizontal' component of our experience blends with the 'vertical' component. The creation and the withdrawal are simultaneous in the eternal 'Now', yet even the concept of simultaneity represents something which we are incapable of knowing while we exist as moments in the temporal manifestation. Our thinking is a process in time, and until we can step outside the process into mystical experience we cannot overcome the limitations set upon us by virtue of our existence, that by which we stand apart from the One.

Time as process, contrasted with time as eternal duration (*Khanda Kāla* and *Akhanda Kāla*), is as much an integral part of the manifestation as are separateness, movement and knowing, because the making of things manifest demands a process, and process moves in time. It is not a series of separate moments, but rather the one moment of the eternal present between the Subject and Object poles of being in which potentiality becomes known as actuality and passes to accomplishment. We can say either that the one moment of awareness moves through potentiality, or that the potentiality moves through the moment. 'It moves and it moves not.' Nevertheless, Time is not the process in itself, but the experience of process.

No matter how important it may be to scientific enquiry to measure the sequential relationship of objective events, unless those events are ultimately related to an experiencing subject, their before and after, their speeds and frequencies are meaningless. The essential subjectivity of the universe inwardly shines in every atom, simultaneously holding the whole being in its enduring grasp. Every subjective viewpoint is both linked and separated by the moving energies which make up and are observed as processes in time. Such viewpoints do not belong only to the physical level; they extend throughout the manifest levels which, as we have seen, represent different degrees of subjective identification with form.

The One Subject is essentially the experiencer of the eternal present, but when identified with form his experience of process is limited by the very process with which he is identified. Thus, our feeling-perception of Time, our personal time-scale, is inevitably bound up with those nervous mechanisms of sensing which form a part of the physical world to which they relate us.

Even this personal time-scale is variable, but from the viewpoint of the inner worlds, the worlds of after-death, the faery worlds of Celtic lore and Hindu fable, 'a thousand years in thy sight are but as yesterday'. Thus it is only when we make our present time experience the standard of measurement that the ages of the cosmic evolution prior to man's advent on this earth seem so overwhelmingly immense, just as interstellar space is only immense in relation to man's six-foot body. The truly great thing in the universe is the Mind which embraces those immensities of spatio-temporal existence in a single moment.

'When' the Father-Mother, Subject-Object polarity is withdrawn, the limited space of this universe is dissolved in metaphysical 'Space'. Not only the human observers then cease to exist but also the Witnessing Consciousness in whose grasp the whole universe is held. Consciousness, form, energy and time are all reduced to unity. Then what happens? There is no time in which any events can take place, so how can a universe re-appear?

If we push such human logic too far we shall find ourselves denying the self-evident fact of our own being. This universe is. Other universes 'have been' and 'will be', even though the order of their sequence is not measurable in terms of time as we experience it in manifestation. In fact the processional aspect of time is somehow rooted in the timeless sequence of 'events' in the Darkness of non-existence.

We have previously described the 'Space' of the Matrix as infinite potentiality, but it is a metaphysical potentiality in Timelessness, devoid of that suggestion, implicit in our minds, of potential futurity. It is a potentiality which includes not only 'future' possibilities but all that has been realised in the 'past'. If, therefore, it is sometimes described as bearing within it the memory-traces (*samskāras*) of past universes, traces which determine the patterns of the future, it is only another way of pointing to a cosmic fact: that, whenever the One Ray of consciousness flashes into the infinite potentiality of the Matrix, the patterns of manifest events always follow a similar course, and the energies are *re*-awakened. The determining patterns are not 'past' in time, for they do not exist in time, but they are inherent in the situation and metaphysically precede the manifestation.

So long as we are in Time there is always a yesterday to every today, cosmic or microcosmic. Only when we are out of Time is there no yesterday but only the ever-presence of the One.

But is this endless series of universes leading anywhere? No; not in the sense that we expect a series of steps to lead to a desired end. We have to speak of a series because of the limitations of language, but their 'sequence' is in Timelessness, and in that dimension there is nothing equivalent to a cumulative progression. The totality of Being has nothing to achieve in the universal series as a series. It is in itself complete and lacking in nothing. It has no purpose and no goal. It is entirely self-sufficient.

Many philosophical systems have laid so great a stress on this aspect of the absolute source of Being that it has over-shadowed their evaluation of events within the manifest universe. Because there is no purposeful progression from one universe to the next, from one outbreathing of the Brahman to the next outbreathing, the unwarrantable conclusion is made that there is therefore no purpose inhering in the manifestation of any universe at all, a conclusion which is flatly contradicted by the purposeful striving towards self-expression which infuses every living particle within our sphere of experience. Thus the whole wonder of existent being, the Cosmos that the Greeks called 'the adorned one', comes to be considered as unnecessary to its Creator, empty of purpose, and in fact a thing that should never have been. It is fantastic that in the face of the utter glory of the divine harmony, the wonder of the evolutionary process, and the near-perfection of natural forms, anyone should impute purposelessness to the power which brought them forth.

Such negative evaluation of the Cosmic process makes nonsense of our own position in it. If we believe the universe to be meaningless and aimless, our lives become essentially similar; and in choosing to accept such a view we are reducing to meaninglessness the most wonderful thing in the Cosmos, Man.

The misunderstanding seems to have arisen largely from thinking of the unmanifest source of being as the Real, and then placing the manifest universe in opposition to it as the unreal or illusory. What we experience is certainly illusory in the sense that it is not what it seems to be, nor are we what we usually think ourselves to be; but that is not all there is to it. The universe we experience is the manifest expression in Time of the unmanifest Being, 'Time is the moving image of Eternity.' But we are blind to its true nature. Seen with the Wisdom Eye of true perception it is the Divine Form, the *Vishvarūpa*, of which Sri Krishna says to Arjuna:

'Hard, hard is it to see what thou hast seen;
This Form of Mine that even the gods all long to see'.[1]

The Unmanifest is prior to the Manifest in order of divine values, yet the two are a mutually dependent pair; rather as mother and child, or lover and beloved, each is necessary to

[1] *Bhagavad Gītā*, XI. 52.

the other. 'Eternity is in love with the productions of Time.' The Unmanifest bears much the same relationship to the Manifest as does the so-called 'unconscious' part of our psychic integration to the conscious; a personal 'unconscious' into which we withdraw in sleep, a realm of death of which most of us are presently unaware and into which we are withdrawn between periods of living, and, by the same token, an Unmanifest into which the Manifest is withdrawn in periods between manifestations. The meaning of the one is to be found in the other. Neither by itself has meaningful significance.

The popular presentations of the Eastern philosophies (though not their actual teaching) would have us believe that these states of withdrawal are spiritually superior in themselves; but that is to place value in abstraction as such. If that were true, we would be essentially greater in the blankness that constitutes ordinary sleep or in the dreamy desire-motivated drifting that constitutes the average after-death experience than we are in the exercise of our most highly developed human faculties in waking life.

In the darkness of non-existence there is no differentiation, for the Father and Mother poles are fused in blissful union. Their living relationship demands to be exteriorised; there is a desire to know and be known. 'It' seeks to know itself, and the result of its seeking is a manifestation of itself in a universe of form. It *seeks* to know itself; but how does it do it? Are we going to invoke an anthropomorphic figure somewhere up in the heavens who watches his creation from 'outside'? Has 'he' produced a race of men whose joys and sorrows he views dispassionately, like a scientist experimenting with guinea-pigs, animals whose intelligence is insufficient to understand the scientist's purpose? No. The Divine Power seeks to know itself from within its own creation, but the object of its search is no more easily achieved than is that of any other striving towards fulfilment.

This is another place where the extrapolations of human reason have gone astray. The Absolute Divinity is all-powerful.

It says 'Be', and it is—just as easily as that. Taken literally, this is nonsense. Undoubtedly, the Absolute Divinity is all-powerful, or, more correctly, all-potent, but in us and around us we do not see anything appearing 'hey presto'—and the rabbit comes out of the hat. On the contrary, we know very well that the rabbit had first to grow and then be put into the hat. Around us we see nothing but a striving towards growth: plants, animals and men struggle for space in which to live, for food to sustain them, and for means to continue their species. In ourselves we find a still further struggle for means of self-expression. All our creative advance is characterised by effort to overcome the obstacles between vague ideas and their clear expression either in language or in artifacts.

The struggle we see is that of living consciousness to express itself in form. It is the creation, the evolution or unrolling of the unmanifest and timeless divinity in time. We, with all our limitations, are the spear-head of the evolution, the growing point of 'the root that grows in the water of life'. We are its products and its instruments, not its rulers. It has given rise to our human state, though in itself it is independent of it. In us and through us the luminous consciousness of the lower forms of life has come to incandescence: a shining flame of consciousness capable of soaring up from time to timelessness, a spark that can become a Sun in which God and Goddess, lover and beloved, are eternally one, joying in the conscious knowledge of their union. We, among all beings, have it within us to pursue the evolutionary aim, not now with blind strivings but with conscious intent. We can, if we will, cease from running after the phantom forms of externalised desire and find the living reality within the calmness of the ever-present.

Without doubt, we have to beware of confusing egotistical with essential values, of confusing our personal, ephemeral aims with the divine purpose. But neither must we hang back from accepting the divine charge that has been laid upon us, the charge to perfect ourselves as Men.

So long as we hold ourselves separate from divinity we must be sacrificed to a purpose that is beyond ourselves. To some people this seems a sufficient evaluation of life that in being our smaller selves to the best of our ability we fulfil ourselves as moments of the divine purpose. But is this the purpose for which we were brought forth: that we should continue unquestioningly as we were born, refusing the pain of further struggle towards the greater Selfhood? To what end can the pursuit of temporal aims lead us and the universe? Looking ahead we see that the physical conditions which have given rise to and sustained life on this planet must come to an end; nor, in a steadily cooling universe, could we do more than postpone the end by transferring the seeds of our present culture to another world, even if that were possible. In the realm of forms, what grows must decay.

Further progress of forms, further technological advance, is overhung by the certainty of its ultimate destruction. Whereas previously the sacrifice of the individual for the preservation of the race, of culture, and of progress, or, correspondingly, the domination of the race by a few men whose intelligence and psychic development were superior to the racial average was essential to total human progress, now, with the spread of cultural development and the high degree of control exercised by man over the environment, the sheer preservation of the race and of the hard-won cultural status of man is no longer the primary problem of life. The early manufacturer of stone implements may be considered to have fulfilled his evolutionary purpose in adequately contributing towards the maintenance and advancement of his society, for early tribal society was concerned with the immediate problem of existence. But for the modern man it is not enough that he should submit his intelligent appreciation of his personal relation to divinity to the external rulership of King or State or code of ethical behaviour (*dharma*) as prescribed by an early 'law-giver', a Moses, a Manu, or a Zoroaster. If the race is to continue to evolve, it must aim to become like the 'race without a

King'[1] in which every individual is his own ruler, governing himself in accordance with his direct perception of the divine harmony.

The spirit of life and consciousness which shines in the individual soul is made neither greater nor brighter by producing an aggregate of souls, for the race is no greater than its greatest individual. The perfected man of the universe is not a mere aggregate of racial consciousness, the highest common factor of the herd, but a clear window through which the ever-existent universal sun is shining. The evolution of the race is no longer in the realm of mass phenomena. It is something to be individually achieved by each man, an achievement as utterly individual as is birth or death.

Thus far the living forces of the evolution have brought us. They continue to press up within us, urging us to effort, but it is now we who have to make the effort, for the divine purpose cannot be effected except through its highest creation, Man. It is indeed the divine will that we should surrender our egotistic aims to the service of the divine purpose, but that will is, at the same time, present in us. It is the spirit of the flame that burns in our lamps, our true Self, and it is by that that we must choose. Man is indeed the measure of all things, but if we refuse our manhood, if we renounce our birthright for the flesh pots of ignorance, then the ultimate purpose of the universal process will not be achieved through us, and our lives will become as meaningless as the pessimistic philosophies say they are.

Other than this, divinity has no aim. If a universe or a thousand universes of suns and galaxies go out into oblivion, what has been lost from the plenitude of the All? Nothing. Only in the heart of man is there anything to be gained or lost. 'But for thee I would not have created the heavens.'[2]

The goal is to be achieved individually. Each man has to

---

[1] *The Naassene Document.* This 'race' is elsewhere referred to as the 'Self Taught Race' and 'the race of the logos', *i.e.* of all who are conscious of the logos in their heart.
[2] One of the sayings of Muslim Tradition often quoted by Sūfī mystics.

plunge within his own being to find the source of his being, yet not by selfishly seeking a private state of bliss, rather by finding his true self in the universal substance in which all individuals exist. Once the goal is reached, all individuality ceases and there remains only the all-pervading Bliss that was, is and shall be. The drop has blended in the ocean.

But is this all, this disappearance of the individual into the universal? From that Divine Source we came forth and into it we can return. We experience, we joy, and we sorrow. Finally we turn away from the pursuit of transient values to discover the eternal treasure. For us the manifest universe of multiplicity need be no more. In dying to our separateness we shall live in the eternal One. 'I' shall be one with the light that shines in all forms, and because 'I' shall no longer be separate, for 'me' there will be no separateness. But the universe of separate forms will continue to exist. 'My' departure will not have altered the essential situation for anyone but 'me'.

Is the purpose of the universe, and derivatively our purpose, ultimately fulfilled by the sporadic intentional return of individuals to their source? Is this the highest goal, aim and purpose of individualised beings? Are we to assume that because we can return, because that is an indescribably blissful state in which all conflict is resolved and all separateness lost, that that is the end for which we were destined?

Such a goal is certainly a tremendous achievement to which the whole of Being thrills in joy. But do not all beings return to their source at the end of the cosmic cycle? 'I' have returned willingly, conscious of the bliss of union, while those who have not followed this path will be withdrawn from being, un-willingly, conscious only of suffering the destruction of their forms. In the end, neither 'they' nor 'I' remain.

In asserting 'my' identity with the universal, 'I' have denied my identity with the particular. The importance of one aspect of being has been stressed to the devaluation of the other. Yet the particular and the universal are not separate; the former is produced from and sustained in the latter. Is not this present position partial? The ultimate truth must lie not in only one aspect of this duality but in its resolution. Is it not possible to blend the universal with the particular in a single united being, that the divine light should shine in a particular form yet not be clouded by that assertive egotism which cuts men off from the knowledge of divinity by exploiting the divinely based powers for individual ends?

How can such a position be achieved? Can we halt on the threshold of eternity and deny ourselves entry into that transcendently wonderful Being whose glory is now unmasked? When even the palely reflecting moon sends men mad with desire, how can we resist the undiluted source of its light? If we seek the goal blindly and unthinkingly, like a moth we shall be consumed in the open flame. First we must conceive the possibility of such an achievement, then dedicate ourselves to its realisation, and rid ourselves of the selfish longing to surrender ourselves to the passion of self-destruction.

Against the passion of love which draws us on to destruction only love for those around us can hold us back. Our perception of our unity with the universal light must strengthen, not lessen, our sense of unity with our fellows. 'I' cannot withhold from the tremendous force of the inflowing love, for there is no 'I' remaining. If 'I' withhold, then 'I' am separate from that love and the gates will not open. Only when the out-turned love for the divinity in man balances the in-turned love for the divine source can 'I' disappear yet remain, not indeed as 'I', but as a window in the heavens, divine man, uniting the above with the below, eternity with time, for the achievement of the one perfect work, the achievement of the cosmic purpose.

All power and all knowledge now flow through such a man, but they are not his. He is free, yet his freedom is not to act independently but is freedom from separate selfhood. He is bound, not now by the compulsions of desire, not to the wheel of eternal recurrence, but by conformity to the cosmic harmony. In him compassion is manifest, 'it is the law of laws—eternal Harmony . . . the law of love eternal'.[1] The drop has entered the ocean and the ocean is contained within the drop.

Only by thus resolving within himself the apparently irreconcilable elements of a paradox can the individual survive beyond the time span of a manifest universe. Those who enter the unmanifest womb of the cosmos pass away never to return, but the few who have attained to perfection keep their long vigil on the threshold of the unmanifest. They are at one with the universal essence, their life is surrendered, their sense powers pass into latency; yet, for the sake of the love which transcends separateness, and by its power, they hold themselves awake throughout the dark night of withdrawal, in order that Compassion may again bring the universal process to fruition in the perfection of man. For, if we, who have been raised to self-conscious being, are deprived of our Instructors, the Sons of the Fire, from whom shall we learn of our true nature, to whom shall the orphans of existence turn for guidance?

By no other power but that of self-abrogating love can individual survival be prolonged into a new universe. The hard shell of human egotism can be preserved beyond the death of the physical body and even beyond the withdrawal of the physical universe, but such self-preservation merely in the interests of personal survival is piracy on the ocean of being.

There are many such monsters of self-interest around us whose egotism destines them thus to remain, even if they are now unaware of the implications of their behaviour. They have to survive because, having been raised to selfhood, they have never re-asserted their unity with the universal Self. They have enclosed their Spark of self-conscious being within a concrete shell of separateness and refused to let it go. At the universal withdrawal they remain, but there is no manifest universe in which to remain and they are cast into outer darkness where there is 'wailing and gnashing of teeth'. When the one Ray of unity again flashes out into manifestation they are destroyed

[1] *The Voice of the Silence:* The Seven Portals.

and their life is diffused in the waters of the new existence. It is from this life that, in the second set of Stanzas on Anthropogenesis, the Earth creates the 'Water-Men, terrible and bad' without calling the Sons of Heaven to her aid.

This verse marks the transition from the transcendent principles of the unmanifest levels—shown here by the use of numbers to represent abstract terms—to the same principles in the 'thought' of Universal Mind, in which mode they are better represented by names. And as each level is capable of being viewed from several aspects it may be described by a variety of symbolic names. Each level, except perhaps the lowest, is for instance capable of being regarded as a Subject, and each, except the highest, is capable of being regarded as an Object: they are all subjects to those below them, objects to those above. In another aspect, the archetypes become hierarchies of living powers, the gods or angels of the religious traditions, which can be known both within the heart of man and, phenomenally, as objective, though subtle, beings.

From the Ever-Darkness comes the unitary uncompounded 'Ray', the effulgency of light or Father. The movement to manifestation is from within outwards and from above downwards: the creative powers or energies spring into outwardness, into the space of the Mother. The Egg is the delimited area within the limitless Mother, without whose enclosure there would be no restriction and so no build-up of energy. The One from the egg is the Son, Universal Mind, which, among other names of the Hindu *Brahmā*, is also known as *Aṇḍaja*, the Egg-born, the power that holds the manifest universe within its unity.

As Pythagoras taught, the simple Geometry we all learnt at school has great symbolic significance. The extent of the 'circle' or Egg of Being is determined by the Ray of unity, just as the radius determines the geometrical circle. And just as the length of the radius marked off as chords round the circumference divides the circle into six parts, so the first natural relationship between the dimensionless central 'point' of effulgence and the circumferential 'Space' of the Matrix is expressed in a sixfold pattern. This is the first pattern carved out in the space of manifestation by the one light of consciousness. It is the first pattern in Divine Mind and the first rational division projected from the mind of man upon the circle of the heavens.

The twelvefold division of the year undoubtedly derives from the lunar months, but there is ample evidence for the importance of the number six in the formation of early calendars. The Chinese numbered their days in sequences of sixty days, approximately one sixth of the year, and Fu-Hi, 'the Adam of China', kept six kinds of animals in a 'park'—surely the paired animals of the zodiac. Again, in the Jewish legend, the Lord God laboured for six days in the creation and rested on the seventh. In India there are further instances of this sixfold division in Kārttikeya's six faces, for Kārttikeya is the leader of the heavenly hosts of stars from the time that the lunar asterism of Krittika (the Pleiades) marked the beginning of the year. Another trace remains in the basic figure of 4320 used in Hindu and Chaldean calculations of cosmic cycles, for the equinox moves through two zodiacal signs, or one sixth of the circle, in approximately 4320 years.

The doubling of the six into twelve corresponds to the change from the androgynous Adam-Eve, Male-Female, state of the first bi-polar individualisation in Mind, to their divided and differentiated Adam and Eve, Male and Female condition when, under the influence of the third Logos, the points in Mind rush out into separateness. More will have to be said about this later, but it is worth mentioning here that the separative movement occasioned by the third Logos replaces the ideal geometry of the Euclidean symbols we have been using by the imperfect geometry of worlds in movement where the single centred circle becomes the twin centred (approximately) elliptical, egg-like, figure of the planetary orbits.

From the sixfold division of the circle also comes the interlaced triangles or 'Solomon's Seal', the upward pointing triangle representing the Subjective triad of conscious powers in Universal Mind and the lower triangle its reflection in the waters of form. This is the manifest duality, as the Father-Mother was the unmanifest duality. Now as a pair they stand for Heaven and Earth, Light and Shade, Spirit and Body, Good and Evil. They are the perfectly balanced union of Knower and Known.

In the *Poemandres* there is a parallel account of the reflection of the higher in the lower, the union of the unmanifest archetypal triad with its reflection in the waters of life. 'So he . . . bent his face downwards through the Harmony . . . and showed God's fair Form to downward Nature. And when she saw that form of beauty . . . and him who possessed within himself the energy of all seven Rulers besides God's own Form, she smiled with love; for it was as if she had seen the image of Man's fairest form upon her Water, his shadow on her Earth.'[1]

Whatever distinctions may have to be made for the sake of clarity of exposition, the manifest and the unmanifest forms of Divinity are in fact one, and one only, undivided being.

All powers and all qualities whatever derive from the interplay of these two triads, for from them flow the creative, preservative and destructive powers of the universe. In ourselves we find the upper triad present, for instance in the powers by which attention is given, by which it is sustained, and by which it is withdrawn. The lower triad consists of the three modes of Nature present in all phenomena, whether gross or subtle, as the peaceful or serene, the active or even turbulent, and the passively inert or dull.[2] Again, the male or upward pointing triangle is the pattern from which derive comparatively immaterial psychic modalities such as the dialectic triads of some systems of philosophy—stable and regenerative, but tending to rarification. From the feminine triangle derive those triplicities of emotion and power which build up and govern both our personal relationships and the movements of power in politics; an unstable but productive flux, uniting

---

[1] *Poemandres*, v. 14. Adapted from G. R. S. Mead's *Thrice Great Hermes*.
[2] The three *Gunas* of *Prakriti*: *sattva, rajas, tamas*.

N

two friends against a common foe, making a child the bond between its parents only to have it usurp the affections of one to the sorrow of the other, or forcing the child to struggle for its independence against the parental ties.

Up till now the Stanzas have been speaking of the Three and the Four; the subjective trinity and the four modes of projection. As we have seen, however, there is not merely a need for the content aspect of being to be projected into externality, the Three into the Four, but a need or desire to know and experience the content.

And to experience the content in externality, the creative power must first descend or 'fall' into 'matter', then thrust upwards in the effort to produce forms capable of sensing, and finally must pierce the sense openings outwards so that Mind looks out upon the forms in which it is itself embodied. The pressure of life towards the achievement of this purpose has given rise to the five major avenues of sense in an animal form of five limbs with five fingers, etc. This basic fivefoldness of the sensible universe is the Five of this verse.

The sensible universe is the universe as we experience it through the avenues of sense. It is not the structural or energetic abstract which exists independently of human observation.

From the viewpoint of numerical symbolism, the Five springs from the interplay of the two triads making up the previous Six. The development of this relationship then gives rise to the Dodecahedron, a regular solid with twelve faces, each of five sides, in which fiveness and sixness find their reconciliation. In Pythagorean symbolism the Dodecahedron represented the Universe, presumably because it contains three and is reciprocal to the fourth of the regular solid figures symbolising the Elements.

Fiveness thus becomes synonymous with the differentiated sense mind; and the world analysed in terms of sensible qualities is the world of the five Elements of antiquity. Both Eastern and Western traditions recognise four Elements:

Earth, Water, Fire and Air (the order in which they are taken varies), and the East adds Space (*Ākāsha*) as the transcendent fifth element, corresponding to what in the West is known as the Quintessence. The first four are correlates of the four lower levels of being already described, and Space, the fifth, is equated with the extensive and pervasive nature of Universal Mind. These five elements have been symbolised in other ways, by colours, for instance, and by the five Platonic solids, all of which have their peculiar interests and applications, but the allocation to the five 'elemental' states of matter is perhaps the most common.

We must beware here lest our minds get carried off by the modern associations of the word into assuming the Elements of antiquity to be our forefathers' simple-minded description of the same phenomena as the elements of physical science. It is only too easy for us, in the pride of our new-found knowledge, to ascribe our failure to understand the drift of antique or 'traditional' thought to its ignorance of what we call facts. More usually it is we who are ignorant not only of the modes of that thought, but also of its conclusions concerning the nature of reality and 'facts'. To the initiated Teachers of those times the inner worlds had as much reality as, if not more than, this physical world. Consequently, the solidity of Earth was for them a symbol of the state of physical experience in which the aspect of permanence is markedly present, as seen in the distinction between, and mutual impenetrability of, subject and object. That the solidity of material objects is not an ultimate truth was at least as apparent to them, though differently described, as it is to a nuclear physicist. Any man who is prepared to devote his life to the understanding of the nature of his own being can have as convincing a proof of the psychic or immaterial nature of sense objects as can be given by physics of their energetic nature.

In this way, by its fluidity, transparency, and miscible nature, water represents the next higher state of experience in which the subject-object distinction is less marked. The changing nature of the objects of experience is more apparent, and there is a mixing and interblending both of appearances and of values, analogous to our experience of dream. Lacking the inertia of corporeal restraint, desires exert their power, more or less unchecked; it is for this reason that the watery mid-region of magical effects is sometimes called the Desire level.

This subtle state of being, symbolised by the Elementary Water, is of considerable significance in the understanding of the creative process. It acts as an impressionable intermediary between the descending powers of the Spirit and the ascending forms of 'Matter'. It is indeed the 'Water of Life in the Great Mother' (III. 9) without whose presence the world of physics and chemistry would be incapable of supporting the psychic powers of life and intelligence.

The objective appearance of the desire level may be likened to the mirage of water shimmering over a heated surface. And if we can imagine the shimmer changing to the flickering of myriads of tiny tongues of flame, we can have some conception of the state of matter at the level equivalent to the lower or sense mind, with its flickering attention leaping from point to point as it grasps each individual facet of experience separately.

Air, whether in the East or in the West, is taken as the symbol of the Self of man, the Higher Mind or *Pneuma,* which, like the wind, 'bloweth where it listeth' in any direction; not held down like earth and water; clearer and more mobile than water; without whose presence the fire of the sense mind cannot burn; the inter-space between the desire-motivated worlds and pure Space, or Universal Mind. It is in the space of air that we get our panoramic vision, representing our ability to grasp whole areas of experience together; and it is this last faculty that gives us the power to relate the individual points of sense experience into a consecutively integrated whole. In this too lies our perception of the flow of time, and so too of memory.

Beyond this lies the Universal Mind equated with Space, the description of which has already been given under Stanza III, verse 7.

Many attempts have been made to equate the levels of being and the five Elements with the five sense powers. Of these, the Hindu system relates earth to smell, water to taste, fire to sight, air to touch, and space to hearing. This order is derived from the arguable fact that while Earth is perceptible to all the senses, Water (pure water) has no odour; Fire has in itself neither odour nor savour; Air in addition is invisible; in 'Space' only sound is heard. Each element in order is thus perceptible by those sense powers that stand above it, but not by those below it. Earth can then be an object of experience to all the senses, while Air can be known only by touch and hearing. Whether or not this ingenious arrangement can bear close scrutiny is not our point here; but it can be experienced, when passing into a state of intense inner contemplation, that the outer senses one by one go into abeyance in the order given, and in a manner similar to the absorption (*laya*) of successive elements, one within the other, described by *Kuṇḍalini Yoga Shāstra*.

In the Western system of allocations Fire is usually given supremacy over Air because it is the upward-striving element, the most subtle of them all. We must also take note that in the Stanzas Fire is often used in a quite different sense from the Elemental, for instance, as the Divine outbreathing.

The foregoing numbers are the primary pattern marked out by the One in metaphysical Space. The clue to the next list lies in Stanza VII. 3 where we read 'When the One becomes two, the threefold appears, and the three are One.' The 'three' in the present verse are thus the upper three unmanifest Principles which unite as the triune basis of all perception. As the subjective aspect of Universal Mind they can be considered as one, the next 'One' of the verse, which, as the One Subject of the Universe, is again One Number that has issued from No-Number, the Father who has become the Son.

The Four (into which the three fall) are the major modes in which content is projected, as discussed under stanza III. 4. But, again, these are modes of the One Power, not separate powers. The One thus pervades the whole of manifest being, holding it together as a unity of living consciousness—a Universe. It descends from 'Spirit' into 'Matter' and ascends from 'Matter' into 'Spirit', seeking, desiring, knowing, grasping, multiplying and dividing, bringing into being, releasing, and finally withdrawing, yet never for a moment losing its essential unity. It is unity wherever we find it, both the unit from which the series of numbers is constructed—the unity of one tree in a forest of trees—and the unity of all being.

Below the Four lie the Waters of the One Mother in which the effulgent spirit seeks the fulfilment of its passions. Formless in herself, she is the material source and sustainer of all forms brought to birth in her Being as she strives upwards with feminine yearning to meet the descending powers of the Spirit.

How, we may be asked, can the Maternal principle re-appear here, when only a moment ago we were treating her as a member of the unmanifest trinity? But she must be here; and if it seems illogical it is because we are trying to confine the wonder of living Being within the inadequate limits of schematic arrangement. The web of the Universe is spun out between Spirit and Matter (III. 10); not the complex physical matter of daily experience, but the basic objectivity which clothes with forms the Spirit's imaginings. This material aspect of the Mother here underlies the Cosmos as the permanent substratum of phenomena. The same idea was expressed by Eliphas Levi when, drawing on Kabbalistic sources, he explained the meanings of the sacred four-lettered name of God: 'Then the mother letter appeared a second time to express the fecundity of nature and woman, and to formulate the doctrine of universal and progressive analogies descending from causes to effects, and ascending from effects to causes.'[1]

[1] *Doctrine and Ritual of Magic*, p. 356 (A. E. Waite).

The Spirit first flows down to clothe itself in its reflected image, and then strives upwards to perceive the reality of which its form is but a reflection. Both are modes of the divine interplay of powers, for the last cannot be achieved without the first. Both modes manifest in their appropriate season—creation and withdrawal, life and death. We have to conquer our fears of independent existence, to find our feet in the world and accept the suffering that is our lot before we are fit to turn away from the substitute reality, which seems so attractive to the out-turned mind, and seek the real source of the reflected image.

The list of the Cosmic levels is complete. Between the unmanifest poles of Ever-Being lies the active range of manifest existence; nothing manifest can lie outside that web of power, and nothing can be manifest within it that is not of it. This is the sum total: the seven unmanifest or inner levels and their manifest counterparts. Yet one thing remains unmentioned —the last number five of the verse—whose being is so paradoxical that it both is and is not within the almost closed circle of manifestation, and for whose experiencing the entirety of material worlds has been unrolled.

Divine Man, the Quintessence, stands as the middle term of the extent of Being. His essential Self is the unmanifest and transcendental Root of Self, the Father Light; his Self is the wonderful all-knowing Person of Universal Mind; and again his Self is the individualised spark of incarnating mind. On whatever level we speak of the Self it is only in ourselves that we can find any experiential point of reference; never by any means can it become an object to the senses. Whatever we see 'outside' lies on the surface of the sphere of being, and not until we stop groping over that finite but unbounded surface and plunge into the heart of all things through the gateway of our own hearts can we gain direct knowledge of reality. In our hearts, in the hearts of men, the entirety of the Divine nature is more essentially and more wholly manifest than it is in any other single or collective being.

The Root of life is in every drop of the Ocean of Immortality (III. 6), it is in every grain of sand, every blade of grass and in every animal; but only in man, the sacred animal, does the divine spark become incandescent, turning animal into man and establishing the essential wonder of self-conscious or reflective being within the conscious and living, but limited, substance of the body.[1] He who looks out of the troubled eyes of men is the same as he who looks out of the calm eyes of the Divine Man of Universal Mind; and the glorious light that shines within those divine eyes is the unmodified essence of all things. It is for this reason that man is a paradox and above all things dual.[2]

That which is man's very self, that by which he is man and not animal, is the divine spark flickering in the core of his being. In so far as he identifies himself with that spark, man is free and his race is of heaven alone; but when he drops down to self-identification with his thought structures, his desires, and finally with his bodily sensations, he is a child of earth and is subject to Necessity. The material history of the evolution of anthropoid forms, fascinating though it is, is not the history of man but only of his physical vehicle—a form thrust up from the matrix by the will of the Spirit. Not until that form was ready could the ingression of the divine spark into the universe take place, nor could man's prior, archetypal or Divine Man, be existent until Universal Mind was embodied in its Macrocosmic vehicle of the four lower levels.

The fifth or central point of our fourfold psychic nature represents the original unity from which the whole has emerged, and it is therefore the power which relates the elements into an integral whole. Without the presence of this

---

[1] This is the 'Couplement' of Plotinus: 'The Animate or living-being is mingled in a lower phase, but above that point lies the beginning of the veritable Man distinct from all that is kin to the Lion and from the multiple brute.' Plotinus on *The Animate and the Man*, I. i. 7. (Turnbull).

[2] Cf. *Poemandres:* 'And this is why beyond all creatures on the earth man is twofold; mortal because of the body, but because of the essential Man immortal, though deathless and possessed of sway over all, yet doth he suffer as a mortal doth, subject to Fate.' *Thrice Greatest Hermes* (G. R. S. Mead).

derivative of the primal unity, experience would be diffuse and separate and, there could be no coherent structure of material, or of thought, or of sequence in time. It is only in so far as we share experience that we recognise any common criterion of reality, and there could be no shared experience at all if the foci of experiencing that we think of as our separate selves were in fact unrelated by the unity of conscious being. When, under the compulsion of the smoky desires of self-interest, we turn away from the unity of the sea of light and assert our separateness both from that unity and, therefore, from others like ourselves, we substitute the empirical self for the higher Self, the quintessence. Man's higher Self is a point or spark in the sea of light, but whether that point is or is not distinguishable in the sea is a question over which too much time has already been wasted in argument. Suffice it to say that we both can and do have personal and apparently individual relationships with those who have won to the goal of the inner path, those whose being is established in that sea.

The list of names is a repetition of the same list of cosmic levels already represented by the numbers. Numbers, for most of us, carry a more abstract connotation than do the more concrete symbols of names; and here, besides referring us to their use in earlier stanzas, the names fittingly represent the transition from abstract idea to concrete form that is being described. The radiant Essences or inseparate beings of Universal Mind; the bright Flames of the out-pouring powers which bring the inner patterns to separate manifestation; the differentiated qualities of the natural Elements; the effectuating powers of the causal hierarchy which build and model the outer forms. These are the Numbers or multiplicity that have issued from No-Number by the blending of the unitary Father-Light with the infinite potentiality of the Matrix. They manifest first as a subtle (*arūpa*) universe of empatterned energies from which the concrete worlds of form (*rūpa*) are produced. Finally the verse mentions the self-becoming nature of the Darkness manifesting as the Force of Divine Man, the one free element in the fixed patterns which arise like crystals from the sea of potential being.

As in the list of numbers, so here, the descent of man is traced separately, lest we should make the mistake of materialists and confuse the wonderful upward evolution of man's compound and material body with the spark of pure spirit. For this reason, in the stanza of instructions spoken by the Sons of Fire, the Source of all things is called Divine Man; for man has not evolved from something less than man, nor is he a chance by-product or off-shoot of some arbitrary and purposeless concatenation of forces. The source of Man is Divine Man, and their natures are identical if we will but see it.[1] From Divine Man, says the verse, emanated the Forms or stages by which the ever-spotless divinity descends to dwell in the manifest levels of material form. The Sparks are the multiple individualities, one in essence, multiple in form, into which that one Divine Being scatters himself.

The Sacred Animals are men; sacred by virtue of the spark of divinity they inherit from Divine Man, animals by virtue of the psycho-physical organism in which the spark is housed. We may also note in passing that in another context the term 'Sacred Animals' can refer to the types of the formative powers symbolised by the zodiac (literally the circle of animals), conscious but not self-conscious powers of the universe. They are gods, but not extra-cosmic nor even extra-mundane gods; they are powers that work from within outwards, controlling the patterns of the zodiac as much as they control the patterns of the world. From within our psychic complex, for instance, they determine that we shall see the archetypal patterns of the zodiac in what might otherwise seem to be the random scattering of stars.

The Messengers are the sons of those previously mentioned fiery and sacred Fathers who dwell within the formless square

---

[1] 'Man is, therefore, a noble creation, as perfect as the scheme allows; a part in the fabric of the all, he yet holds a lot higher than that of all other living things on earth.' Plotinus, *On Providence* III. ii. 9. (Turnbull)

of the Holy Four on the uttermost limits of the Cosmos. This square[1] marks the magical point of transformation between the unmanifest and the manifest, between non-being and being. For this reason it is there that lies certain knowledge of the mystery of creation, and from there that come the Messengers of the Fathers who have that knowledge, Messengers who are the Sons of Fire and who, like the angels on Jacob's ladder, pass up and down the rungs on the ladder of the Cosmic levels, both establishing the Divine Powers on those levels and carrying the message to all who will hear it that 'All is one Number issued from No-number.'

(4) *This was the army of the voice—the divine mother of the seven. The sparks of the seven are subject to, and the servants of, the first, the second, the third, the fourth, the fifth, the sixth, and the seventh of the seven. These 'sparks' are called spheres, triangles, cubes, lines and modellers; for thus stands the Eternal Nidāna—the Oi-Ha-Hou (the permutation of Oeaohoo).*

The list of Powers given in the last verse is here termed the Army of the Voice, a phrase which reminds us of the Biblical 'angelic hosts' and the Qu'rānic 'they who stand in ranks'. These hosts of divine powers have as their external symbol the hosts of shining stars which are the gods (*devas*, literally shining ones) of some traditions and the angels of others. Their hierarchical arrangement is one reason for the army symbol, while another is to be found in their almost infinite multiplicity. The list given is certainly complicated enough, but it is only a schematic outline and the actual reality is far more complex.

The Voice or Divine Mother of the Seven is the Matrix. This is the Sound (II. 2) or, to use another Hindu symbol, the goddess *Vāch* or Speech. The power which forms sound into speech is sometimes considered as male, as in the Sanskrit alphabet where the consonants are male and the vowel sounds female. But the voice is the producer of sound and is thus the 'mother'

[1] Cf. discussion on the four poles of being under Stanza III, 9 and 10.

of the seven vowels or archetypal energies which are the permutations of Oeaohoo discussed under Stanza III. 5.

Later in Stanza VI we shall come across the same maternal, productive side of the androgynous Universal Mind as *Kwan-Yin*. This is said to be the Chinese Buddhist rendering of the Sanskrit name of the Bodhisattva *Avalokitesvara*, the Lord who looks down in compassion; but some eastern scholars[1] maintain that the original term was *Avalokita-svara*, literally the looked-at-sound.[2] This 'sound' which is 'seen' reminds one of the Vedic Rishis who were said to have 'seen' the *mantras* of the *Veda* while in a state of ecstatic meditation. This does not mean that they saw a prehistoric form of writing, but that their vision was at a higher level than that at which sensing is differentiated into five different channels. At that level—the level of Universal Mind—there is truly neither seeing nor hearing, but the experience has to be translated into such terms when relating it to this environment. Those Vedic *mantras* were not merely the collection of hymns so carefully handed down to the present day, but the whole body of the Divine Wisdom, the Wisdom content of Universal Mind, the very truth itself which, in more or less modified forms, all the religious doctrines of the world (Hinduism amongst them) seek to present.

The vision of Divine Wisdom can only be attained when the self is lifted, by effort or by grace, beyond the lower levels of differentiated psychic process. There, the 'sound' of the Wisdom which is the teaching of the sons of Fire can be 'seen' as well as 'heard'.

Ancient writers were not so intoxicated with wonder at the phenomenon of ordinary speech that they worshipped it as divine, as some scholars seem to have thought. Speech, even ordinary speech, is in truth a wonderful thing, but what we

---

[1] See *The Bodhisattva Doctrine* by Har Dayal, p. 47; also *Manual of Zen Buddhism* by D. T. Suzuki, p. 33.

[2] There is much evidence in support of the latter term, but in neither case can the past participle *Avalokita* (+ *Iswara* or + *svara*) mean he who *looks* down or the down-looking: it has to be *looked, seen, viewed* or *observed*.

know as speech was considered by those ancients to be but
the outer rind of real Speech which was described as having
four forms.[1]

The Voice here spoken of is the highest of these four forms,
the creative Word (*Shabda*) that sounds forth the universe in
space. All linguistic occultism, all use of *mantras* to produce
phenomenal effects, their power to 'summon spirits from the
vasty deep', yes, and even the familiar power of words to
evoke thoughts, depends ultimately on the fact that what we
know as sound and speech is a manifestation of that Creative
Sound, the Voice which ever thunders forth the hidden
'Name of God' to all the worlds.

It should not surprise us that sound, as a symbol, should be
considered to carry connotations of a more primary nature
than does light or any other basic phenomenon of sense
perception, when we recall that hearing is the last sense power
to go into latency when we pass into a state of deep concentration or, for that matter, when passing under the influence
of an anaesthetic. A not insignificant fact to be considered in
the evaluation of the primacy of sound as a psychic experience
is that the deaf are seldom happy in their isolation, though they
are at a lesser disadvantage in terms of adaptation to the
material world than are the blind. The latter suffer more
greatly from the physical aspect of their disability, but are not
denied the joy of participation in the psychic life of their
fellows, so much of which depends on the power of rational
communication. This last is one of man's most fundamental
psychic distinctions and derives from that universality of
consciousness which is the dominant quality of Universal
Mind.

The seven archetypes begin as abstract determinants deriving
from the combinations of the three transcendent principles,
Source, Father-Light and Matrix. These are the Primordial
Seven of verse 1 and the Seven Inside of Stanza III. 4. Their

[1] *Parā, pashyantī, madhyamā* and *vaikharī*, corresponding to the *turīya, sushupti, svapna*
and *jāgrat* states of consciousness.

derivatives, the Seven Outside, are the thought patterns or images which control the effective operations of the out-flowing energies. The Sparks of this verse, the Sparks of the Primordial Flame, are thus the mass of individualised quanta of energy which, as it were, bear the imprint of the thought-forms whose patterns they build or model. The geometrical names given to them show them first as the structural elements of three dimensional form: Points (the dimensionless loci of the Sparks or Modellers); Lines (relating point to point), Triangles (plane areas), Cubes (the first solid arising from the square) and Spheres. Not counting the dimensionless point, there are only four figures given instead of the seven we might have expected. These correspond to the four determining qualities of the space into which the Sparks are projected and also to the four lower levels of existence on each of which 'Sparks of the Seven' produce their effects, for they control not only the physical structures of minerals, plants and animals, but also the patterns of thought, feeling and action.

Even by analogy it is difficult for us to get an idea of their actual mode of operation, because the illustrations we have to use—thought patterns, images, etc.—lay too great an emphasis on the conscious component of their action. They have been described as blind powers, but if blind, they are still vehicles of reason; they are not unconscious but un-self-conscious. They are also the angelic Messengers of the previous verse, and are in some sense the Spirits of the Elements—Gnomes, Undines, Sylphs and Salamanders.

They are Sparks of awareness, sons of the Father-Light, yet, unlike man whose *essential* allegiance is to the One alone, they are subject to and the servants of the seven archetypal energies whose qualities they carry. They are subject to the Seven because the patterns of form which are built around them are determined by the Seven, but they are also their servants because they are moments in awareness through whose agency those Divine Patterns achieve expression. In some sense they are not merely acted on but are themselves active agents.

Each has a primary characteristic deriving from one of the Seven, yet at each point all seven powers are manifest in varying ways and in different proportions. Each level, for instance, is a manifestation of one distinct Power or Energy, but that is only what may be termed its dominant character. 'Reflecting the "Self-existent-Lord" like a mirror, each (level) becomes in turn a world'. But in addition to that unity each level reflects every other level, for

> 'Nothing in the world is single,
> All things by a law divine
> In one another's being mingle—'

We must constantly remember that Reality is One. The Levels are not so many drawers in a chest, or even so many skins of an onion; they are levels of experience, and each level is an experience of the whole, but in a given manner or with a given emphasis of attention. Consequently, on any given level of experience, the whole of manifested reality will be present in some form or other, though because of the quality of attention characteristic of that level, certain aspects will dominate the pattern or form its groundwork. Those aspects are termed the characteristics of the level itself; but, at the same time, all the other moments of Reality will be, as it were, embroidered on them, and it is to this embroidery we refer when we say that each of the seven reflects all the others.

As an example, let us consider our familiar 'physical' level. On it, the Father and Mother are represented by the subject-object mode of all experience, the Universal Mind is represented by consciousness and its unity, the higher mind by the limitation to one single sensory point of view, and the lower mind by the element of perceptual recognition (as opposed to mere sensation). The Desire nature (*kāma*) comes in as the attraction felt for the sense-data which themselves represent the seventh or lowest level.

The same is true, *mutatis mutandis*, on all other cosmic levels, each divine type or pattern having its counterpart on every subsequent level and every subdivision of a level. Let us take an example from another scale: Day-dreaming or reverie is a sub-level of the waking state; it is related to dream, but, whereas in dream we have little or no control over events (a characteristic of the dream level), in reverie we have a fair degree of control over events (a characteristic of waking). But the dream state we normally experience is in itself only a sub-level of the total physical consciousness (waking, dreaming, deep sleep), above which lies the normal state of consciousness of the after death (disembodied) state, whose dominant characteristics have much that is in common with our dream.

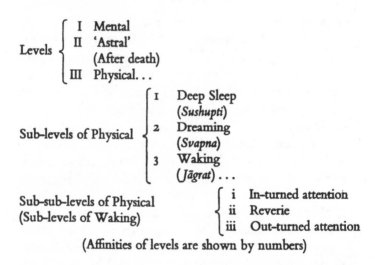

Levels {
I   Mental
II 'Astral'
    (After death)
III Physical...
}

Sub-levels of Physical {
1   Deep Sleep
    (Sushupti)
2   Dreaming
    (Svapna)
3   Waking
    (Jāgrat)...
}

Sub-sub-levels of Physical
(Sub-levels of Waking) {
i   In-turned attention
ii   Reverie
iii Out-turned attention
}

(Affinities of levels are shown by numbers)

Each level can be divided into sub-levels and each sub-level into sub-sub-levels, of which only one example is given above. The process can be continued almost indefinitely and, usually, fruitlessly. Nothing very much is to be gained by thinking of the Cosmos in terms of a detailed rigidity of structure. The point to be seen is that it is a Cosmos, an orderly arrangement, and not a chaos.

Having completed the list of the hierarchy of cosmic powers and stated the subjectedness of the outer universe to the inner, the verse ends by saying that this entire pattern of levels and powers is what it is because all things are ultimately determined by the First Cause (*Nidāna*), the very nature of the Darkness itself, the Will of God.

The enumeration of the moments of causation is set out in the next verse which reads straight on from the present one.

(5) (*The Oi-Ha-Hou*) which is:
Darkness, the Boundless or the No-Number, Ādi-Nidāna Svabhāvat: the ○ :
I. *The Ādi Sanat, the Number, for he is One.*
II. *The Voice of the Lord[1] Svabhāvat, the Numbers, for he is One and Nine.*
III. *The 'Formless Square'.*
And these three enclosed within the ○ *are the sacred four, and the ten are the Arūpa Universe. Then come the 'Sons,' the seven Fighters, the One, the eighth left out, and his Breath which is the Light-Maker (Bhāskara).*

The Cosmic Elements listed in the preceding verses are present in various ways in all experience. Their particular ways of manifestation on any given scale of experience, their comings and goings, are all controlled by a principle which is what we know as the principle of causality, and which the verse refers to as the *Nidāna*. The latter is a Sanskrit word which primarily means a band or rope and which is used to signify the type of linkings we term causal, and so is the root of all causality in the Ever-Darkness.

Causal efficacy suggests to most people that there is some special power residing in things by which they *cause* other things. Ages before Hume's famous criticism of such a notion, however, the inner teaching stated that there is no such

---

[1] Two readings occur in the *S.D.* First where the Stanzas are printed all together we get a reading as above, but later, on I. 98, the reading is '*Voice of the word, Svabhāvat*'. If this latter reading be preferred we must take Word in the sense of Logos or Father which manifests through the Voice or Mother. The different readings are thus identical in meaning.

causal efficacy resident in things.[1] No *thing* causes any other thing, for causality resides not in things but in the whole. Particular events take place not because of any power in some other events which are said to be their causes, but because of an organic linking of the whole of cosmic experience, a linkage which is such that all events in the Cosmos are bound together in one harmonious correlation. Movement of any one 'part' or element of the Cosmos necessitates movements of all the other elements, not because of any direct 'causal power' exerted by the first but because all exist together in one seamless garment that is the Whole, the very Darkness itself. This, however, is a subject that we shall have to return to in connection with verse six of this stanza. Here it is only necessary to point out that the principle which governs the correlated manifestations of the Cosmic Elements, the principle we know as causality, is placed by the stanzas, not in the Elements themselves, but in the Whole of which they are but moments; for, as we read: 'Thus stands the Eternal *Nidāna*—the Oi-Ha-Hou'. That is to say, the differentiations of the outer Seven must act in the way they do, because such is the *Nidāna* or causal principle in the One Darkness.

Let us remember the words which prefaced the stanza, the teaching that all is One, issuing from the Dark Mystery; just as all the bright images that fill our minds are one in the dark background of our psyches. Like those private images of ours, the Cosmic Images come forth and change and vanish. Forever the unceasing flow goes on, changing its form and shape continuously. Nevertheless, in all those changes, changeless regularities can be observed. As the Buddha, who is the first historical figure to have enunciated this principle, phrased it: 'This being, that also is; this not being, that also ceases to be.'

It is on account of this principle that we are able to describe and mark the patterns in the Cosmos, to talk of 'laws of nature' and to forecast the future. 'Coming to be! Coming to

---

[1] Nāgārjuna, to quote only a well known example. *Mādhyamika Kārika*, Chapter 1, Examination of Causality.

be! Ceasing to be! Ceasing to be! Ceasing to be!' These were the words which many a Buddhist in those early days meditated upon as he walked the countryside or sat in the shade of trees; words with which he strove to penetrate to the heart of the mystery of the world. *What* comes to be or *what* ceases to be we cannot say. Something appears, glitters for a moment, and then vanishes into the abyss. Its duration may be a moment as we count time, or it may be a hundred million years, which yet is but a moment in the Cosmic Day. But, moment or age, the problem is the same. It came, it was, it vanished, and is gone—'like drifting clouds, like the waning moon, like ships that sail the ocean, like shores that are washed away.'

Such is the Power which rules the Cosmic play. If we will meditate deeply on its manifestations, on the comings and goings, and on the law which binds them together, we shall come to see that in very truth nothing comes and goes. All that surrounds us, atoms or men or mighty solar systems, are but the bright and changing images of dream. Even the images themselves, if scrutinised, melt away to nothing before our eyes. We gaze right through them, and our spirits strain and lose themselves upon the edge of a great gulf of blackness. Strive as we will, we can go no further; yet, as we hang poised upon the edge, something seems to be issuing forth from the black gulf, a formless image of a mighty rhythm, and, as the images crowd back on us, we know that it is by that rhythm that they come and go; or, rather, that the images are somehow just the rhythm itself, a shining magic that is and yet is not the magic of '*the Eternal Nidāna*'.

The verse commences by giving an analysis of the separable moments within the Darkness, the unmanifested Powers that together make up the Sacred Four. These we may understand as the first of a series of causal quaternities, 'The Sacred Four', then, 'The Formless Square', and we can see that this is the fourfold pattern in causation of what will later appear in manifestation as the 'Lower Four'.

We first met the 'seven-vowelled word' Oeaohoo in

Stanza III. 5 where we saw that it represented the one and undivided creative power, the Source, Sustainer and Cause of the sevenfold universe. Oi-Ha-Hou represents a change of Oeaohoo into three separable moments of the causal linkage, the aspirate representing the outbreathing which brings the powers to manifestation.

Enumerating the principles of causation, the verse first mentions the Darkness itself, Oeaohoo, the No-Number and Primal Self-becoming Cause (*Ādi Nidāna Svabhāvat*). This first moment of the Sacred Four is the O or all-container which holds all together in its Boundless Circle and to which the following three are subsidiary. These three moments are equivalent to the three creative Logoi or utterances of which an account was given under Stanza III. 3.

I. The Primal Eternal or 'Ancient of Days' (*Ādi Sanat*), the Unity which initiates the whole series of numbers or manifested Powers. This principle, the Father or transcendent Self, is the very Self-nature (*svabhāva*) of the Darkness and therefore bears the same name, *Svabhāvat*. In many accounts, indeed, the two are not counted as separate, being taken as substantially the same.

He is One, the Number, because he is the principle of unity, the self-affirmatory first integer, 'I am One', and so the cause of all individuation.

II. The Voice is the Mother, the fecund not-self nature of the Darkness, who is the principle of multiplicity. She is called the Voice because it is her power which gives the Father's silent Word (logos) expression as Sound (cf. II. 2). The Word (according to another version, the Lord) *Svabhāvat* is, as we have seen, the Self-nature of the Darkness and, because of his unity, is the rational determinant of the series of integers, 'the Numbers', from One to Nine which he calls forth from the not-self of the Matrix. It is he who determines which among the infinite possibilities of the Mother shall become actual.

The One Father, the *Ādi Sanat* or First Cause, is thus the primary 'Lord of Hosts' (*Gaṇapati*), General of the Army of the

Gods (*Devasenāpati*), notwithstanding that these and other like terms have been devalued and misunderstood. Though it may appear as if it is always he who causes, determines and leads the hosts and multitudes of gods, yet, without the Mother's power, his 'Voice', no word of command could be effective. We must be careful, therefore, not to belittle the part played by the feminine element. As *Prakriti* she may be 'blind', irrational, but, like Penelope, by Day she weaves the web of the universe and by Night unravels it again. Without her consent the Father's Will cannot create.

If the Father is the source of Reason, the Mother is the source of Life, an instinctive, irrational life, it is true, with no conscious adaptation of means to ends, but when the universe sleeps, Life pulsates 'unconscious in Universal Space' (I. 8). It is like a dog, sleeping with one eye open. Then, at the slightest stir of the Spirit rustling the dry leaves of the dormant tree of Life, 'spring in Space the re-awakened energies'.

The Lord *Svabhāvat* is, as we have seen, both One and Nine. One in himself as the fertilising 'effulgency of Light', Nine in union with the Mother, for it is her multiple nature that enables him to multiply and divide. Both are aspects of the Dark Source whose ineffable 'Unity' enfolds them. They are inter-dependent and share the burden of giving birth to the Universe.

That the Source of all things is One, is, or should be, self-evident. As Ibn-ul-'Arabi said, 'even an ass knows more than he who merely knows something about the unity of God'. But that the Source is also multiplicity is not so often perceived. For this reason it has been necessary to stress that not only the One Lord of unity is an aspect of the Darkness, but also that all the nine integers, the Numbers, symbolising the whole series of cosmic powers, are implicit in the same Darkness. The transcendent Unity is therefore not merely O, the Void, but also the combination of the One and the Many, the 10, the Plenum.

III. Lastly we come to the 'Formless Square' or immaterial

quaternity of powers which are the peculiar property of the Son. The Four moments of this 'square' are the now familiar four modes in which unmanifest content is objectified, whether in the inner, imaginal worlds or in the outer worlds of sense. They are placed in the causal hierarchy because they are the means by which the transition is made from the Unmanifest to the Manifest, from the archetypal worlds of the inner Seven to their counterparts in externality. They are determining modes of projection, not the projections themselves, and are therefore Formless (*Arūpa*).

'These Three, enclosed within the O, are the Sacred Four', the divine Tetraktys. The principles enumerated have been the familiar Source, Father, Mother, and Son, but arranged as a quaternary which represents an extremely important moment of Reality. In it is rooted the essential balance and harmony of the Universe, the divinely harmonised interaction of the cosmic powers.

The interaction between the Father and the Mother represents Fohat, the power aspect of Reality; the tension between the poles being the essential dynamism of the Cosmos. Were it not for the Divine Creative Will of the Darkness, which holds Heaven and Earth asunder, the Poles would fuse together and the manifestation come to an end. That Will is a fiery out-pouring, the 'Wrath of God', which, after separating the two Poles of being, passes through the Father to the Mother and brings the qualities of both to birth in the Son. Then through the Son it first individualises, then differentiates, then flows into, and finally exteriorises its Being. It is the only Will in the Universe, and if any individual thinks to oppose himself to it by virtue of his seeming independence, he will be destroyed as ruthlessly as the mass will of public opinion can destroy a man who outrages the standards of the community.

It is in this quaternary, too, that we must seek for the hidden source of what we perceive down here as the causal linkage of all phenomena. The actual motive power of causality, so to speak, resides in this mysterious balance that lies at the root of and controls all manifestation. It is because of its dynamic, living energy that any movement, any alteration of equilibrium occasioned in the phenomenal worlds, brings about an answering movement that we term its effect. One billiard ball impinging on another does not directly cause that other to move; the harmony of the Tetraktys brings it about that the disturbance of equilibrium occasioned by the first is answered by an appropriate and balancing movement elsewhere. The locus of the 'effect' is governed by relationships, or what may be called psychic affinities existing in the Universal Mind. In the case of the low grade existents which we term purely physical objects their inner relationships will manifest mainly as spatio-temporal contiguity. But where higher or more spiritual levels of being are involved, as in man, the 'contiguity' involved may be of quite a different nature. This is seen in the phenomena of Kārmic effects which may be separated widely in time and space from the 'causes'.

The Ten of the *Arūpa* universe are the ten 'Numbers' mentioned in the verse which, together with the Sacred Four, make up the total of fourteen energies listed in verse 3 of this stanza. This *Arūpa* universe is neither the entirely unmanifest state of the transcendent principles, nor the worlds of concrete form, but the totality of empatterned energies which spring to birth in the 'Space' of the Mother and form the subtle energetic background out of which the visible universe is built.

The Fighters are the (seven) differentiated powers which externalise the inner content and impress the patterns of the archetypes upon the outer levels of form. They are Fighters because they are the effective forces of the divine Army, as opposed to the 'non-combatant' directive forces of the Army Staff who remain unmanifest in the background. They are thus the efficient cause of the universe, having the power to act on the plastic objectivity of the outer worlds and so to reveal the archetypal nature by external tokens.

The worlds of form are in fact the worlds of symbols. All

their concrete forms, whether those of sense or the subtler ones of thought, are in truth symbolic of the formless realities of the Ten. He who cannot make the intuitive transition from the symbolic form to the symbolised reality remains shut up in the closed worlds of symbols from which he is quite unable to escape. The intuitive power to pass beyond the symbol is thus not a luxury with which we can afford to dispense; it is an absolute essential if we are to pass out of the circle of mental concepts into the living universe beyond. This is another reason why the teachers of the inner path prefer to use concrete symbols which exhibit their symbolic nature upon their very faces, rather than the abstract ones which are so popular in modern times and which, with their deceitful promise of precision, lure the mind into remaining within their charmed circles.

These Fighters, whom *The Secret Doctrine* calls Architects,[1] are also Builders, 'The luminous Sons of the Manvantaric Dawn' (II. 1). Themselves under the dominion of Father-Mother they are the 'Producers of Form from No-Form'.

These, then, are the Seven Sons; but the One Son is the Universal Mind, 'the Eighth left out', the eighth (or first) note of the octave of the Sound. He is left out or rejected (IV. 6) because, as has been previously pointed out, he is the bright image of that Darkness, the eighth and transcendent level which is no level.

> 'You might ask on Olympus
> Where the eighth also dwells
> Whom nobody thought of.'[2]

Finally the verse mentions the living outbreath of the Darkness, that 'Ceaseless Eternal Breath' (II. 2) which causes all things to ex-ist in the radiant light of consciousness. The reference to the Light-Maker (Sanskrit *Bhāskara*) shows the identity of the Breath with the Effulgency of verse 3 and the

[1] S.D., I. 101 (Stanza IV. 5. d.)
[2] *Faust.*

'Ray', both the latter terms being meanings of *Bhās*. But, as we have seen, there is a lack of distinction between the Darkness and the One Son, Universal Mind; the Breath of the one is the Breath of the other. In the context of this verse, the Light-Maker refers to the effulgent radiance of the Son, the Sun of the universe, which, as Mind, makes clear (*Bhāskara*) the Divine Ideas.

The seven 'Planets' of ancient astrology are almost exact parallels to the effectuating powers of the seven Fighters. Each and every one of the Seven ingresses into each and every integration of being in the outer worlds, imparting to them their characteristic properties of sensible form and the patterns of their psychic nature. They govern the patterns of events and determine the fixed framework within which even mankind's inherent freedom is confined. Their influences ingress most particularly at the moment of any birth or coming-into-being, and the patterns they impress at that moment govern, in a manner equivalent to fate, the possible patterns of the native's future. The medium through which they govern events is, however, as impossible to objectify as is an electric potential or a psychosis. This is the meaning of the detailed statement about the subjectedness of the Sparks in the previous verse, and this too is why the attempt to classify phenomena by their Planetary types raises such difficulties and gives such variable results. In astrological terms, the influence of every 'Planet' is effective simultaneously at every point on the 'Earth', but the intensity of each one's influence and whether or not it will be 'beneficent' is dependent on time and place expressed in terms of the patterns of relationship both between the Planets themselves and between them and the point (Spark) under consideration. If in place of 'Planet', we read 'Fighters' we can get some idea of the latter's causal efficacy. The planets of astronomy are, of course, no more the influential Powers than the hands of the clock are Time.

In the effort to understand the powers of the Fighters we are having to anticipate the circumgyratory movements of the temporal universe which belong to the next stanza. In the a-temporal and 'static' universe of the Inner Seven (3+4) archetypes, those divisions of being which will later be manifested as qualities of form are, as it were, evenly distributed. They are orderly but impotent patterns, houses without occupants. They may be likened to the twelve (3×4) divisions of the zodiac which seem to circle the earth smoothly and majestically, but whose attributes are inert until modified and transmitted by the 'Planets', those erratic Wanderers which, as we have seen, represent the effectuating powers of the Fighters.

The zodiac seems to revolve. Seems, for it is the earth and the planets which move, and the fixed patterns of the eternal archetypes which stand unchanging behind the flux of events. It is this circumgyratory movement which replaces the static patterns of perfection by the ever-changing flux of events in time and produces both the intermingling of qualities and their degrees of intensity which is Life's infinite variety. This mixing of powers is what produces those inequalities between creatures of the same category which often seem to us an injustice. 'God is the Compassionate, the Merciful', we say, yet we cannot reconcile the concept of a merciful Person with what we observe of the powers of Life which both raise up men from the dust and trample them back into it again with the heartlessness of a child playing with flies. 'He is the Quickener and he the Giver of Death.'[1]

The 'Unity' of the Darkness is, as we have seen, not a mere sameness, a dull monotony. Unknowable though it is in itself, we know it through its manifest nature. Everywhere around us we see inequality, the vast ranges of difference which are partial expressions of the Plenum. So long as these differences are on the sub-human scale we raise no objection; we even praise the Creator for the infinite variety of his creatures. Only when these same differences appear among men as inequalities of innate ability, circumstance and opportunity do we cry out 'injustice'. Why?

[1] *Qu'rān*, LVII. 2.

Neither is a mountain merciful nor a tiger cruel, nor is a river unjust when it erodes one man's land and deposits it on another's. Compassion, mercy, justice, righteousness, *dharma*, are human qualities, qualities of person deriving from the Person of Divine Mind. They are qualities implying a purposeful necessity to establish and maintain a harmonious relationship between individuals. More, their application to life is an expression of a felt need to raise ourselves above our animal passions and to identify ourselves with the spark of divinity within our hearts. Even our ability to perceive the apparent injustice inherent in the patterns of life derives from the presense of that divine spark of Mind within us.

But how to reconcile these conflicting perceptions of 'Allah, the Compassionate, the Merciful' and the Allah of the *Hadith* who drew forth the posterity of Adam from his loins in two handfuls and said, 'These are in Paradise and I care not; and these are in Hell-fire and I care not'?

The great out-pouring Breath of the Ever-Darkness is an impersonal Power which, like a great animal, storms out along its wrathful path, trampling whatever comes in its way. Verily—

'Through fear of Him the Wind blows.
Through fear of Him the Sun rises.
Through fear of Him both Fire and Indra
And Death as fifth do speed along.'[1]

The inequalities carried on the Breath originate as the 'Numbers' sounded forth in Space by the 'Voice'. They are thus an essential element of the Cosmos, the all-inclusive Harmony of which good and evil, justice and injustice, mercy and ruthlessness, are mutually complementing modalities. But this is not all:

'Other than *Dharma*, other than *Adharma*; other than both Cause and Effect; other than also Past and Future; That which thou seest, tell me that.'[2]

[1] *Taittirīya Upaniṣhad*, II. 8.
[2] *Kaṭhopaniṣhad*, II. 14.

In the Son of the Divine Parents there is the reconciliation of conflicting forces. He is the Divine Person, the Hermetic Androgyne, *Prajñā* and *Karuṇā* united as *Avalokiteśvara*, the Christos, the Compassionate, the Merciful Vishnu, the sustainer of Order, Adam Kadmon, Kabbalistic symbol of Divine Man.

In so far as we are creatures of the Breath, we are born on its outflow and die with its inflow; and our hereditary characteristics, our environment, our opportunities, our successes, failures, joys and sufferings will be ruthlessly determined by its seven archetypal modes. But when we look within and distinguish our essential humanity from our animality we find a nobility and freedom of the Spirit that is subject neither to the first nor the seventh of the Seven but to the Eighth, the One left out, the bright, Compassionate and Merciful Son of the Darkness.

(6) *Then the Second Seven, who are the Lipika, produced by the Three. The rejected Son is One, the Son-Suns are countless.*

The Lipika, a word deriving from the Sanskrit word of that form, are here the Second or outer Seven, the written characters (*lipi*) or impressions of the archetypal patterns in the outer though still invisible worlds. The patterns of phenomena are impressed, written, or structurally constituted in correspondence with the ideal or archetypal structure of the inner Seven. This is what is meant by the statement in verse 4 that the 'Sparks of the Seven', their derivatives in outwardness, are subject to them. The manifestations and movements on all levels of the cosmos are governed from within outwards.

The transition from inner archetype to outer form is akin, as the words of the verse suggest, to the psychic process of translating thought into speech or writing. Thought is a universal 'language', and in the realm of the psychic interchange of thought, thought transference, we do not have to know a man's natural tongue to know his thought. Our psychic process translates his thought into our speech, just as it translates our own; but this process is not always an easy one. Just as we tend to misinterpret the promptings of the psyche, particularly when they run contrary to our egotistic interests, so it is with the outer Seven. Having won a degree of independence, they follow their 'interpretations' of the divine injunctions and build structures which are only approximations to the ideal perfection. On the human scale, for instance, these misinterpretations may lead to such bestiality in the name of divinity as is exampled by the Inquisition. The inner Warriors not only build the outer worlds but have to fight to save them from the near-chaos into which they fall.

What happens when we try to give expression to the 'internal' content of our psyche? There is a feeling-charged flow of ideas or images demanding to be exteriorised, an inner pressure manifesting as a need to act. In some cases thought is the predominating influence, in others it is feeling, but the process of transition from idea to action, the power of effectuation, is something we cannot objectify. We perceive the causal pattern and we sense the result; we can even watch the muscular movements, themselves effects, which mediate the process, but nothing more. The subtle link of living is there; we move and are moved by it at every moment, yet, like knowing, it can never in itself be known. In the microcosm of man this is the triune emotive power of creation, the 'Three' which produces the outer 'Seven'. The 'Seven' compare with the thinking-feeling complex which governs the pattern of our actions.

How seldom, however, do the results of our actions seem adequate expressions of our intentions. Wherever we put the blame for our failure—on the material, on the tools, seldom on our own skill—imperfection is inherent in the process of transition from unmanifest content to manifest expression.

The archetypal universe is the realm of perfection. There, there is nothing to mar the beauty of the divine conception. Here, however, in the outer universe, on whatever scale of being, there is nothing perfect; the best is near-perfection. What has gone wrong? If this universe is the existent image of perfect priors, then why is it not also perfect? Perhaps the fault lies not in the universe, but in our conception of what constitutes perfection. We tend to think of beauty in terms of the frozen forms of statuary and architecture, instead of the living and changing forms of reality, for change is an essential feature of the outer universe. If the divine Will was seeking perfection in the classic sense, it would long ago have locked itself into a static pattern of fixed forms and qualities. But it does not and perhaps cannot, for the infinite potentiality of the Matrix does not lend itself to precise definition, the circle of being will not submit to exact measurement, and so all forms must differ from their conceptual priors by an imperfection that is an essential characteristic of the outer Seven.

We know from human experience that the very same forces that establish a family may also disrupt it, for attraction and repulsion are different modes of the same power. In any youth, also, there is a conflict between the desire to retain the safety and protection of the parental atmosphere and the desire for independent manhood. The tensions produced by this conflict act upon him independently of his understanding and tend to make him quarrelsome, over-vehement, and unreasonable. Similarly with the growth of the cosmic family of levels. The Sons on the outermost manifest levels—the outer Seven—are in what may be termed a state of vehemence; there is a constant turmoil of forces both outflowing and returning. Desire forces and their resulting movements are strong, vigorous, and erratic; experience is vivid; forms are clearly defined. There is no longer any easy interchanging and fusion of identities, but progressively hardening limits make possible the impact of separate integrations. In fact, separateness and conflict are mutually dependent concepts. The manifest universe is inevitably a realm of discrete bodies, acting and reacting upon one another under the influence of conflicting flows of energy.

Just as inevitably, and for the same reason, the living content of the outer worlds is inferior and degraded in comparison to that of the divine archetypes. The outer worlds are sick with the ferment of pent up desire forces; the flow of life thrusting, now up, now down, seeking but never finding an unrestricted outlet.

But what is this sickness of the universe? Why must we live eternally dogged by the shadows of evil, illness, misfortune —our own and others'? Why cannot heaven be established here on earth? Why have we been created slaves to evil passions?

The lower worlds of manifestation cannot be without conflict. When the Father-Light of the cosmos is himself seeking the experience of outwardness and himself sustaining the manifest universe to that end, how can his creatures escape the compulsion of the out-turned forces acting in and through them, forces manifesting under the pressure of the Creator's out-turned seeking. So long as the parents of the universe are utterly at unity in themselves there can be no creation, for no forces can be generated between them, so complete is their mutual absorption. The very powers that bring about the primal separation of the Father and Mother poles are mutually repulsive; powers, as it were, seeking satisfaction outside the primal relationship. From these separative forces, then, arises the outward looking consciousness, the out-turned flow of desire, whether cosmic or human—and conflict.

The out-turned experience of separateness and conflict in multiplicity is complementary to the inturned, unitive and peaceful state of primal being. In the outer universe there can therefore be no cure for the sickness of life; for only if the divine consciousness were to return to that in-turned and peaceful state of unity (*pralaya*), the sustaining consciousness of the universe thereby being withdrawn, then only would all separateness and all manifestation cease to exist, and with it all conflict would disappear.

Within man, and within man alone, the bright spark of self awareness stands essentially free from all compulsions save that of the primal duality. He alone of all the universe can travel the return path to psychic health, the path of self-transformation, in spite of and, perhaps, because of the sickness of the surrounding world. But to do this, he must find and then become that spark by withdrawing the gaze of his soul from external preoccupations and seeking within himself the source of his own and, indeed, of all being.

The archetypal universe of the Inner Seven is that Eternity of which Time is the moving image, yet it is not like an insubstantial version of an architect's model of which the temporal image is an inferior copy. It is rather the sevenfold scale of musical tones from which all themes, harmonies and variations are produced. The first externalised patterns, the Second Seven or Lipika, are 'produced by the Three' causal determinants of the preceding verse. That is to say, the outer universe is a tissue of empatterned energy structures made up of the triune outflow from Father-Mother-Son.

It is in fact the abstract, formless or archetypal nature of those Three (and Seven) which acts as a controlling Power, governing not only the events on any one level, but also the correlation between different levels. The entire universe is thus woven into one web of *karma*, mental events being correlated with physical ones and *vice versa*.

This is why any event or sequence of events can be explained with apparent adequacy from any one level. A neurosis, a physical disease, or even an 'accident', can be accounted for in terms of its correlations with other purely physical-plane factors. It can also be accounted for in terms of its psychic correlates on higher levels. The former is the method pursued by ordinary medicine, while the latter is, or should be, that of psycho-therapy. Because of the inter-plane correlation, any fact in the universe, physical or psychic, *can* be reduced to its physical-plane correlates. He who is determined to find the cause of everything on the material plane alone will always be able to find, not indeed its 'cause', but at least a set of material correlates which will appear to explain the particular phenomenon. Nevertheless, the opposite method, that of accounting for physical events in terms of their psychic correlates, is a truer and more fundamental one. The lower levels hang from the higher, and we should therefore make it our task to see all outer events and all characteristics of our material environment in terms of the inner psychic events which are their higher correlates, higher because the universe expands from within without. Psychic events are thus nearer than the physical to the Source of all and partake more in its creative power.

Standing behind and uniting all consciousness, all experience and all being, is the ever unmanifest, timeless and spaceless root of all Being and all Cause, *Ādi-Nidāna-Svabhāvat*, the Darkness, in relation to which all things are as they are. Only by virtue of their coming from that common source do phenomena, on whatever level, come into relation with each other. Only, then, in that source can there be a moment in which cause and effect unite. From there, too, descend those jointless yet flexible bands of sequential relationship that manifest around us as apparent causality and in us as our feeling of being initiators of action.

Ibn-ul-'Arabi held that the real cause of every effect is 'non-existent' in the sense that it does not exist objectively anywhere. A similar view of causality is that taught by the Buddha in what is termed *pratītya samutpāda* or Correlated Origination; the general formula of which is, not 'such and such causes so and so', but 'this being, that manifests; this not being, that vanishes'. Those who seek to probe deeper into the mysteries of causality and *karma* will have to come to grips with the complicated structure of the Three as outlined in the first part of the previous verse. The Lipikas are produced by the Three, as we have read, but the understanding of their structure and of the interactions which take place between them is frankly beyond the competence of the present writers who can do no more than point out that there, in the very heart of the Sacred Four, is the place where the answer must be sought to those problems of causality which have baffled even the greatest thinkers.

P

Perhaps those who trace all real causality back to the divine Will are wiser and nearer to the truth than those who scoff at them. The 'Will of God' is certainly a more apt symbol of the mysterious power-structures in what is here called the Sacred Four than are the fortuitous collisions of the miniature energetic billiard balls of, not the best scientific, but popular materialist thought. We may do well here to remember the words of the Sūfi Jalalu'ddin Rumi: 'From beginning to end the Qu'rān is teaching the abandonment of belief in phenomenal causation, but the understanding of this is not for the merely practical intellect. Perform service (of the teacher) that it may become clear to thee'.[1]

The Rejected Son refers us back to the 'Eighth left out' of the previous verse, the eighth and transcendental level which is no level but the source and root of all levels. But, as has been shown above, the quite indescribable unity of the Source reappears as the self-nature of Universal Mind. The unity of the dark Source, which was perceptible in the relationship of the Father-Mother pair, sprang into radiant manifestation in the being of their Son—the Son who is the manifest Source, as the other is the unmanifest Source.

In this Son lies the only means we have of obtaining knowledge of what is otherwise utterly unknowable. It is a unity which embraces the whole manifest universe with all its separate Solar and other systems. Nevertheless, the Sons of that Son, or, as the verse terms them, the Son-Suns, are countless in number, just as though the heaven is one, it is filled with countless stars. They are in fact the countless central points of any of the sevenfold differentiated systems, sub-human, human or astronomical, that occur within the embrace of the Universal Mind.

Indeed, the so-called astrolatry of the ancients was not the open-mouthed wonder-gaping at the starry sky, grand as the latter is, that some have supposed it to have been. Their 'suns',

---

[1] *Mathnawi*, III. 2525-26. Note the similarity to *Bhagavad Gītā*, IV. 34. 'Understand this by service and humility'.

'stars', and 'planets' were not the ones seen with telescopes
but their counterparts in the psychic worlds. Their 'astronomical' schemes of concentric heavens have more in them than
hasty critics realise, for their astronomy dealt, not with this
physical level alone, but with the mighty cosmos of the
Seven.

Every man had his Star: yes, and still does. But the movements of that Star are not chronicled in the *Nautical Almanac,*
though those that are so chronicled are undoubtedly correlated
with 'the Stars', as are all events whatever. It is on these
correlations, the *Lipika* or writing on the heavens, that the
true astrology is based. This record or writing, forming as it
does the law of structure of the levels, is the power which
operates as manifest causality or *karma,* the power which binds
the movements on all levels in regular sequences of cause and
effect. That certain 'effects' should follow certain 'causes', that
a given course of action should necessarily be followed by a
given result, all this is due to the existence of that writing, a
veritable 'writing on the wall' or book of Fate.

Every Power and Principle in the universe, formless and
formed, inner and outer, reacts on and interacts with every
other. Yet all Power comes from the one Source and, if any
movement on any level be meditated on sufficiently, it will
prove to be an Ariadne thread that will guide us back to the
One which is its Source.

It has been said before, but it will bear repetition, that in
talking of matter and motion we are not talking of the 'dead
matter' and mechanical motion of last century science and
present day popular thought. What is here termed matter is
something that can only be described as living psychic content;
while what is termed motion is the manifestation of living
psychic power, akin to such powers as we exhibit in imagination, will, sympathy and the like. From top to bottom the
Cosmos is alive; nowhere is there anything that is dead. Its
movements are the movements of life, effected by a hierarchy
of living, creative Powers, and its content is the image-content

of the Cosmic Mind. The whole is one vast organism in which every part is organically related to every other. Scientists have told us that the striking of a match has consequences in the remotest stars, and it is no less true that the wanton killing of an ant has consequences which wander through infinity and are reflected back upon the slayer.

It was no silly superstition of the ancients that peopled all the world with gods. The common people may not have understood their true nature any more than do they now the nature of the mechanical 'forces' which have taken their place. The trees and rocks, the ocean waves, the moving air, and the far-shining stars are all the vehicles of living, spiritual Powers, as living as the powers which mould and wield the thoughts within our minds. Everywhere in the ancient world these powers were known and worshipped by the common men as gods, and everywhere, too, in Greece, in Egypt, and in ancient India, those who were initiated in the mysteries knew and sometimes proclaimed that these same gods were but the aspects of one protean Power, the great creative power of Life which ensouled, nay, which was the cosmos down to its tiniest 'atom'.

Let us conclude this section with the words of one of the greatest of modern philosophers, Professor Whitehead: 'Apart from the experiences of subjects there is nothing, nothing, bare nothingness.'[1]

---

[1] *Process and Reality*, p. 234.

STANZA FIVE

Being the fifth of seven Stanzas from
The Book of Dzyan

1. *The Primordial Seven, the first seven Breaths of the Dragon of Wisdom, produce in their turn from their holy circumgyrating Breaths the Fiery Whirlwind.*

2. *They make of him the messenger of their will. The Dzyu becomes Fohat: the Swift Son of the Divine Sons, whose sons are the Lipika, runs circular errands. He is the steed and the Thought is the rider. He passes like lightning through the fiery clouds; takes three, five and seven strides through the seven regions above and the seven below. He lifts his voice, and calls the innumerable sparks and joins them together.*

3. *He is their guiding spirit and leader. When he commences work he separates the sparks of the lower kingdom that float and thrill with joy in their radiant dwellings and forms therewith the germs of wheels. He places them in the six directions of space and one in the middle—the central wheel.*

4. *Fohat traces spiral lines to unite the six to the seventh—the Crown; an Army of the Sons of Light stands at each angle; the Lipika—in the middle wheel. They say, 'This is good'. The first Divine World is ready, the first (is now) the second. Then the 'Divine Arūpa' reflects itself in Chhāyā Loka, the first garment of the Anupādaka.*

5. *Fohat takes five strides and builds a winged wheel at each corner of the square for the four holy ones . . . and their armies.*

6. *The Lipika circumscribe the triangle, the first one, the cube, the second one, and the pentacle within the egg. It is the ring called 'Pass Not', for those who descend and ascend (as also for those) who, during the Kalpa, are progressing towards the great day 'Be with us' . . . Thus were formed the Arūpa and the Rūpa; from one light seven lights; from each of the seven, seven times seven lights. The Wheels watch the Ring. . . .*

THE FIERY WHIRLWIND

In the last stanza we saw how the second Logos resulted in a multiplicity of powers and centres of awareness. This stanza describes the third stage in the cosmic process whereby the inner, imaginal content of Mind begins to be exteriorised as a universe of form.

The vortical outflow described as coming to manifestation is a mixture of the three principles which gave it birth. The Breath of the Father mingles with the Waters of the Mother, and to that flow is added the gyratory movement of the Son which blends the roar of the voice of the Lord with the roar of the Waters of the Deep, as all three principles flow out together, forming the *prima-materia* of manifestation, the fiery whirlwind.

(1) *The Primordial Seven, the first seven Breaths of the Dragon of Wisdom, produce in their turn from their holy circumgyrating Breaths the Fiery Whirlwind.*

In the earlier stanzas, dealing with the unmanifest cosmos, symbolism permitted us to speak of a rectilinear and unidirectional flow of the creative Breath, because all such directions and dimensions were metaphysical; but, as the Breath, the Light-maker of stanza IV. 3, passes to manifestation, the metaphysical becomes physical, or as Rumi has said, 'This spatial world has been produced from that which is without spatial relation. The world has received place from placeless-ness'.[1]

We are here introduced to the concept of rotation, a circumgyration of the Breath. It is as if the direct linear out-thrust, originating in the Father-Light, called out a circum-gyratory response in the Waters of the Matrix, an incubatory circulation about the Ray of the One Darkness, which gave birth to and enfolded the Son.[2]

We can also regard the primal division in the Ever-Darkness as a rotation of Being about itself, giving rise to a polar tension between centre and circumference. This image gives a symbo-lic explanation of why the two poles of Being do not rush together and fuse as soon as separated, because the same movement which brings them into being also holds them apart.

The peculiar significance of the circumgyration is therefore its power to relate, to integrate, and to separate. The separate, abstract principles of consciousness can thus be integrated into a system of reflective awareness, a Mind; single concepts can be united into logical wholes; an inchoate mass can be divided into related organisations. The manifestation of a field of perception in which the unitary content of the Absolute Being will stand forth as discrete objects of experience is thus depen-dent on this circumgyration of the creative Breath.

Universal Mind as an integral being can thus be identified with the great light-filled vortex in the Waters of the Matrix. It circles about its own centre of awareness, and the rim of the vortex is the limiting ring of its unity. The circumference reflects the radiating consciousness back upon itself and fills, or seems to fill, the revolving content of the circle with archetypal or ideal images. These are the 'writings' (*lipika*), the first objectifications in Mind of the ineffable content of the Ever-Darkness, images of the Primordial Seven which, with

[1] *Mathnawi*, II. 6 & 7.
[2] It may be of some significance to note that a 'linear flow' of electricity is surrounded by a circular field of force. In the human sphere one may also note the circular arrangement of psychic content, the revolving of thoughts brought about by the direct thrust of an idea.

the out-turning of Mind, will be projected into externality as the fiery Breath of the Dragon of Wisdom.[1]

We are now in a better position to understand the Web of the Universe described in Stanza III. 10 as deriving from a fourfold interplay of powers, the Web that is the field of perception.

Around the primary outflow of the creative Breath is generated the vortical movement of derivative energy which results in Mind's self-related awareness, the unitary blend of Knower, Knowing and Known.

Seen from a slightly different angle, this appears as the alternating weft which crosses the warp of the Breath and weaves the whole into a web of experience.

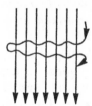

This combination of the three types of motion, outflow, inflow, and gyration, produces those alternations of stress which, superimposed or 'written' on the direct flows as

[1] Cf. The Greek Ouroboros; the 'Flying Fire Drake' of the Alchemists; Nārāyana surrounded by the Cosmic Serpent Ananta whose coils represent the 'cyclic' eternities of the macrocosm; the constellation of Draco (the dragon) encircling the apparently starless region of the unchanging pole of the ecliptic, which symbolises the unmanifest, eternal pivot of the universe surrounded by the limiting and manifesting circle of the Dragon of Wisdom; the Lion-headed Mithraic Kronos in the coils of the Serpent, and his roar which is the sound of the creation; the Fiery breath of the dragons of western traditions.

vibrations or waves, makes them perceptible as manifest phenomena, for no unrestricted or unmodulated power-flow can ever become an organised integration in itself, nor can it become an object of perception.

The gyration, in giving rise to sequence, also gives rise to time; and, by virtue of the sequential nature of time, the simultaneity of the Unmanifest is spread out as a series of separate phenomena.

The Fiery Whirlwind, the out-breathing of the sevenfold archetypal contents of the coiled dragon, is thus the outward universe born into independent ex-istence. The linear, unmanifest energy of the Cosmic Breath continues to pour into it, but the rotary component of its movement is what sustains forms in consciousness, neither bringing them into being nor dissolving them. The rotation sustains forms by integrating objective content into unitary wholes, and is thus responsible for the integration of all systems of psychic content from atoms to galaxies, from the centring of man's emotions to the circling of his thoughts about his interests. Just as the electrons whirl about the nucleus of the atom, or as planets whirl round the sun, so do the principles of man whirl round the central point which is the human monad[1], and this whirling constitutes our life. As the Gita says, 'the modes of objectivity (gunas) roll round within each other'.[2]

Now, with the fiery outbreath of the Dragon, the cirrus clouds we likened to the Curds of Stanza III are afire with the light of the risen sun.[3] 'And I looked,' says Ezekiel, 'and behold a whirlwind came out of the north, a great cloud, and a fire infolding itself, and a brightness was about it.'[4]

[1] Cf. the *Poemandres* of Hermes, I. 11: 'Then the Formative Mind (at-oned with Reason), he who surrounds the spheres and spins them with his whirl, set turning his formations, and let them turn from a beginning boundless unto an endless end.'

[2] *Gunā guneshu vartante* (*Bhagavad Gītā*, III. 28). The *gunas* are the three components or moments of *prakṛiti*, 'matter' or the content aspect of experience. They are the three objective cosmic elements and they manifest in our experience as the *buddhi* or content half of the Universal Mind (*sattva*), the lower mental level (*rajas*), and the physical (*tamas*).

[3] *Supra*, p. 130.

[4] *The Book of the Prophet Ezekiel*, I. 4.

(2) *They make of him the messenger of their will.* *The Dzyu becomes Fohat: the Swift Son of the Divine Sons, whose sons are the Lipika, runs circular errands. He is the steed and the Thought is the rider. He passes like lightning through the fiery clouds; takes three, five and seven strides through the seven regions above and the seven below. He lifts his voice, and calls the innumerable sparks and joins them together.*

Not until the Mind of the Universe turns outward, and the bipolar bliss of the androgyne is exchanged for the differentiated emotions of outwardness, does the potential dynamism burst out as kinetic energy, the Dragon of Wisdom give its first seven fiery breaths of independent life. Then the moments of eternity stand apart as past, present and future, and the inner seven archetypes shine forth as existent images in the divine imagining, clothed in the living waters of externality. The moments of the inner unity are separated; synthesis and analysis, attraction and repulsion, good and evil, structure and power. Every allurement of sense has its corresponding repulsion hidden in our psyches and every disgust its attraction.

This exchange is what is meant by the Dzyu becoming Fohat. The former represents Power in its calm or latent state within the inturned, self-absorbed Mind, and the latter, the active or kinetic energy of the outwardly creative plastic Power.[1] The change may be conceived after the pattern of the potential energy in a seed, an energy which must be supposed to reside in its structure, remaining latent for years before being transformed by a change of conditions into the manifest energy of growth.

Fohat is described as the Swift Son[2] of the Divine Sons, or Inner Seven archetypal powers, and, as the messenger[3] of their

---

[1] Contrast the Greek *dynamis*, strength, might, power, with *energia*, act, operation, energy.

[2] Compare the 'Swiftly Speeding' (*Ashuhemen*) Vedic and Avestan God *Apām Napāt*, Son of the Waters, who is 'a fire god born from the cloud of lightning' and is said to have 'seized the brightness in the depths of the ocean'.

[3] 'The living intelligence is Thy swift Messenger.' *Sanai.* (Quoted by Margaret Smith in her *The Sūfi: Path of Love.* Luzac).

active, outgoing will, he is the 'parent' of the Lipika or Structure-Images of the cosmic levels.

We must assume H.P.B.'s intention, behind her use of the otherwise unknown term Fohat, was to produce the effect it has done, namely, to set us all wondering what she was talking about. Had she used any one of the dozens of conventional alternatives, most of us would have thought we understood her meaning merely because the word was familiar. But to understand Fohat we should as usual seek first within ourselves till we find that power which brings forth, holds in being, and again withdraws, the multiform contents of our psyches. Only then shall we be able to understand the real nature of that Brahma-power which moulds the universe, and of which the Stanzas say that Fohat is the steed and thought the rider.

We must be on our guard, however, against conceiving Fohat as either a mechanical force or a deific personality. Fohat is not a personal being but a power; nevertheless he is not a mechanical power but a living one, as are, indeed, all the Powers in the Cosmos. Fohat *in principio* springs from the tension relating the first unmanifest Father-Mother duality which is the origin of all power, and in this sense is the self-nature of the Ever-Darkness. As a manifest power, however, he derives from the similar tension between the 'Brother-Sister' duality within Universal Mind. His continual downward movement follows the dialectical pattern whereby each new product of the synthesis of Subject with Object becomes again a subjective thesis that in turn posits an opposition in an objective antithesis. The antithesis of the outflowing urge of the Father-light and its derivatives is always the seemingly desirable receptivity of the Matrix in her various forms.

Fohat passes like lightning through the Fiery Clouds of the cosmic levels, clouds in their lack of organisation, fiery with the energy they already contain, the linear energy of the cosmic expansion. With his first three strides he separates the three times, past, present and future, and he manifests the three modes of consciousness, waking, dreaming and deep sleep. The five strides can then be referred to the five Elements of antiquity which are the sensible modes of objectivity, and the seven strides to the sevenfold structure pattern. It is as though he strides through the Inner Seven, gathering up their abstract formulae and impressing them upon the fluid energies of the Outer Seven. He then starts again from the Outer Seven and manifests their 'writings' as the structure of the sensible worlds.

These three, five and seven strides do not in fact refer to the manifestation of particular things in experience so much as they do to the generalised moments of the manifesting power which make all resulting structures, whether physical or psychic, correspond to certain basic patterns, represented as threeness, fiveness and sevenness because these are symbolically the male creative numbers.

Fohat is said to lift his Voice and call the innumerable Sparks and join them together. Let us conceive a number of specks of dust resting on a surface of calm water. It can easily be seen that the formation of a small whirlpool round each speck will have the effect of separating the whole into so many units, and at the same time of linking together all the specks so that they interact with each other.

Somewhat on this analogy must be conceived the action of Fohat.[1] His circular errands result in the organisation of vortical systems round each point-like centre in the Universal Mind, converting their homogeneous unity into a number of separate entities linked with each other as the parts of a manifold. Thus by the action of Fohat takes place the 'entification' of the primal oneness, the conversion of its pervading unity into a number of separate points of view; points of view which may be regarded as suns, as human individualities, or as atoms. On whatever scale they are taken, the effect of the circular action of Fohat is to cut off or veil their inner unity, and to replace it by an outer connectedness in which each of them acts

---

[1] It is to be hoped that the reader will remember that all these analogies are only analogies. They are not intended to be descriptions.

upon and is acted upon by all the others in an external manner. Thus, on the astronomical scale, arises what we know as the force of gravity which is the outward expression of Fohat, linking together that which he has separated. It is not a peculiar force in itself, but is inherent in the separation; as soon as the unity of content is divided into separate units by being organised round individual centres, it follows inevitably that those units will 'attract' each other, such attractions being merely the outward expression of the inner unity.

We may note, though we shall not elaborate the point, that a similar gravitation exists upon the mental level, and for the same reason. This mental gravitation ensures that no man can live for himself alone; strive as he may, he can no more escape the pull of the invisible threads which link him with his fellows than the earth can escape from being influenced by the other heavenly bodies. This mental gravitation appears on a lower level as the gregarious instinct, and on a higher one, as the essential solidarity of mankind and, indeed, of all beings. 'Compassion,' says *The Voice of the Silence*, 'is no attribute. It is the Law of laws—eternal Harmony, Ālaya's Self.' In other words, compassion is the effect of the underlying Unity which manifests in the world of separation as attraction, fellow-feeling and sympathy.

(3) *He is their guiding spirit and leader. When he commences work he separates the sparks of the lower kingdom that float and thrill with joy in their radiant dwellings and forms therewith the germs of wheels. He places them in the six directions of space and one in the middle—the central wheel.*

We have already seen that the whirling action of Fohat results in the organisation of experience content in vortices around central points or 'sparks'. It is but natural that the power which exteriorises the universe should be described as the guiding spirit and leader of those sparks, for when this movement begins it results first in their being carried out from the primal unity into the manifest outwardness of distinct, separate being. They were moments of a partless whole, and so neither joined nor separated, for they were one. The whirling movement makes those moments into separate sparks and then links those sparks so that they become parts of a manifold, not moments of a unity.

As moments of awareness within Universal Mind they partake of its androgyneity. Both halves of experience, subject and object, male and female, are at first in-turned towards each other, united in mutual contemplation; Self looks upon Self with neither desire nor fear, 'the Male united with the Female, neither male nor female'.[1] The feeling or energy flow between the two halves of one androgyne is bipolar, so that the beings are in the extremely blissful state of complete harmony. They are related by the unity of the Mind in which they are held, by the sameness of the objectivity they contemplate, and by the bliss which pervades the whole space in which they stand and which is the essence of their self to self relationship. Yet, from the point of view of the urge towards manifestation, their condition is static, for it leads to no further development either of forms or of modes of consciousness. The division between self and other is not sufficiently distinct.

The third logos, 'Create', separates the two halves of the androgynous individuals and drives them out from their state of paradisal bliss: 'The Sons dissociate and scatter' (III. 11). This outflowing moment is the anger or wrath of God which drove Adam-Eve out of the biblical paradise of Eden and then set an angel with a flaming sword at its gate to prevent their return. The separated beings are reluctant to leave their state of beatitude and, if their way was not blocked by the Angel, their nostalgic longings would drag them back again and no manifestation would be achieved. Through being shut out, they are forced to seek outside themselves for the bliss they can no longer find within. The subjective pole of the minds looks outwards, but their ideal content, their paradisal field of vision, is, as it were, behind them. What they see and

[1] Hermes.

what they create 'outside' themselves is the projected image of their inner harmony shining in the outer waters.

When the inner pressure drives us to exteriorise our psychic content in any creative activity, such as writing, painting or building, we seem to be lured out rather than pushed out. Always the goddess of illusion seems to stand 'out there' beyond the doors of sense, sometimes as the fascination of women, wealth and fame, and sometimes as the absorbing passion for learning and scholarship—a passion which may seem to be inward turned, for its slaves may care nothing for worldly recognition and nothing for worldly attractions, yet in the end it is out-turned because it is concerned with objectified knowledge, knowledge of and about things, people and ideas; learning, not wisdom.

The biblical myth speaks of the Angel with the flaming sword as if the power that prevents the return of the souls to paradise is something which stands behind them. But we know that what stands behind us in the darkness of our subconscious being becomes apparent when projected onto the outer world. What prevents our return to the paradisal state of divine bliss —to the actuality which, in a much mutilated form, appears as the mythological heaven worlds of popular religion— therefore appears to us as something separate and external. The Angel with the flaming sword, as an image projected into externality, thus becomes the tempting Devil, personified desire; for what shuts us out from the gates of paradise is the tension between the primal poles or gateposts of being, the Ring Pass-Not. And it is this tension, the divine Eros, which is the dynamism of the whole universe, urging us outwards in the fever of desire, *demon est deus inversus*.

Mind is thus led out by the promise of seeing more outside itself than is present to its own inner light. The inner brilliance is transferred to the outer image and the great illusion of the outer worlds stands forth in seeming reality. It is this attractive promise of the outer world, the daughter of the great Mother, which seems to lure the divine child from the mother's lap and carry it off to the adventure of the moving Cycle.

As we have seen in Stanza IV. 3 the waters of the One Mother, impregnated by the Ray of the Father and alive with the Light of consciousness (III. 6), lie as the material substratum of all phenomena and as the possibility of all form. These are the living, energetic waters in which the Sparks clothe themselves, organising the potential objectivity around them into forms that correspond to the patterns of ideal content in them.

On whatever level of experience, all the material objects of experience, great or small, are the organisations of those waters around the empatterning Sparks of Mind. Life is inherent in every particle of matter; for at the centre of every particle is a Spark capable of experiencing, but only of such a degree of experience as is possible to centres on that particular level.

On the lowest level are the simple atomic organisations which are in turn integrated into more complex molecular structures around centres of a higher order, finally rising by similar steps to the levels of plants and animals; each succeeding order incorporating and sometimes transforming the lower organisations out of which it builds its more complex structures. The Spark of a plant, for instance, is capable of acting as the focus of a higher organisation than that of a mineral; the Spark of a 'Sacred Animal' (man) than that of an animal.

Their radiant Dwellings are their ideal content, radiant because manifest in Mind, and charged with the energy of Fohat. They thrill with joy because all being and all consciousness, in its divine aspect, is suffused with the bliss (ānanda) which springs from the union of the two primal aspects of divinity and is itself Fohat, the self-nature of the Ever-Darkness.

In other words, a Dwelling is an organisation of energised experience content around a given centre in consciousness. It is on account of that organisation with its whirling bliss that

the centre or Spark becomes attached to and identifies itself
exclusively with that particular dwelling. Each of the systems
thus has a soul and a body, the former being the point-like
Spark or centre in consciousness, and the latter the content
or empatterned energy which revolves around it and to which
the soul becomes attached by the experience of bliss. Note that
we do not speak of the soul or Spark as its (the dwelling's)
consciousness, but as that point in the universal ocean of
consciousness which identifies itself with that particular
dwelling. Sever the attachment to the particular, and the
consciousness is once more one and universal.

Just as a word originates in the secret recesses of the psyche
and proceeds outwards till it issues in overt speech, so does the
rotary movement issue from within and proceed to well up
within the structure of outwardness. It is a process analagous
to that in which the unstruck strings of an instrument pick
up, each for itself, the appropriate vibrations from the sounded
notes. The entire Universe is in this way bound together in
one Cosmic Dance, electrons answering to stars above, and
both reflected in the human soul;[1] this is the mighty inter-
linkedness of all that is, the *rita* or harmonious order of the
cosmos. Touch an electron and you touch the furthest stars;
study those stars and the book of the Divine Wisdom lies
open before you. In the leaves of the tree are concealed the
secrets of the gods, and not alone in the dark groves of Dodona
does the sacred oak speak of the hidden wisdom to him that
has ears to hear.[2] As an old Greek verse—said to have come
from Egypt—puts it:

> 'Heaven above, Heaven below;
> Stars above, stars below;
> All that is above is also below;
> Understand this and be happy.'

[1] *e.g.*, the discovery by Kekule through a dream of the arrangement of atoms in
the Genzene ring.
[2] Does not the *Bhagavad Gītā* say that the leaves of the *Ashwattha* tree, the tree of the
world, are the Vedic mantras? This truth is not confined to the realms of allegory.

Q

Above us is the infinitely great, below us the infinitely small. Deep calls to Deep, and in the human heart is traced in mystic symbols the pattern of the sublime Cosmic Harmony, the harmony in which the Morning Stars danced together in the luminous dawn of the world, a harmony which lasted till the human egos with their divine freedom descended to distort, but not to shatter, its indestructible and shining golden web.

We may remember here the Vedic teaching that the Strides of Vishnu were filled with honey, as also the words of H.P.B. that Fohat was the prototype of the Orphic Eros. We may also note the rapture caused by speed, the child's love of whirling motion (*e.g.* on a roundabout), the ecstasy of the whirling dervish, and indeed the thrill of dancing in general. Such parallels are by no means forced or trivial, for they give symbolic expression to a whirling creative process in our psyches, and it is fundamentally on this account that they bring with them the sense of bliss. This feeling of the universe as an ecstatic divine dance has been wonderfully caught in the South Indian images of the Dancing Shiva, images which, along with the seated contemplative Buddha and the enigmatic Egyptian Sphinx, are among the greatest artistic expressions of the world process that the heart of man has brought to birth.

The uniting power of Fohat, the divine Eros, joins the Sparks together to form the Germs or prototypes of Wheels. These Wheels are the first swirling organisations in the clouds of Sparks which will gradually settle out into galactic systems. The circumgyratory motion characteristic of the third Logos is imparted to every Spark, and it is through the interaction of the energetic vortices surrounding each Spark that the rotary motion is transmitted to the aggregate. But the forces linking the Sparks are too tenuous to permit of the whole revolving as one gigantic integration; the Clouds therefore split up into numerous revolving systems of a flattened or wheel-like structure, placed throughout the whole volume of Space—the six directions (4 cardinal points, above and below). Indeed it is not until the circumgyration begins that there can be any meaning in direction. The above and below as physical directions lie on the vertical axis of each gyrating Spark, while the cardinal points are, as it were, marked out around the axis in relation to the separated points in space.

The unique 'central' wheel is not a material organisation, but is the archetype of all Wheels—the 'circular' content or Egg of Universal Mind. It is a wheel of self-born light and, though its one centre is in the middle and very navel of all the Six Directions, yet its circumference embraces all of them within its rim, the rim of Light which shines through all the Suns. Sustaining all plurality, the wheel itself is ever One, unstained by all the worlds that swim within its Light. As Krishna says in the Gita: 'the support of beings, yet not rooted in beings, my very Self, the nourisher of all'.[1]

And, since the Light of the Worlds is also the Light which lighteth every man, that stainless central Wheel is to be found within ourselves as well. In the very centre of our being dwells that eternal all-beholding Wheel. There and there alone can we resolve the duality of our nature; there only can we harmonise the many voices that sound within our hearts. It is only to one who can unite himself with his 'Father in heaven', who can poise himself within that inmost unity, that those voices will cease to seem conflicting and will unite in sounding forth the harmony that the Chinese called the Great Tone of Nature, the voice of a river rushing towards the sea, or that of the wind wandering through mighty forests.[2]

In the central Wheel is the resolution of every discord, the answer to every puzzle, the healing for every ill; but only he is able to enter it who has passed from all the wheels of self, he, in the vivid words of Light on the Path, whose eyes have become incapable of tears, whose ears have lost their sensitiveness, whose voice has lost the power to wound and whose feet have been washed in the life-blood of the heart.

This, too, is the door in the heavens (janua coeli) through

[1] Bhagavad Gītā, IX. 5.
[2] See The Voice of the Silence: The Seven Portals, n. 10.

which the creative power—call it by whatever name one pleases—flows out from the Unmanifest into manifestation, mediated as it goes by the archetypal modes.

The circumgyration of the Breath is what produces the varying mixtures of the modes of being out of which all forms are built according to their rank in the manifest hierarchy—inorganic, organic, sentient, etc. This is what distinguishes the archetypal from the physical universe, that the former consists of unmixed principles, while the latter is compounded of a mixture of all the former.

The period of creative outpouring continues until the conscious powers have completed their self-externalisation, after which the outer universe continues to exist by virtue of the impetus given to it. The Ring Pass-Not shuts it out into independency, just as the new-born child is shut off from the womb of gestation. The inner aspect of Mind, having emptied itself of its creative potential, remains like the workshop of God from which the workers have for a period gone forth.

The unmanifest principles on whose presence the whole manifestation depends never for a moment cease to uphold the being of the universe, but no further energy is pumped in, and the universe continues to exist as a closed system, on any level of which the total energy can be accounted for.

In the Six Directions, then, revolve the gleaming Wheels throughout the Day, and, as they turn they sing the Song of Life, the song that is the Music of the Spheres. 'Listen to the song of life' says the *Light on the Path*; adding that from it may be learnt the lesson of the harmony of life. That song in its completeness is heard in the heaven of the heart. It is there that we must go if we seek the Divine Wisdom, for it is there, in the midst of all, that Fohat placed the central synthesising Wheel.

It is of this Song of Life that Plato writes in the Republic. Speaking of the eight revolving concentric whorls (the Wheels of our stanzas) he says that the central spindle of the whole turns on the knees of Necessity, a phrase which reminds us of the Son of Necessity mentioned in Stanza I. 6. 'And on the upper surface of each circle is a Siren, who goes round with them, hymning a single sound and note. The eight together form one harmony'.[1] 'Even here', says a speaker in a symposium of Plutarch's, 'a dim murmur of that music reaches us, rousing the inner memory'. As for the Sirens, they are, as Proclus well said, 'a kind of Souls living the life of the Spirit', in other words, conscious but not individualised Powers; Powers that, in Homer's words, 'know all things that shall be upon the fruitful earth'.

(4) *Fohat traces spiral lines to unite the six to the seventh—the Crown; an Army of the Sons of Light stands at each angle; the Lipika—in the middle wheel. They say 'This is good'. The first Divine World is ready, the first (is now) the second. Then the 'Divine Arūpa' reflects itself in Chhāyā Loka, the first garment of the Anupādaka.*

The preceding verse spoke of the Germs of Wheels or first organisations of the clouds of Sparks in dimensioned space; but no differentiated qualities have been impressed in their energetic dwellings. Those were the 'Sparks of the Lower Kingdom', but above them stand the Sparks of the higher levels, Armies of the Sons of Light, who will plunge down into the shadowy clouds and build up structures which reflect their respective qualities.

These Sons of Light are represented as standing at the 'angles', the angles or points of the six-pointed star which symbolises the 'Divine Arūpa' or archetypal pattern of the universe. The six angles are thus the six metaphysical 'directions' or psychic properties corresponding to the six physical directions of the sensible universe.

In the centre, that metaphysical, dimensionless and placeless centre of the circle of being, the centre of Divine Mind and the centre of every Spark, is the triune subject of the universe

---

[1] *Republic*, 617 b. (Jowett). The references which follow are taken from Jane Harrison's *Prolegomena to the Study of Greek Religion*.

surrounded by the Lipika, the first objectifications of the entirely unmanifest cosmic patterns of the Inner Seven.

The circumgyratory outflow of the third Logos now pours through the centre of Divine Mind, the central seventh wheel or Crown,[1] carrying the imprint of the empatterning Lipika out to the six directions. The triune power goes out in an expanding spiral, setting the whole content of space in motion and, entering the heart of every individualised Spark, it forces them out from their androgynous in-turned bliss by exerting an expansive pressure from within.

We have already referred to the fact that the Sparks thrill with the bliss of the vortical movement. It is this thrill of approval as the creative process commences that is expressed by the exclamation 'This is good' which comes as they give themselves to the dance. 'And God saw everything that he had made, and, behold it was good'.[2] Looking at the actual condition of the world, many have thought these words of the Lord God's quite unwarrantably optimistic, and so they would be if they bore the meaning they have been given by theology and expressed the self-satisfaction of any extra-cosmic creative *tyrannos*. But it is not so. Consciousness itself creates the universe and, having created it, itself enters into and ensouls it. It is not the self-gratulation of a potter who has made a fine pot—at least in his own eyes—but the thrill of consciousness itself as it sets out on a new adventure which will lead it into strange and unknown lands; lands in which even the stars will be different and only the Sun and Moon remain the same to remind it of its permanent identity. It is by its own will that consciousness sets out on the adventure of descent and not as the result of any external fiat. It is therefore quite entitled, irrespective of the dangers and discomforts it may subsequently encounter, to pronounce the adventure 'good'.

The Divine Worlds are the objective or content aspects of the universe corresponding to the Logoi or creative outpourings.

---

[1] Kether, the highest of the ten Sephiroth of the Kabbala, is also called the Crown.
[2] Genesis, I. 31.

The first Logos flashed into the Mother-Deep and demarcated the extent of the creation, the 'Egg' (III. 3). This is the first Divine World. The second Logos described in Stanza IV fills the Egg with the hosts and multitudes of Sparks and Energies —the second Divine World. The third Logos, however, does not produce a third Divine World; it produces instead a world of shadows (*Chhāyā Loka*) in which the bright spiritual shining of the Sparks is masked by concretions of the cooling energy, the Breath of the Mother, which surrounds them.

The third outpouring itself produces the 'reflection' of the 'Divine *Arūpa*', for the very separation of the Sparks brought about by its churning motion produces the first form (*rūpa*) on the pattern of the point-like archetype. The fiery clouds of this stanza become the fiery dust of the next, and the now separated orphans of existence, the *Anupapādaka*, are clothed in their first garment of 'material' form.

The great outburst of energy rushes down, as it were, to the very bottom of the lowest level of outwardness and builds the first garment of the universe in the Element of Earth. Above, behind, or within, stand the ranks of higher powers, ready to call out their images from the now manifest matrix of impressionable 'matter'.

No longer do the Sparks stand in their own independent natures but must bow their heads to the necessities of the cosmic correlation or law. In place of their former state of constant omnipresent ideal shining, they must now submit to being born again and again of Time and Space, appearing and disappearing in accordance with the Cosmic Law, for such is the nature of the adventure on which they have embarked. Nevertheless their real nature is not touched. In all the shadows of time and space their inmost nature remains for ever what it always was: 'constant, all-pervasive, steadfast, immovable and eternal'.

The 'Divine *Arūpa*' is said to be 'reflected' because the manifested forms are but representations of the divine reality. Like shadows, too, there is a certain inversion in the image, for what is inner and eternal manifests as outer and ephemeral. However far we extend the range of our out-turned faculties of sense, whether into the infinitely great dimensions of astronomical space or into the infinitely small dimensions of atomic structure, they can never give us direct knowledge of the inner reality, never can we perceive the light of consciousness inwardly shining behind its dark mask of power.

The whole universe of objectified patterns is the dark form of God, the shadow image of the immaterial Divinity. It seems to proclaim its independence from the spiritual powers which brought it forth, for we who look outward through the doors of sense see only the outer surfaces of the power structures, surfaces which reflect the light by which we see, yet in themselves are invisible fields of energy, energy which swirls around, separates, unites and interrelates the points in consciousness blissfully shining within the entirely unmanifest field of the Matrix.

In itself this dark mask of God is not 'evil', for even the ruthless violence of the animal world is an inherent part of the divine striving towards total self-expression. But when we take the image for the reality and worship the outer glitter of reflected light—the glittering images of pleasure, wealth, fame and power—then, indeed, the mask becomes the mirror of our evil passions and the divine forms seem to glare back at us in malignant opposition to our aims. For this and this alone is evil, that we, the Sons of God, assert our independence from the cosmic harmony.

The whole unfolding of the divine self-nature has not been brought about that we might pleasure ourselves with trivial delights. Our civilisations, our cultures, and our sciences, stand upon mountains of human skulls, the countless generations of men who lived, suffered and died that we might reap the harvest of their experience. If we are not to betray their trust in the meaningful significance of life, then we must try to see phenomena through the inner eye of understanding, for thus only can we pass beyond the shadowy mask of appearances to the divine light that shines both in our hearts and in the hearts of all.

Behind the shadows, coming and going, dying and being born in the magic play of outer worlds, behind them or within them stand the Players, the Realities of the Divine Archetypes, 'without cessation, without origination, without an end, yet not in endless time; without self-identity, yet not lost in differentiation, without movement, whether of coming or going'.[1]

(5) *Fohat takes five strides and builds a winged wheel at each corner of the square for the four holy ones . . . and their armies.*

The 'square' of this verse refers us to the Formless Square of Stanza IV. 5 which is the same 'square' of powers that gives rise to the fourfold Web of the universe (III. 10 and 11) in which 'the Sons dissociate and scatter', a dissociation or separating of individuals which, as we have seen, is the effect of the third out-pouring. It is to be noted that 'Formless' in this context does not mean totally unmanifest, but non-physical. This follows the usage in Buddhist philosophy where *Arūpa*, formless, refers to subtle states of manifest being.

The 'Armies' also have to be understood in connection with previous references. We can distinguish between the 'Army of the Voice, the Divine Mother' (IV. 4), and the Army of the Sons of Light' (V. 5). Both these 'Armies' or ordered multitudes derive their multiplicity from the effect of the second Logos, the 'Numbers' (IV. 5); but whereas the former 'Army' is made up of the energies of manifestation, Sons of the Mother, the latter is made up of the spark-like centres of awareness, Sons of the Father-Light, the Selves of the integrations on any scale.

In the preceding verse the 'Sons of Light' were assembled at the 'angles', while here the 'winged wheels' are placed at the 'corners of the square'. The 'angles' refer us to the sixfold division of the circle by the 'One Ray' (see under IV. 3) which

---

[1] The opening verse of Nāgārjuna's *Mādhyamika Kārika*.

gives rise to the six-pointed star. This figure represents the 'Divine Arūpa', the archetypal or nöetic universe; the seven archetypal modes being distributed, as it were, one to each of the six 'angles' and an integrating or central seventh. The 'Square' then represents the qualities of the Space into which the patterns are to be projected.

When this figure is projected into the solid, the interlaced triangles become two mutually interpenetrating tetrahedrons (solids with four triangular faces and four vertices) whose eight vertices (4+4=8) correspond with the eight vertices of the cube (a solid with eight vertices and six square faces) which has been developed from the Square. The twelve edges of the tetrahedrons (6+6=12) also correspond with the twelve diagonals (6×2=12) on the six faces of the cube.

Thus, as the symbols show us, when the subtle qualities of the inner universe (the six-pointed star in the square) are projected into the solidity of spatial dimension (the tetrahedrons in the cube) the Three and the Four, Spirit and Matter, find their reconciliation.

The Armies of Sparks, Sons of Light, empatterning powers of the Archetypes, stand, then, at the 'angles', and the Armies of Energies, Sons of the Mother, are arrayed at the corners of the square. When the outrush of the third Logos thrusts them into externality, the 'angles' and the 'corners' coincide and the cosmic battle begins. The bright Fighters plunge into the dark Energies which conquer and imprison them, yet, in conquering, they are themselves transformed. Rank by rank the hosts and multitudes of Angelic armies descend, trampling upon the bodies of the living slain and fighting until they in

their turn are conquered and shut within prisons whose bricks
are the bodies of fallen comrades. Thus life is built on life,
form devours form, until the long series of transformations
produces a fit vehicle for the bright power of Understanding,
and Man looks forth upon the world.

The massed armies also represent the tremendous build-up
of pressure, the out-thrusting pressure of the Divine Breath,
which will now explode into outwardness, 'the bursting forth
of the ardent desire in Nature'.[1]

The single Subject that looked out and breathed out in one
metaphysical direction now breathes out in all physical
directions and looks out from a multiplicity of subjective
points, each viewing the same objective existence from
spatially different positions, and all still held together as a
universe by the unity of their source. The unmanifest creative
Breath manifests, therefore, in a multitude of experiencing
spheres—spheres that are the three dimensional expressions of
the dimensionless points. Just as the circle represented the
delimited area of Universal Mind, so the sphere represents the
spatial restriction of each separated point, its 'skin' or, in more
abstract terms, the co-ordinates of its spatial identity.

The Four Holy Ones similarly refer to the four controlling
moments listed as the Sacred Four of Stanza IV. 5, the Powers
or causal determinants which rule the energies of manifestation.

We must also remember that the total energy of the manifestation springs from the primal division in the Darkness
into the Father and Mother poles. Father-Mother then spin
a 'Web' between Spirit and Matter (III. 10). These four
moments of the Web are the same as the four causal determinants of Stanza IV. 5 and are therefore the controllers of the
energies of which the Web of the universe is woven.

When we said that a point of the divine awareness exists
in the heart of every atom, it was not intended to convey
that individual atoms are vehicles of high-grade psychic
process. A conscious and formatory power acts in every

[1] William Law.

atom, but it is convenient to regard this as a trans-individual power or hierarchy of powers governing all the 'atoms' on every level or sub-level. These formative powers are the Four Holy Ones and their Armies of derivative powers, one for each mode. They are 'holy' because they are primary modalities of the creative consciousness, living Gods, who dominate the modes of manifestation in much the same way that the powers or 'gods' of sense perception dominate the modes in which we perceive phenomena. They are in some sense connected with the five Dhyāni Buddhas of Mahāyāna Buddhism and have also been termed the 'Consciousness of the levels'.

Their armies are, as we have seen, the hosts of conscious but not of self-conscious powers which empattern the vortices and whose awareness looks out, like the eyes of Ezekiel's dreadful rings, from whatever material form they invest.[1] When any man's inner vision is opened to the perception of these universal powers he is indeed struck with awe and dread, the dread of the personal self for the universally diffused impersonality in which he fears to lose his hard-won manhood.

Fohat's first 'stride' is the leap with which the creative energy bursts into externality, the circumgyratory outburst of the third Logos. It is as if Space itself is externalised, for, until Mind looks outwards, spatial dimension is only potential. We can have a concept of infinite space, but we cannot demonstrate it. As soon as phenomena manifest in space, that space is limited.

This out-turning of Mind is equivalent to the externalisation and separation of the Sparks of awareness around which the vortices of energy are then organised.

The next four 'strides' externalise the fundamental modalities of existence which characterise the universe of experience, modalities which correspond both to the four lower levels (the Four into which the Three have fallen) and to the remain-

[1] See Ezekiel I for a visionary description of these Four Holy Ones and their wheels of conscious powers which emerged from the fiery whirlwind.

ing four elements, Air, Fire, Water and Earth. If, however, intellectual symbols are preferred, these modalities can be classified approximately as spatial limitation or individuality, differentiation of qualities, relatedness, and change or motion. Continuity of being or duration belongs to the fifth Element or level, Universal Mind, the 'Space' in which all other modes exist.

We may also note that the 'corners' and 'angles' represent the mysterious points of interaction between the levels where the relatively unmanifest formative powers of higher levels ingress into their manifest forms. On the human level the strange moment between our waking and our sleeping is an example of a border-line condition between two states of being where things outside our normal range of consciousness can ingress or become manifest to us. It is through such a metaphysical 'corner' in the psychic square of our being that the soul enters and leaves its physical vehicle.

This aspect of the square as mediator between the inner points of awareness and the outer qualities of form has given rise to the symbol of the four-faced *Brahmā*, the demiurge, who discovers by in-turned meditation what is to be created outwardly. He 'looks' both inwards and outwards, bridging the gap between inner patterns and outer forms.

Each level is a whirling integration of energy or Wheel, 'winged' because it is flying in Space, the supporter of the lesser integrations which swim within it but not itself supported by anything external to it.

(6) *The Lipika circumscribe the triangle, the first one, the cube, the second one, and the pentacle within the egg. It is the ring called 'Pass Not', for those who descend and ascend (as also for those) who, during the Kalpa, are progressing towards the great day 'Be with us'. ... Thus were formed the Arūpa and the Rūpa; from one light seven lights; from each of the seven, seven times seven lights. The Wheels watch the Ring. ...*

H.P.B. has pointed out that the numerals and figures both

of this verse and of Stanza IV. 3 can be construed to represent 3.1416, the approximate value of π, the ratio between the diameter and circumference of a circle.[1] This has its significance when the universe is regarded as the circle of being, while the fascination which such calculations have for certain types of people shows that they are not merely problems of applied mathematics, but are highly significant symbols of archetypal ratios in the human psyche. Such problems as the value of π, the squaring of the circle, or the trisection of any angle, have no perfect solution in this world. So long as we are content with working approximations, we can project the theoretical exactitudes of Euclidean Geometry on to our environment and find fascinating correspondences between the patterns of thought and the patterns of matter. Provided we are not too fastidious with our measurements, the whole world can seem to glow with a magical perfection of harmonious interrelations. Sun, moon and stars mark with wonderful precision the intricate cycles of time whose details, some say, were embodied by the 'ancients' in the canon of measurement of temples, pyramids, and statuary. The medicinal values of plants, the patterns of society, the molecular structures of the elements of chemistry, the very body of man, the most disparate elements of experience, all blend their complex affinities into a cosmos, a unified harmony of being. But, when we check these perceptions of exactitude against their material counterparts within the finest possible limits of accuracy, we find everywhere our perfect scheme is marred by irregularities whose approximate quantities are calculable but irrational, with an irrationality that seems to be an inherent part of the material order. Such are the values of π, Planck's constant and

[1] The Triangle = 3. The first one = 1. The Cube (the development of the square) = 4. The second one = 1. The Pentacle = 5 or 6.

Some will perhaps think that it is incorrect to describe the six-pointed star as a pentacle, a term they would reserve for the five-pointed variety. Both the Oxford and Chambers dictionaries, however, are against them and so is H.P.B.'s *Theosophical Glossary* which defines pentacle as 'any geometrical figure, especially that, known as the double equilateral triangle, the six-pointed star . . . called also Solomon's Seal.'

the square root of minus one $\sqrt{-1}$. The order is still there, but nothing is exact; with the result that many people feel unable to reconcile the two views. They feel that if the first is true it should fit external facts exactly, and, if it does not, then its values are imaginary. And so they are; they are the values of the Divine Imagining. Their reconciliation is not to be found in a mere external agreement of mental patterns with material details. The universe is not, and rightly is not, entirely rational either in its origins or its material limits. There is an irrational, or more properly trans-rational, element which finds its resolution in the ultimate unification of Being and Non-Being in the unmanifest Darkness.

This irrationality, the signature of a living process, never permits the Divine imagining to lock itself into a logically perfect union with its material counterpart. The Spirit both is and is not identified with the forms in which it manifests itself. If it was entirely identified, the universe would be a closed system with neither the need nor the means either of evolving or of being transcended. If the Spirit was not identified, and if the Upper was not veiled by the 'shoreless Sea of Fire' (III. 7), the illusory nature of phenomena, and the contrast between the absolute values of divinity and the relative values of the world, would be so apparent that no 'Spark of the Parent Flame' could be induced to accept the substitute for the Real and so continue its separate existence.

The power of life which relates our central consciousness to our circumferential environment never quite fits; and in the endless and non-repetitive series of numbers which is π one can see, not only the guarantee of the continuance of life in the endless succession of changing forms, but also the manifest promise of the ultimate freedom of the Spirit from their enclosing limitations.

The writings (*Lipika*) whose patterns are impressed on the outer levels derive, as we have seen, from ideal patterns held in the inner (*Arūpa*) universe. They are, as it were, the perma-nent structures of the divine 'consciring' which contain and modify the changing flux of power. The vowel powers of the 'Oeaohoo' flow through and are directed by the consonantal structures of the logos, the divine reason.[1] It is in this sense that they circumscribe or delimit the geometrical figures symbolising the progressive stages of manifestation, and are consequently the delimiting outlines of all forms and all images of sense. We are reminded of William Blake's insistence on the thin, wiry outline which he opposed to Joshua Reynolds' blend of light and shade (chiaroscura) as a representation of nature. In the Upanishads the Universal Mind (*Mahat Ātman*) is called 'Light and Shade' (*Chhāyātapau*) and it is understandable that the diffuse 'all over at once' nature of its experience-content can only achieve the discreteness of manifest forms through a process of delimitation and definition.

It is this delimitation of experience-content which is referred to as the Ring 'Pass-Not'. Just as every individual form on every level of manifestation has its 'outline', so has every sphere of experience its limiting 'Ring' beyond which any particular grade of power cannot pass. Our unaided sight for instance can neither pass the limits of the horizon, nor the limits of the finite but unbounded space of modern relativity theory. In other words, our physical powers are restricted to the confines of the physical universe; our after-death integration is restricted to the confines of that more subtle world; even our most abstract thought is confined by the symbols of its expression.

There is also a sense in which the final Ring of the universe is the consciousness of the Father-Light, the all containing Ring of Being. 'Space is boundless by re-entrant form, not by great extension. That which is, is a shell floating in the infinitude of that which is not. We say with Hamlet, "I could be bounded in a nutshell and count myself a king of infinite space".'[2]

There is a 'curvature of space' which limits our desires; a

---

[1] Compare the manner in which the Semitic languages change the meaning of a fixed group of consonants by modifying the included vowels.
[2] *The Nature of the Physical World*, Eddington, p. 81.

curvature, rather, which ensures that they return upon our heads after many days. If we cast bread upon the waters it will return to us some day and so, alas, will those poison fruits which we are so much more ready to project. Our thoughts, too, 'these thoughts that wander through eternity', compelled by the Ring Pass-Not of their level, must return to us, their thinkers. 'If thou wouldst not be slain by them, then must thou harmless make thy own creations, the children of thy thoughts, unseen, that swarm round humankind, the progeny and heirs to man and his terrestrial spoils.'[1]

These considerations show us the connection between the Ring (or Rings) Pass-Not and the law of Karma which brings it about that all our acts, our desires, and our thoughts, come back to us in the end. Just as, if a man walks straight on in this world he will inevitably return to his starting point, so do our acts and thoughts, compelled by the Ring Pass-Not, return to us with an equal inevitability.

On all levels there is a Ring, imposing limit and finitude on its experience. Those Rings, however, exist only on and for their own levels. They are, so to speak, open on top, so that only on the level itself is experience bounded: there is no obstacle to ascent and descent from one level to another.

It is otherwise, however, with the ultimate Ring, the Ring on the level of the Father, the Logos itself, which acts as an impassable boundary between the manifested universe and the Darkness of the One Reality. Beyond that Limit none can pass. It is the 'shoreless Sea of Fire' of Stanza III. 7. The ultimate Ring of the cosmos cannot be transcended by any differentiated power so long as the Cosmic Day lasts. The creative powers have gone out into the manifestation where, passing between life and death, between growth and decay, between coming into being and passing out of being, they descend to the lowest level of the universe and ascend again in constant alternation; but they never return to their ultimate source until the great day 'Be with us', the day of the final withdrawal of

[1] *The Voice of the Silence*: The Seven Portals.

R

the whole manifest universe into the non-existence of the Ever-Darkness.

Those who are 'progressing' are the souls of men, the *Jīvas*, who also ascend and descend in constant cyclic movement from life to life. Not even the greatest of liberated souls, however, can pass beyond the Light of the Father to the Darkness until that final Day, because to do so would involve the transcendence of the Father-Mother dualism, a dualism which is kept in being by the Breath of That which is the Darkness and cannot be transcended by any individual however strong.

Thus were formed the subtle inner worlds and their concrete forms, the *Arūpa* and the *Rūpa*. From one Light, the Light which to us is Darkness, came the seven inner Lights, and from each of those seven came a vast number of outer ones. The phrase seven times seven, like the biblical seventy times seven, signifies an indefinite number on a septenary base. Each of the Inner Seven is reflected in *each* of the outer Seven and then again in each of those sub-levels throughout the gamut of seven scales. Each 'Son-Sun' or individual Spark from stars to electrons, moreover, is a centre of just such a septenary system of 'Lights' which reflect or are lit from the Inner Seven as, indeed, are the seven principles which form each human being.

The verse and also the stanza concludes with the statement that the Wheels watch the Ring. The Wheels are spheres of experience, and all experience is centred in the Father-Light, the Ring which is the pure and unstained Root of all consciousness, the famous Circle with its centre everywhere and circumference nowhere. It is in this sense that the Ring is the centre as well as the outward limit of all experience in any sphere whatever. Never can anything that is manifest pass beyond the fiery bounds of its all-encompassing circle, a circle which is itself the transcendent basis and the utmost bound of all cosmic experience.

It is a characteristic of experience that it forever strives to pass beyond itself, and indeed it is this characteristic that sends the waves of evolution pulsing up and down the ladder of the cosmos. Strive as it will, its surges are reflected back from the Ring as from some mighty sea-wall against which they hurl themselves in vain. The Wheels watch the Ring: their consciousness strives, now to the utmost edge of outwardness, the fringe and utmost shore of all the worlds, now to the very centre of its being, but in both cases the result is the same. Circumference or centre of the magic circle, both are alike and confront with an invisible barrier, an implacable 'thus far and no further', the Light which seeks to pass beyond.

The Fiery Whirlwind, the 'Messenger' of the divine Will, was sent out on its errand of creative activity, its adventure of ideas. The universe was born into independent being; integrated into the circle of existence by the circumgyration of the Breath; defined and limited by the Writings of the divine reason. It evolved its multiple forms of living being; developed its central theme of self-consciousness in the person of Man; and finally, like all things that are born, returns to the womb that gave it birth. The Messenger completes his circular journey, the great cycle of creation, and returns, loaded with his burden of experience. Ahead of him, ahead of the returning Whirlwind, the souls of men who have heeded the voices of the inner teachers reach the innermost limits of the manifest universe. Beyond that limit nothing can pass until 'Heaven and Earth shall pass away'.

STANZA SIX

Being the sixth of seven Stanzas from
The Book of Dzyan

1. *By the power of the Mother of Mercy and Knowledge, Kwan-Yin, 'the Triple' of Kwan-Shai-Yin, residing in Kwan-Yin-Tien, Fohat, the breath of their progeny, the Son of the Suns, having called forth from the lower abyss the illusive form of Sien-Tchan and the seven elements.*

2. *The Swift and Radiant One produces the seven Laya Centres against which none will prevail to the Great Day 'Be With Us'; and seats the Universe on these Eternal Foundations, surrounding Sien-Tchan with the Elementary Germs.*

3. *Of the Seven—first one manifested, six concealed; two manifested, five concealed; three manifested, four concealed; four produced, three hidden, four and one tsan revealed, two and one half concealed; six to be manifested, one laid aside. Lastly, seven small wheels revolving; one giving birth to the other.*

4. *He builds them in the likeness of older wheels, placing them on the Imperishable Centres.*

   How does Fohat build them? He collects the fiery dust. He makes balls of fire, runs through them and round them, infusing life thereinto, then sets them in motion; some one way, some the other way. They are cold, he makes them hot. They are dry, he makes them moist. They shine, he fans and cools them. Thus acts Fohat from one twilight to the other, during Seven Eternities.

5. *At the fourth, the sons are told to create their images. One third refuses—two (thirds) obey.*

   The curse is pronounced; they will be born on the fourth, suffer and cause suffering. This is the first war.

6. *The older wheels rotated downward and upward ... The Mother's spawn filled the whole. There were battles fought between the Creators and the Destroyers, and battles fought for Space; the seed appearing and reappearing continuously.*

7. *Make thy calculations, O Lanoo, if thou wouldst learn the correct age of thy small wheel. Its fourth spoke is our mother. Reach the fourth 'fruit' of the fourth path of knowledge that leads to Nirvāna and thou shalt comprehend, for thou shalt see. . . .*

ESTABLISHMENT

The last stanza dealt with the beginning of the movement by which the inner patterns are established in outwardness. This stanza takes the process further and deals with the embodiment of those spheres of experience which are the manifest and material universes enformed upon the four lower cosmic levels. Our 'world' is one such sphere of experience whose limits extend throughout the universe of physical sense experience. The sphere of after death (and before birth) experience is also a world and a material world, but the experience is of a modified sort and the 'matter' is more subtle.

It is necessary to repeat that the *experience* we term 'matter' has very little connection with scientific theories of the structure of matter. However verifiable those theories may be, they rely finally on sense experience for their confirmation, notwithstanding that scientists exclude, so far as is possible, all psychic factors from their observations.

The present enquiry is concerned with the manner in which the objects or phenomena of sense experience arise out of an undifferentiated source of consciousness. Solidity is thus not the signature of a 'Thing', but the end result of the progressive identification of the subjective pole of being with the objective. Our awareness of solidity arises from our subjective self-identification with the physical body and its sensory apparatus, so that our finger significantly differs from the stone it touches only in its capacity to act as a vehicle for a higher grade of psychic process. Part of the experience of the finger becomes perceptible to us, whereas ordinarily the experience of the stone does not.

When, therefore, we speak of the subtle material of other manifest levels, we are intending to suggest the presence in the universe neither of regions of rarefied gas in which float the souls of the departed, nor of those weirdly environed 'astral' worlds of spiritualistic reverie, but of levels in consciousness in which the subject-object identification is less marked than it is here. There are still barriers of impenetrability which appear as 'solid', though that solidity is not the same as ours.

It is in this sense that we say there are no sharp divisions in the cosmos between Spirit and Matter, but a series of gradual steps, a rainbow bridge, whose conventional distinctions are clearly perceptible, though they blend under analysis into a continuum of imperceptible differences. This bridge lies between our present individualised state and the unitary consciousness of Divine Mind.

Without knowledge of these intermediate subtle worlds we have difficulty in relating the facts of our sense life to our less tangible 'spiritual' values. This tends to a lessening of our inner certainty and to an overvaluation of materialistic theories extrapolated from the factual findings of the material sciences.

This stanza, then, deals with the manifest levels of being, culminating in our 'material' universe. The terms used in the commentary are often the same as those used in describing transcendent levels (Father, Mother, Son, etc.), but these now have to be understood as the moments within Divine Mind which derive from those transcendent principles. The purpose in retaining the same terminology is to retain at the same time the sense of an interrelated structure sprung from one source.

Up to this stanza everything has been considered from the viewpoint of the descending hierarchies. Now, as the creative powers begin to clothe themselves in the outwardness of the universe of form, the viewpoint shifts, and there are references to the residual impressions in the Matrix derived from previous manifestations. The meeting of the individualised modalities of consciousness with their corresponding forms that rise towards them from the depths of the Matrix is the meeting of the ever new with the ever old. The substance of forms is always old; they are always built up from the remains of previous forms and are variations or repetitions of things that have been before. Newness lies in the experience of living being. To every living being that opens its eyes on this ancient world the experience is that of an entirely new adventure.

In this stanza also comes the first mention of man's birth, and at the end comes the mention of that knowledge which finally frees him from the wheel of birth and death. Looking downwards on the road to birth, man sees the multiplicity of forms and of individuals; then, in his earthly vehicle, he must look upwards with the power of his awakened intellect and strive to hear the voice and see the splendour of the One.

(I) *By the power of the Mother of Mercy and Knowledge, Kwan-Yin, the 'Triple' of Kwan-Shai-Yin, residing in Kwan-Yin-Tien, Fohat, the breath of their progeny, the Son of the Sons, having called forth from the lower abyss the illusive form of Sien-Tchan and the seven elements.*

In this first verse there is a certain confusion of terms which makes it clear that the subject is not being handled from an exoteric Buddhist viewpoint; the ordinary meanings of the words and their standard associations will therefore not suffice to reveal the intended meaning. Indeed, H.P.B. states that she has resorted to Chinese Buddhist terms because she found none suitable in Sanskrit to express the ideas contained in the original stanza. It seems, however, that she has used even the

Chinese terms in an unusual sense, and regards *Kwan-Shai-Yin* as the male and *Kwan-Yin* as the female aspects of an androgynous principle, whereas these two terms are more usually regarded simply as variant translations of the Sanskrit *Avalokiteshvara*[1] (or *Avalokita-īsvara*).

The mention of the 'Triple' of *Kwan-Shai-Yin* implies that we are not dealing with the accepted division of Universal Mind (*Mahat*) into the soli-lunar, Father-Mother, Brother-Sister duality represented in classical Hinduism as *Mahat-Buddhi,* or in Buddhism as *Prajnā-Upāya* (the Knowledge and Mercy, *Karūṇā*, of this verse), but with a triplicity of which two elements may be considered to be the usual pair, and the third element the relating power which is Fohat. In Stanza V, and again here, Fohat is described as the son of the Inner Seven; he is the product of their 'holy circumgyrating breaths', but he is also their 'breath' in the sense that it is he who gives them their life, for he is life itself. As we have previously seen (III. 12), Fohat is the unifying and relating power between the transcendent Father and Mother of the Cosmos, and represents the self-nature of the One Darkness. Here too he appears as the productive life power flowing between the two halves of the androgyne.

Here we may quote Thomas Vaughan: 'God the Father is the Metaphysical, Supercelestial Sun; the second Person is the Light, and the third is Fiery Love, or a Divine Heat proceeding from both.' And again: 'The subject of this Art . . . is no mineral, no vegetable, no animal, but a system—as it were—of all three. In plain terms, it is the seed of the greater animal, the seed of heaven and earth, our most secret, miraculous hermaphrodite'.[2]

It is this triadic division in Universal Mind that makes us what the modern teacher G. I. Gurdjieff called three-centred beings: a phrase that finds its parallel in the Hindu *Jnāna,*

---

[1] *S.D.,* I. 139. II, 195 and *Theosophical Glossary.* See also discussion of this term under Stanza IV and note in text of Stanza III. 7.
[2] *Anthroposophia Theomagica.* (A. E. Waite.)

Bhakti and *Karma*, the three modes of thought, feeling and activity. Another and important relation of this triad is to the three *gunas* of *Prakriti, sattva, rajas* and *tamas; sattva* being the moment of knowledge and harmony derived from the Father, *tamas* its own passive, absorptive, or inert nature as content-potentialities, and *rajas* the moment of creative life derived from the one Power.

Fohat is the active power, and he is said to work by the power he draws from the feminised androgyne, *Kwan-Yin,* not merely because power (in Hinduism) is thought of as feminine (*Shakti*), but because the power to enform has to be drawn from the Maternal aspect of the Logos which has within it the potentiality of all forms and is therefore able to lend to Fohat the power by which the ideal inner structures may be clothed in 'matter'.

The heaven of Kwan-Yin, the 'melodious Heaven', as H.P.B. translates it, is the 'Bright Space' of Universal Mind (III. 7) in which is sounded forth the ideal Melody or Song of Life that is to be the manifested cosmos.[1] The reason for its being mentioned here is to contrast this higher Space of established harmony with the dark inchoate Space of the Lower Abyss, rather as one might contrast the day sky with the night sky, for out of the qualities of these two spaces will the phenomenal universe be built.

Sien-Tchan is the noumenal or higher universe, the illusive form or shadow of which was called (V. 4) the first garment or 'material' covering of the formless divinity.[2]

The lower abyss from which the form of Sien-Tchan is evoked is the unmanifest root of all forms, the 'Waters' of the creation. It is that aspect of the Matrix to which we have previously referred as standing at the bottom of the whole

[1] For the connection between Kwan-Yin and sound see Stanza IV. 4.

[2] The terminology of the whole verse is confused and ambiguous, but the meaning is clear enough. If, however, our reading of the word 'Sien Tchan' is at variance with the Chinese language, the authors offer their apologies. In *S.D.*, V, p. 379, n.1. (*An unpublished Discourse of the Buddha*) Sien Tchan seems to refer to the noumenal universe of Brahma, while *Nam Kha* refers to the phenomenal universe of illusory appearances. The brackets in the note are misplaced.

system of levels. Out of this Fohat is now said to call forth the manifest reflection, shadow or garment of the unmanifest pattern of the universe, the phenomenal forms of the higher or noumenal realities. These forms are projected like the bright images that seem to spring into independent being in the darkness before the closed eyes of a meditating seer, thrust out by the Fohatic power from within.

There are, as it were, two abysses, one 'above' and one 'below' the phenomenal universe, abysses which can be likened to the darkness enshrouding the state before and the state after our transient lives here. They are the two dark and unmanifest extremes from which the two aspects of the manifestation are produced.

From the unmanifest darkness of the upper abyss comes the ideal structure pattern of the universe—the pattern described in the previous stanzas which comes to manifestation in the Universal Mind or Melodious Heaven. From the unmanifest darkness of the lower abyss comes the externality with which those patterns are made manifest.

The lower abyss is the root of all objectivity, yet the Matrix whose Waters fill that abyss and clothe all forms is never in herself manifest. That abyss is like the dark invisible background of the night sky against which appear the shining stars that are worlds, spheres of experience, whether galactic, human or atomic. The slow tides of the Mother's life underlie all movement, while Fohat superimposes his more rapid and erratic rhythms. Without this darkly contrasting background no differentiation of form would be possible, and so, though unmanifest, it becomes as it were manifest by default, like the print on this page.

As for the Seven Elements, the Stanzas, like all ancient writings, use the term element in its metaphysical sense of elements of experience. Fundamentally they are the seven archetypal moments of experience whose grandest and primary manifestation is to be found in the seven Cosmic Levels. Of those Elements, all, absolutely all, is composed, and into them all can be resolved. On an understanding of this point hangs the golden key of inner knowledge. Those who analyse a phenomenon, say a tree or a river, in terms of chemical elements will arrive at a knowledge of chemistry. He who analyses them in terms of the occult Elements will attain real insight into the phenomenon and will understand how it is that a tree exists on all planes and extends its being throughout the length, breadth and depth of the entire universe. From the little spheres of the human sciences he will have crossed the frontiers of the all-embracing sphere of Divine Magic.

Lastly, 'Mercy and Knowledge' refer to Universal Mind seen as two halves, the Solar-Lunar or Father-Mother aspects known as *Mahat* and *Buddhi*. There has always been confusion in these terms;[1] they are in fact two aspects, since both Father and Mother are present in the Son; and it may be said that the feminine *Buddhi* serves as the vehicle of the masculine *Mahat*. Nevertheless, they are both aspects of the unitary Universal Mind, and it is because of their intimate union that the uncertainty and difference of opinion has arisen. From some points of view they may be reckoned as one, from others as two.

In this verse Mercy, though we usually think of it as a feminine quality, is the Solar aspect of *Mahat*. It is the unity which links all beings, and is responsible for what we know as compassion. 'Compassion is no attribute. It is the Law of Laws—eternal Harmony, Ālaya's Self.'[2] 'Knowledge', on the other hand, is the feminine or lunar *Buddhi*, of which word it is indeed a translation.[3] It is symbolised by the Buddhists in the feminine image of *Prajnāpāramita*, by the Hindus as the goddess *Saraswati* and by the Gnostics as *Sophia*. The Sun shines and attracts, the Moon knows and understands.

[1] The classical *Sānkhya* for instance holds them to refer to the same principle, while other systems such as those found in the *Kathopanishad* and the *Pancharātra Āgama* count them separately.
[2] *The Voice of the Silence*: The Seven Portals. *Ālaya* here signifies the Universal Mind.
[3] The word *Buddhi* means both the intuitive faculty by which knowledge is gained (the 'faculty that gives certainty') and also the Knowledge itself. It is sometimes used in one sense, sometimes in the other. Here it is the Knowledge.

(2) *The Swift and Radiant One produces the seven Laya Centres, against which none will prevail to the Great Day 'Be With Us'; and seats the Universe on these Eternal Foundations, surrounding Sien-Tchan with the Elementary Germs.*

This verse now goes on to deal with the method by which the two aspects of the universe are brought together, a method which, as we have seen, primarily consists in the out-turning of the universal consciousness under the influence of the third Logos. By that integrating power of gyration the potential objectivity of outer space, the darkness of the lower abyss, is then made to conform to the bright inner patterns. The centres through which the inner patterns are projected, around which the outer objectivity is organised, and through which it is again withdrawn at the Day 'Be With Us' when all things return to their transcendent Source, are here called Laya Centres.[1]

We have previously referred to these centres as Sparks or *Jivas*, the individualised points of the cosmic consciring. Here a wider view is taken, the seven Laya centres being the generalised modes of the multitude of individualised centres which fill the whole of space. So long as the Inner Seven continue to breathe out their 'Holy circumgyratory Breaths', those seven typal modes of externalisation will remain as the Eternal Foundation of the universe—'eternal', because they last throughout the 'seven eternities' of the cosmic Day. No individualised centre, no human soul even, however great or spiritually advanced, can prevail against the creative outflow of those seven centres until the flow itself returns.

We may compare them to the points in our psyche round which are organised the structures in our psychic life on any level, whether of sensation, feeling, or thought. On the level of sensations those points are represented by our sense organs

---

[1] The Sanskrit word *Laya* from *Li*, to dissolve, is used to signify dissolution. *Laya-Yoga* is a yoga system in which each element or principle of experience is consecutively dissolved in the next higher one. The latter half of the word *pra-laya* is the same; the whole word being used to signify the universal withdrawal. Also see *S.D.* I. 140 where *pralaya* is said to be used as a synonym for *Nirvāṇa*, that state being understood as a withdrawal of consciousness from forms.

which remain constant through all the changes of sensation fields; and, though less easily indicated, there are similar points, organs or *laya* centres on the levels of feeling and thought as well. Through or in connection with those points, all the experience of the day will manifest.

Sien-Tchan, the archetypal pattern of the universe, is surrounded by the Elementary Germs. This is the same process as was described under Stanza V where the Sparks (*Laya centres*) were distributed, according to the archetypal modes, to the six angles and seventh central point of the interlaced triangles; the latter figure representing the noumenal universe. When the archetypal figure is projected into externality, it is as if its single form was multiplied indefinitely so that the lower space becomes an interlinked network of hexagons, like a stretch of chicken netting. In the centre of each hexagon is the unmanifest central point through which the power flows to the surrounding six points of the figure. These latter now carry the power outwards in a network of mutual relationship which links the whole of manifest space into a unity of structure, the World Net in which all beings are held.

Around each point in this widely extended network the inner patterns are first projected and then organised into progressively more 'material' coatings, corresponding to those archetypal modes of being, the Seven Elements first appear as Germs or semi-manifest potentials in the centre before passing outwards to full manifestation at the six outer centres. These further stages can be represented as the development of the plane six-sided figure into the cube or six-faced solid.

All manifestation follows a similar course. Whether we consider a mineral, a plant, or the body of man, the inner pattern has governed the external result and has been exteriorised in a living process of growth from within outwards.

Such Laya centres form the hearts not only of every Cosmic plane or level but also of every sub-plane in the whole gamut of scales. Difficult as it may be to form any adequate conception of their nature, it is a fact that upon a knowledge, not necessarily a conceptual knowledge, of their whereabouts, or rather of their relationship to the 'matter' of the level or sub-level in question, depends the possibility of producing the psychical phenomena known as materialisation and de-materialisation. If, for instance, it is required to cause a material object to pass into a closed box, it is necessary to know the laya centre of the 'matter' in question, to cause it to become unmanifest by re-entering that centre, and then to allow it to manifest again through the *same centre* inside the box. It need hardly be said that this phenomenon is merely cited in order to illustrate the nature of a *Laya* centre and to show that, metaphysical though it may be, it yet has an intensely 'practical' reality.

The limitation of the space of manifestation is inherent in the power which fills it, for the withdrawing moment of the threefold Logos predetermines the outflow in time to turn back upon itself. The effect is as if the earthy hands of the Matrix reached up and spread her woven screen of objectivity over the windows through which Mind looks out, so that Mind's experience of space is modified by the conformations of the windows through which the Light of consciousness passes and returns. Space therefore seems to conform to the patterns held in the Light; its dimensions are, as it were, determined by the shape of the windows through which the Light flows. The square (or cube) of the lower quaternity, the four-dimensional 'curved' space-time of experience, is a limited enclosure within the utterly undimensioned and a-temporal space of the Matrix—the spatial aspect of the Ever-Darkness —where there is neither light not object to reflect light. In this latter undimensioned space no creative outflow could come to manifestation unless it was first conditioned to turn back upon itself as the object of its own experience.

The limitations of the enclosure are therefore set by determinants flowing from within, and not by any restriction imposed by external forms. Within this enclosure occur all the phenomena of the cosmic manifestation.

(3) *Of the Seven—first one manifested, six concealed; two manifested, five concealed; three manifested, four concealed; four produced, three hidden; four and one tsan revealed, two and one half concealed; six to be manifested, one laid aside. Lastly, seven small wheels revolving; one giving birth to the other.*

This verse gives us the general pattern of the stages by which the subtle (*arūpa*) universe is progressively exteriorised. It is a pattern which will be as applicable to any part as it is to the whole, for as we read in Stanza IV. 4, the Sparks of the Seven are subject to each one of the Seven.

The first point to be noted is that of the seven only six are to be manifested, one is 'laid aside'. This One is the seventh and central mode of being deriving from the Father-Light, the one universal Subject to which all the other six modes become manifest as phenomena. All that is, is manifested to that one Subject which is both the all-pervasive awarenesss of Divine Mind and the awareness of the experiencer in the heart of every integration in being. Whether we look inwards or outwards, the Subject can never become an object of perception, for it is he in us who looks; 'He who looks through the eye, but the eye does not see.'[1] For this reason the seventh is said to be laid aside.

Of the six to be manifested, however, the verse only goes as far as four and a fraction (*Tsan*). The reason for this is that the universe of form is limited to its four modes of spatial existence. Within the Lower Four of the exteriorised universe, only four of the archetypal modes can come to full expression —four are 'produced', the other three remaining 'hidden'. The fraction which is 'revealed' is that part of the perfect, spiritual self-consciousness of Divine Mind which finds limited expression in and through the minds of men: the 'fraction' for which the Chinese Sages in an old myth were busily engaged in seeking.

Divine Man is the fifth, the Quintessence; but, because of

[1] *Brihadāraṇyaka Upanishad*, III, vii. 18.

the limitations of form, this can never ingress in all its glory into the physical vehicle. It is for this reason that the perfected Seer, the Buddha, always remains limited by the accidents of birth and circumstance. This limitation is expressed in the Buddhist saying that, from the enlightenment to the *paranir-vāṇa* (death), the Buddha never spoke a word. The speaker who taught was called the Bodhisattva.

It is this mysterious 'fraction' which, breathed into man, changes him from a static point of divinity within the harmony to a dynamic but inharmonious being, through whose struggles to reconcile the incompatibility between himself and his environment it becomes possible for a vehicle of consciousness capable of transcending the limitations of physical form to be raised.

Midway between the upper Three and the lower Four a semi-tone is sounded in a minor key. The great 'I am' of the Father-Light is echoed by the self-conscious Sons who are to become men, and they plunge downwards into the joys and sorrows of physical existence, seeming to themselves to have won full independence from their heavenly parents.

The egotism with which we affirm our separate existence is a necessary adjunct to the evolutionary outflow and only becomes our enemy when we seek to progress beyond its limitations. It should be clear that neither the body, nor the sense powers, nor the thinking-feeling complex are in themselves necessarily ego structures. Egotism is a particular mode of feeling by which all these aspects of personality are exploited for the preservation of separateness.

Let us now consider an aspect of the three which remain 'hidden'. We have seen that the second creative emission filled the unmanifest space of the Matrix with a multitude of experiencing points. The consciousness of these points was, however, in-turned. With the outbursting of the third wave of creative energy, an energy which consists of the Triad of creative outflow, inflow, and gyration, each of these points now becomes a creative centre in itself, a Laya centre or, more properly, a sevenfold Laya centre through which the divine principles are brought to manifestation.

The first thing to happen is that each in-turned, androgynous point is thrust out from its narcissistic state of self-enjoyment and compelled by the inner pressure to seek experience outside; but outside there is as yet only darkness, the sheer darkness of the womb in which the creative process gestates. The Light flows out from every point, as from stars in a night sky, but there is no means of perceiving that Light, for only one aspect of the subjective triad is manifested. The points are aware of seeking in darkness but not of finding.

Having spent its quota of energy, the polarity of the points changes, and, instead of thrusting out into darkness, they become receptive to the returning inflow of the Light and they manifest the second, feminine or receptive mode of the triad. This receptivity to the Light gives rise to perception, and the space now seems to be filled with a uniformly glowing mist, the fiery clouds of Stanza V. 2. This mist is the manifest or external aspect of the Curds of Stanza III. 4; it is the intimate mingling of subject with object which is the basis of our experience of matter.

The gyratory power of the outflow, by setting all the points in rotation, produces a blend of both modes of experience, outflow and inflow, so that the energy, instead of flowing either out or in, now circulates around the points, enclosing each in a separate sphere of the radiant mist, while relating each to every other through a mutual interchange of attraction and repulsion, each acting and reacting upon the others. Space has now become the 'Fiery Dust' of the next verse. It may be remembered that one of the Upanishadic names for the Universal Mind is Light-and-Shade, and it is the power stemming from that source which organises the mist of Light into contrasting patterns of Light and Darkness and therefore into a state in which there can be discrimination between the separate points.

This field of manifest externality, which is the field in

S

which we 'live and move and have our being', is thus neither purely subjective nor purely objective but a blend of both, held in being by love, perception, time, movement, life, or anything else implying actual as opposed to theoretical relationship. This actual relationship is a pulsating interchange between the poles of being; it is the shuttle which weaves the 'Web of the Universe' (III. 10). The forces which bring about the outflow and the inflow, projection and reception (*pravritti* and *nivritti*), are simultaneously upholding this fluctuating web of power. Deep in the Cosmic Heart the stress of attention falls first on one mode, and a universe is created; then on the other mode, and that universe is withdrawn. Deep in the heart of man the same stress turns outwards and we wake, then it turns inwards and we sleep. Between these two lies the region of dream, an uncertain region of changing polarities.

These are again the three modes of consciousness manifesting within the fourfold web of the universe. And this web is the field in which the Subject of the universe ploughs his furrow, sows his seed, and reaps his harvest of experience. The whole complex process of creation comes in fact from a Will to produce a field of experience in which the self-knowing may be achieved, a field of images which reflects the light of knowing back upon the knower.

Just here lies the awkward point where the 'occult' sciences part company with the physical sciences. These three modes of manifest power, manifest yet 'hidden', constitute what has been termed Etheric matter. They are subtle physical states bearing much the same relationship to physical forms as the three inseparable moments of self-related awareness do to the four psychic modes of handling experience.

Throughout the gamut of manifest levels the upper three levels of any septenary on any scale have thus a subjective or formatory status in respect to the lower four. They are subjective to the levels below them, objective to those above. The reason why their presence is not ordinarily perceptible to us is that our *organs* of sense, though not the sense powers themselves, belong to and function exclusively on levels of physical objectivity.

In the relationship between this triad of manifest powers and the lower four levels lies the all-important link between forms and the formative powers of life which ebb and flow in them. These are the powers which, in harmony with the seasons, flow through the Laya centres of seeds, infuse them with their life, bring them to maturity, and then withdraw, leaving dead structures behind them.

Just as the self-conscious powers of man gain access to his psycho-physical organism through his 'subjective' triad, so do the formatory or life powers of the lower levels gain access to form through their corresponding etheric triads.

On any level of being the triple ether appears as the particular power function of that level. This is why there are said to be seven Laya centres, because the triad of manifesting power appears differently on each level, from electromagnetism to will. Further, just as the power is locked into the electromagnetic structures of atoms, so in its appropriate mode is it embodied in living cells. In this way the energy in cells becomes assimilable as food for the sustenance of more highly complex forms, while the forms develop in complexity to become vehicles for the manifestation of higher degrees of conscious power.

Bringing to birth, sustaining, and withdrawing into death, are the three modes of what is fundamentally one power. In itself the power is hidden from our eyes, but, as with electricity, we know it by its effects.

When we regard this triad of powers as three moments of one power, we see that the three upper levels of each manifest septenary can be regarded as one level. It is in this sense that there are said to be five Elements, Earth, Water, Fire, Air, and Space (*Ākāsha*) as the fifth, the triple Ether.

We must repeat here that the levels are not arranged like a chest of drawers, or even like the skins of an onion; they are co-extensive with each other. All the conformations of Earth, Water, Fire and Air are produced in, swim in, and are pervaded by the Ether of their scale, and all are held within the fourfold power-filled Space which is the manifest field of consciousness, the Space of the Goddess who is Mother, Nurse, and Devourer of all forms.

In order to gain an actual understanding of the nature of this power we must look into our own subjective psychic life and discover there the power which brings forth, holds and withdraws the manifold thoughts and feelings which fill our inner world.[1]

The seven small wheels are the actual rotating integrations of energy on the physical level. Whether we think of the processes by which the clouds of 'Fiery Dust' become suns and finally planets, or by which the most simple atom is built up into the most complex, they are chains of events 'giving birth to each other'.

(4) *He builds them in the likeness of older wheels, placing them on the Imperishable Centres.*

How does Fohat build them? He collects the fiery dust. He makes balls of fire, runs through them and round them, infusing life thereinto, then sets them in motion; some one way, some the other way. They are cold, he makes them hot. They are dry, he makes them moist. They shine, he fans and cools them. Thus acts Fohat from one twilight to the other, during Seven Eternities.

The seven small wheels of the preceding verse are said to be built in the likeness of older wheels. There is an ambiguity in the use of the word older which goes back to a divergence of views about the origination of the pattern of the universe.

One line of enquiry into the source of being sees the manifest universe as an unfolding of the self-nature of the unmanifest: being comes from non-being, the existent comes from the non-existent. Particular qualities and forms are temporal expressions of an eternal and ineffable Absolute. Each universe

[1] Some interesting exercises for developing perception of this triple etheric power in outer objects (plants) were suggested by Rudolf Steiner in his early book *The Way of Initiation* (Theosophical Publishing Society).

in the series of creations and withdrawals, if such a series is at all envisaged, amounts to an entirely new event.

The other approach to the subject agrees in general with the first, but stumbles over the logical difficulty of explaining how particular forms can arise from an absolute source of which no qualities at all can be predicated. Refuge is therefore taken in analogy from human experience. The continuity of experience between one waking period and the next, is dependent on memory. When we wake from sleep our thoughts are conditioned by impressions or memories remaining from our experience of the day before; we therefore start living each day on the basis of the life we led yesterday, a basis on which we are free to build further structures with a certain content of newness. It is therefore supposed that during the period of universal withdrawal the memory of previous universes is somehow retained and later used as the pattern for the formation of the new universe. The problem of an original creation is thus pushed off into what amounts to an infinite regress.

In terms of the second way of thinking, the older wheels thus refer to previous universes whose patterns are 'remember-ed' in the creative consciousness. 'Older' here means older in time. According to the first system however, older means prior in order of divine descent. The older wheels are therefore the archetypes or perhaps noumena of the wheels, the patterns held in Divine Mind which are in turn expressions of the self-nature of the absolute source. These pre-existing patterns correspond to the 'Former Heaven' of the Chinese, the 'as it was before' (yathā-pūrvam) of Hinduism, and the Christian 'Thy will be done on earth as it is in Heaven'.

It is quite possible that both systems of thought were originally the same, and the second diverged from the first through a misunderstanding of the terms used. Thus the former divine universe in eternity was understood to mean former in time, following the usual tendency to hunt for human origins along the historical time scale, and the divine Remembering was therefore thought to be a recalling to mind of past universes, whereas it was truly a calling into temporal manifestation of eternal ideal patterns. It is in fact a metaphysical remembering and not a temporal one. In Time there is always a previous universe before the present one, just as in our experience, even our dream experience, there is always a yesterday before today. In Eternity, however, there are no yesterdays nor tomorrows, only the one eternal Now.

The Imperishable Centres on which the wheels are 'placed' are the seven Laya centres, the Eternal Foundation of the universe described in verse 2 of this stanza. In verse 3 it was described how the three movements of the creative energy— outflow, inflow, and gyration—produced a field of fiery mist or dust[1] which was organised into a sphere around each experiencing point.

The dynamism which effects this process is what has been termed Fohat, the power which, as representative of the original state of transcendent unity, relates all parts of the Cosmos to each other and tends to draw all things together into states that, as nearly as possible, re-present that unity— 'colonies of souls bound together by love'. We can just as well call it the Divine Desire, for desire is in fact a creative movement, and it is only on the path of return (*nivritti*) that it is said to be an evil or a hindrance. Even this needs qualifying, because it is a sort of desire which makes anyone want to travel that path. Desire in itself is neither good nor bad, and its almost universal condemnation is not a true judgment of it, but arises from human resentment against a power whose exploitation for selfish ends always leads to disaster, and there is scarcely a man alive who does not wish to exploit it. Indeed, our relation to desire is one of extraordinary difficulty. If the higher ranges of our psychic being were not liable to infection by the fever of desire we would have no incentive to play our parts in the divine evolution, yet under its influence our in-

[1] The Sanskrit word *Rajas* means reddish dust, and, derivatively, is the quality of passion or mobility.

herent human freedom is liable to be swamped by the purely repetitive and monotonous processes of our animal components. In order to understand what it is in itself, the reader should endeavour to grasp the nature of such desires as that for food or sex *before* those desires have created the images of food or a sexually attractive object to which to attach themselves. Particularly in the latter case there will be noticed a swelling or bursting feeling which 'bursts out', as we say, into an attractive image which then acts as an outlet or drain for the desire energy. The natural result of a desire is the creation of images, and it is this which has given rise to Sigmund Freud's over-generalised theories that all dreams are wish-fulfilments. Incidentally, it may here be mentioned that when the appropriate images cannot be projected because of their incompatibility with conscious standards, psychic ill-health or neurosis is apt to result as the effect of thwarting the creative movement which consequently turns inwards in an often disastrous manner. This however is by the way, for we are not here concerned with psycho-therapy. What does concern us is to point out that the desire energy is often confused with the attraction or movement towards the image, or towards the thing which has been found to support that image. The desire is not the attraction but the 'bursting out' energy that created the image; the attraction being but the effect of the latter in draining off the energy of desire. Desire, it may be repeated, is essentially creative.

In saying that Fohat collects the Fiery Dust of the Desire energy that pervades the whole cosmos, we must not imagine him as running round with a sort of gigantic sweeper's basket, any more than we should think that the power of electricity, which, as H.P.B. never tired of pointing out, is both a form and symbol of Fohat, collects in that manner the scattered charges on the drops of water in a thunder cloud in order to produce the lightning flash. The Desire Energy or Fiery Dust is itself an aspect of Fohat, and in saying that he collects it what is referred to is the naturally cohesive tendency of such energy, a characteristic which shows itself in the tendency of our desires to collect or fuse into what psychologists term complexes. The 'collection' of the Fiery Dust means just such fusion into complex aggregates for manifestation.

These complex aggregates, the Balls of Fire, may be structures of any 'size', including, as they do, Small Wheels or individual structures on any scale down to the atomic. What characterises them all, small or great, is their creative tendency, the movement to create images outside themselves and then to flow into those images as the result of what we term attraction. This attraction exists on all scales, manifesting as the 'gravitation' between worlds, the attraction between the sexes, and the chemical 'affinities' of atoms.

It is this process which results in the creation both of Small Wheels and of separate forms within those Wheels. We read that Fohat as Desire-energy 'runs through' each Small Wheel, thus making each new creation a creative centre in turn. Similarly, the desire-charged images in the psyche, becoming in turn creative, give rise to other images in an indefinite succession, until our energies are for the time being exhausted and a reverse flow sets in.

This 'running through' them is the direct outward thrust of cosmic expansion. It is followed by the 'running round' or vortical movement which separates each unitary system from its fellows as well as links it to them. This too may be seen in the psyche when, after the creation of a rapid succession of images as the result of an intense desire, there comes a pause, and the separate images, or some of them, are rounded off, as we say, and made clear and distinct.

The created forms are then set in motion, some one way and some the other. It has already been stated that the experience of attraction (or repulsion) follows *after* the creation of the images to which there may be either a positive flow of energy, which is what we term attraction, or a negative one, which we experience as repulsion. It is these two 'flows' of psychic energy that are here referred to as Motion, inasmuch as it is they that give rise to the experience which we know as actual physical motion of forms towards or away from each other.

It must be emphasised that just as all so-called matter is the content aspect of experience and so is thoroughly psychic in nature, so all motion even of the most trivial and commonplace character is a psychic phenomenon based on the flow of desire. We tend to think of physical motion as something real, while the flow of desire we regard as more or less a metaphor. In fact, the latter is the primary phenomenon of which the former is an expression. The combination of hydrogen with oxygen to make water is a psychic event brought about by Desire; and all the movements of the heavenly bodies, the movements, in fact, of all the 'matter' in the cosmos, are but the living tides of Desire, ebbing and flowing throughout the Cosmic Day. All motion is a divine Son of Fohat who is born again and again as the winged Eros that we know as Desire; and nowhere is there any motion that is not carried by his wings. Just as in dream we move hither and thither, slowly or fast, borne by those tireless wings—and not we alone, but all the moving figures of our dream as well—so in this waking life, however its darkness may blind us to the truth, it is the Divine wings of Eros that sustain and are the motion of the world. By Desire the wind whispers in the grass or soughs among the pine-trees; by Desire the moving waters perform 'their priestlike tasks of pure ablution round earth's human shores'; by Desire surge the great tides of men, massing in battle or ebbing to their homes; by Desire the swift electrons circle on their tiny orbits; and by Desire the planets in the heavens weave gleaming patterns around their Lord, the Sun.

In truth there is nothing anywhere that moves, though all is motion. 'Things' are the images that clothe the viewless path of Eros as he flies. With each beat of his wings an Image flashes into being, to vanish at the next instant and be replaced by another. When such images resemble one another closely we speak of things which move unchanged, while, when they are dissimilar, we speak of changing objects. Whether at rest in seeming self-identity of being, or whether changing like a summer cloud, all things are flashing sparks, the gleaming incandescent path of the invisible lightning cleaving the night. When man shall be able to seize a living flame and seal it in a jar to keep it as his possession, then and then only may he hope to grasp and hold those illusory 'things' that, like a desert mirage, lure his heart's desire. We strive to catch them in our net and, like fairy gold, they dissolve before our eyes, leaving our hands empty and our ears filled by the sound of invisible wings, the laughing divine wings throbbing onwards into the Future.

It is these series of Desire-born flashes that appear to us as the heating by Fohat of the 'cold' wheels. The cool moments of formless being are caught by Fohat's fiery wings to stream like incandescent tracks throughout the worlds of form; Fire thus producing Heat, the Heat of Motion in the waves of space (III. 9).

'They are Dry, he makes them Moist.' The moistening of the forms signifies the plunging of them deeper into the Waters of matter; in short, involving them in the lowest levels of the cosmos, for we have seen that matter is always symbolised as the Waters. As the incandescent tracks of form proceed outwards, they become more and more objective, more and more 'material', until they reach that lowest level, that which we know as the physical world.

Pari passu with this moistening there is a contraction or hardening—'it contracts when the Breath of the Mother touches it' (III. 11)—and a cooling of the heat of Desire which brings it about that the lower and more 'material' a form is, the less it is mobile and responsive to the moulding of Desire. In the end we arrive at this physical plane on which, though the forms which compose our environments are actually moulded and manipulated by Desire, so hidden is the working of the Power that we consider them to be controlled by purely 'mechanical' forces (whatever the phrase may mean). In fact we even take the external world as a type of reality that is uninfluenced by Desire, and contrast it with the obviously desire-moulded worlds of inner fantasy.[1]

In truth there is no such dichotomy. Our external or material environments are no less the creations of Desire than are the inner worlds of dream and fantasy.

Whose Desire? Surely not yours or mine, for that gives no 'public' world but rather a plurality of private worlds as separate from each other as, apparently, are our dreams; the view, in fact, of what is known as Subjective Idealism.

Yes, the Desire is yours or mine; or rather, it is the Desire which works through the individual centres known as you or me. Nevertheless we are not subjective idealists and, beyond the privacy inherent in the fact that 'a fool sees not the same tree (or world) that a wise man sees', the material environment is a public one. Its publicity arises from the fact that you and I are focal centres in the same Universal Mind. Our points of view and hence our environments on *any* level are bound to interlock, just because they are moments of the same Whole. There are no purely private worlds, because none of us are independent of our fellows. We ignorantly fancy that our desires are private and that we can entertain them in complete independence of others. But that is an illusion. It is impossible for any one of us to entertain a desire without its reacting on the desires of all other beings down to the minutest atomic entities. Hence the environment adjusts itself to the moulding of Desire without losing its publicity in any way; for beings are like the knots in a marvellous net, and movement of any one knot is transmitted throughout the whole.

We can see from this how important it is for us to order our desires according to the principles of the Cosmic Harmony; if our desires are harmonious, we pull, according to the measure of our strength, the whole world with us, while if they

[1] Cf. Freud's dichotomy of the Pleasure Principle which rules the subjective worlds and the Reality Principle which, according to him, governs the external world. The names of these principles are not perhaps the best that could be chosen but the idea behind them is fairly obvious.

are inharmonious, separative, and 'selfish', we depress, if only by a little, the general level of the whole.

It should not, of course, be imagined that the view set forth above implies an immediate answering of the world ship to the helm of our desires. That is impossible just because of the interlocking mentioned above. Nevertheless, in the end, Desire does bring about its fulfilment. Willy-nilly we must eat the fruits of our own longing, and, for the most part, bitter is their taste.

By way of showing the universality of this symbolism in ancient times, the following quotations may be of interest. The first is from the Hermetic writings[1]; the italics and comments in brackets are the present writers'.

> 'And Matter *being moved was heated* (Cf. what was said above about heat and motion) and did turn to Fire and Water. . . . And Fire opposed by Water was dried up by it (the "cooling" of the creative Desire by being plunged into waters of matter) and did become Earth borne on Water ("solid" forms borne up on the ocean of formless "matter"). And when it was excessively dried up a vapour rose from the three—from Water, Earth and Fire—and became Air (Cf. here what was said of the backwash or return movement of the creative tide in verse 3 of this stanza).'

The second quotation is from the celebrated *Vision of Aridaeus*. It tells how Aridaeus, travelling in a vision through the other worlds, comes to a great Vortex called the Place of Oblivion. He was not allowed to stay there; his companion dragged him away.

> '. . . explaining how the rational part of the soul was melted and *moistened* by pleasure, while the irrational part, and that which is of a corporeal nature, being then moistened and made fleshly, awakens the memory of the body, and from this memory comes a yearning and a desire which

[1] *Thrice Greatest Hermes*, III, p. 66. G. R. S. Mead.

drag down the soul into generation . . . the soul being weighed down with moisture.[1]'

Returning more directly to our verse, we may note the fact that the fire of a desire, hunger, say, is cooled when its images having been projected outwards on to material objects, food in this case, are then plunged into and taken into the self. The Cosmic Creative Desire is similarly cooled by plunging further and further into the created images or forms. The process is repeated at each level of descent until this physical plane is reached on which, though desire is constantly welling up from the heart of life, it is as constantly being slaked in matter, to well up anew.

'They (the forms) shine, he fans and cools them.' This carries further the previous thought. The forms, moistened in the sea of matter, are further de-energised by being 'fanned'; a term which signifies a still more definite 'cooling' and hence 'contraction'. Each form 'contracts' on its own centre, thus separating from its fellows and becoming a hard, distinct and inert 'thing' existing apparently in its own right in the physical world, one of our familiar objects composed of so-called dead matter.

Thus acts the Power of Creative Desire from Dawn to Dusk of the Seven Eternities of a Cosmic Day.

(5) *At the fourth, the sons are told to create their images. One third refuses—two (thirds) obey.*

The curse is pronounced; they will be born on the fourth, suffer and cause suffering. This is the first war.[2]

In the last verse the action of the creative power was treated from the general viewpoint of its effects in the manifest field. Here it is regarded in its more particular and personal aspect in its effect on the individualised centres of awareness, the 'Army of the Sons of Light' (V. 4).

[1] *ibid.* I. p. 454.
[2] In the main body of *The Secret Doctrine* this verse is split up into two, numbered 5 and 6 respectively. On p. 33, however, it is printed as above.

As we have seen, the production of the individualised centres occurs as the fourth major step of the cosmic unfolding which we refer to as the fourth macrocosmic level. At this significant middle point of the whole process towards manifestation the individuals are thrust out from their static in-turned bliss into a condition of dynamic, out-turned activity.

It is this out-turning, coupled with the outrush of Fohat running 'through them and round them' which tells them to create their images, for it sets them searching outwardly to re-establish their lost state of beatitude.

What do we do when forces beyond our control carry us out from our homes into strange undeveloped lands? We build new homes and establish our cultures somewhat along the lines of the ones we have left behind, just as the Aryan invaders planted out their sacred place-names in India, and the English emigrants in America.[1] The more blissful the memories of the past, the more closely we try to follow their patterns. So it is with the separated beings. They seek to re-establish the condition of bliss from which they have been driven out, though in truth it is not they who seek but the divine power which seeks through them. In search of their lost paradise they look into the outer waters, the outer field of experience, and Narcissus-like fall in love with the forms they see reflected there.

They become aware of the multiplicity of selves, and consequently of their individuality. In seeking to regain the blissful unity of their in-turned state, the selves replace it by an outer skin of separateness; they clothe themselves in the vortices of the lower 'Elements', organising them around themselves by virtue of the energy each has received from the Logos.

The two halves of the Self, consciousness and its content, subject and object, have again united. Soul and body have come together, but not in the bliss of in-turned absorption, for

---

[1] See A. K. Coomaraswamy's *Rig Veda as Land-Nama-Bok* in which he brings out the inner significance of the process.

beyond the periphery of its own vortex of self-hood each integration of being is to some degree aware of the proximity of other vortices. Self-hood is now separated from otherness. Strive as they may, the two halves can never wholly come together in externality.

The central point of the reflected image is the reflection of its own separated individuality, but the form in which it is clothed is the projected image of the inner ideal content attaching to each viewpoint within Mind. The outflowing energy of projection is thus organised into concrete forms corresponding to the inner patterns.

The outer field of experience around each point is now divided into an enclosed area of self-identification—the particular form of each individual—and an external field of otherness. Similarly the inner field is divided into an available content related to the particular viewpoint—the empirical ego—and a subliminal archetypal field whose content only becomes apparent when projected onto or reflected from the external field.

In turning outwards they become aware of the multiplicity of selves and so of their own separateness for they do not seek to unite their subjectivity with the subjectivity of others but to discover the blissful content aspect of Self which they have left behind. This sense of separateness from each other, and so from their unitary source, leads them to make their first inharmonious movement, that of self-protection. On their mental level this is equivalent to a hardening of the skin of the soul. We can see in our microcosmic selves how the intellect analyses, discriminates and defines. In its macrocosmic aspect the intellect has the same effect on all the elements of its content, clarifying the mental limits of the experiencing selves. We can also recognise in ourselves how the effect of the unwelcome intrusions of others can be minimised by intellectual detachment. It is necessary here to recollect that the intellectual level, being the highest of the lower four, though it is the first level on which the souls of all things are first separated in outwardness, must yet be the last principle of man to achieve full expression through the evolution of his psycho-physical organism.

Their primal harmony having been disturbed, a further mixing of the individuals follows, though this mixing will in general (as it were statistically) be controlled by the conformations of the six-dimensional space described in verse 3, and their movements will be energised by the attractions and repulsions which are the separated moments of the blissful harmony.

The primary result of this mixing is the division of the mass of similar beings into male and female, active and passive, positive and negative, dominant and submissive. Division is the root meaning of the word *sex*,[1] and it is this first conflict, the 'first war', which determines which of the two possible polarities inherent in each androgyne will play the dominant part in its further development, which 'sex' it will be. The decision is in some sense already determined by the spatial co-ordinates of the individual point, but it is a potential factor and does not become explicit until this first clash of mental integrations occurs.

The 'first war' begins, then, as a clash of affinities and oppositions first arising between the bipolar individuals. In a sense it is a war between the two armies of the preceding stanzas: the army of the Sparks or Sons of the Father-Light (V. 4) and the army of the Voice, the Energies of the Divine Mother (IV. 4). The energies surround, clothe and separate the Sparks, while at the same time relating them to each other, so that their inner unity is now replaced by an outer separateness and they meet either in love or hostility. But this war is not only between the now separated Sparks; the conflict is also, and perhaps primarily, internal, within each integration. It is the eternal war between Spirit and Matter, Good and Evil, Light and Darkness, *Ahura Mazda* and *Ahriman*, the war of the opposing forces out of which the body of Divine Man, this universe, is built. It is the root of all the outward conflict we

[1] From the Latin *secare*, to cut or divide.

see throughout the worlds of form: between nations, men, animals, and even plants. In ourselves we find it as the clash between the perception of our essential unity with all men in the divine Light, and the personal rights we demand as single embodied beings. In so far as we strive to find our place in relation to the unity, we can bring harmony into our surroundings, but when, as most of us do, we identify ourselves with our physical bodies, our families, our religious sects and our race, we inevitably bring ourselves into conflict with other bodies, families, sects and races. So difficult is the task of reconciling these two opposing forces that it is entirely understandable that many mystics have preferred the relatively more simple alternative of transcending the duality by a world-negating and love-negating denial of value to all but the one Light.

All the first individualised beings are 'men' in the sense that the subjective pole of their being which is first exteriorised is 'male', positive, or out-looking; the 'feminine', content aspect, or objective pole, remains behind or within. When these 'males' meet 'head on', those who are less highly charged with energy, the weaker, play a submissive role towards the stronger. Like two bar magnets being brought together, the stronger induces a reversal of poles in the weaker, so that its inner feminine nature manifests outwardly.

This reversal of polarity does not oppose the creative outflow which carries the multitude of individuals outwards to physical embodiment, but the mode, or attitude towards the movement, is changed. The feminine type is carried passively downwards by the creative wave, while the male type may react either way to the tide, either rushing ahead of it or reluctantly hanging back.

The divisions here spoken of are modes of behaviour not necessarily or directly connected with physical sex determinants. Nor is it meant to imply that the induced polarities permanently determine those modes throughout the period of manifestation. Certainly, amongst the higher forms of life, psychic properties and sometimes even physical bodies are sub-

T

ject to changes of mode. Differing types of education can bring
out either of a child's blend of masculine and feminine qualities,
and man and woman tend to exchange some of their characteristics in old age. Psychic qualities which have been refused
expression during one human life time may demand expression
in another, and so bring about incarnation in a body of the
opposite sex to that of the preceding birth.

We can see from the above description that the movement
of the individual souls is really occasioned by the production
of an unbalance between the two sides of their androgynous
integrations. When both sides are perfectly balanced there can
be no compulsion to move. Such a state of perfection is not
of course present in any newly individualised soul; that is a
condition which can only be achieved by prolonged efforts.
It is in fact the goal of the creative process, not its beginning.
Nevertheless, it is the third possible type of individualised
integration deriving from the total perfection of the Universal
Mind, and is therefore mentioned here. It is not a quantitative
but a qualitative third.

The first movement governs all the subsequent patterns of
relationship. In general, like continues to seek like; *Homo
sapiens* seeks *Homo sapiens* as a mate, and so on throughout the
animal and vegetable worlds. Even the Alchemical concept of
sexual polarities in minerals is not so silly as it has been made
to sound; it arises from the perception that all natural affinities,
on whatever level of being, spring from one fundamental
relating power, the divine Eros.

On the human level the Sons are the selves of men which,
looking upwards in affirmation of their identity with their
source, are the Higher Selves (*Shuddha Manas*), the highest
and most central of the separated moments through which the
Divinity seeks to manifest and perfect his inner purpose.
Looking downwards, however, they become identified with
the transient integration of psychic qualities, the lower self,
which incarnates in the physical vehicle and passes from birth
to birth in a long, though not endless, series of lives. So long

as the selves assert their separateness from their true source, their higher properties are, as it were, dormant within them, and when the energies which support the psychic integration are withdrawn, as they are at the universal withdrawal, then their triune nature dissolves into its component principles and nothing remains.

As will have been seen from the foregoing description, even the Higher Self is not a permanent and indestructible monad. It is the individualised modality of Universal Mind; it is not a thing but a condition of or in consciousness. Throughout the entire universe there is one and one only Light of consciousness, life and power, universally diffused in Divine Mind, individualised in the Higher Self, separated by identification with psychic modalities in the empirical self, manifesting as life in the tissues of animals and plants, and as energy and structure in minerals. One can perhaps describe the Self as a focal point in the Light. Such descriptions, however, tend to detract both from its reality and its glory. Properly understood it is for each of us our personal divinity: He is our Instructor, the Son of Fire, the divine charioteer who will guide us safely through the battlefield of life, if we give ourselves to his charge. He is also Adam or Manu the first man, the progenitor of the race; but if we insist on searching for our human origins along the time-scale, then, instead of the primordial paradise, we find only the greater apes sleeping in the trees of the primordial jungle. We have to turn inwards to a past which is prior in the scale of being, not prior in extension of time. Without the aid of that Higher Self we can never find the paradise we all either seek or despair of finding, for it exists neither in the remote past nor in the remote future, but in the ever-present eternity. He, too, is ever-present, here in our hearts, the very essence of our present being, but we have to find him, to give ourselves to him, and let him fight in us and 'fill the dull void within'.

Throughout the Stanzas there is a play on the correspondences of the number symbolism, so that the 'Fourth' at which the 'Sons' are told to create their images can as well be read as referring to the Fourth of the Seven Eternities of the preceding verse as it can to the fourth macrocosmic level. And because of the actual correspondences between the patterns of all existing things the meaning of the verse will be as applicable to one as it is to the other.

At the fourth of the 'Seven Eternities' (VI. 4) those Sons who bear within them the potentiality of growth into intelligent manhood are told to create their images, which means that they are to invest an otherwise animal form with their divine inheritance of self-conscious or reflective being. The first three eternities are the ages preceding the advent of man, the evolutionary ages from mineral to animal. At the fourth, Mind begins to construct its physical vehicle in the form of man. During the fifth, sixth and seventh ages the evolutionary powers work in and through men in the attempt to achieve the accomplishment of the divine purpose.

The Breath of the Father, the Light-Maker, is essentially free, yet it voluntarily exchanges its infinite freedom in eternity for the limitations of finite form. Each son of the Father-Light receives his measure of the self-affirming Breath; and to each as he is caught by the outflow it seems as if he turns outwards of his own volition into the limited space of manifestation. We have not been compelled to come to birth by the fiat of an offended God; the divine desire acting in our hearts has chosen to bring us here. And because we˘ are essentially moments in divinity, the desire is ours and the choice is ours, for we are the bearers of the two-edged weapon of free-will, the double axe of human sovereignty.

All who descend into birth must suffer and cause suffering, must act and be acted on, must learn to be the instruments of learning. For our task is to learn through experience, to learn how to handle, to harmonise, and in the end to master the elements of experience, until finally the compulsive self-indentification with the form is broken and we come to know ourselves in the freedom of our true nature.

No mere intellectual detachment can give that integral freedom, for it leaves untouched the self-affirming egotism which, in separating one man from another, separates him also from the divine unity. The lesson of mankind's mutual dependency has to be both learned and practically applied if we are actually to overcome the great heresy of separateness.

When the Buddha described all existence as suffering (*duhkha*) he was not displaying ignorance of the fact that most people experience a fair measure of happiness in life, but was pointing to the essential sorrow inherent in all things that have but ephemeral significance. And as he also taught, the suffering that pervades the worlds is rooted in the sense of separate individuality, the state of separateness which makes a 'world' on any manifest level. As long as there is a feeling of separateness, so long will the tissue of life be woven upon a background of sorrow. The inner craving for unity, the lost garden of Eden, can never be satisfied by seeking for it among the ever-changing forms with their inherent impermanence. 'Sorrowful is union with the unpleasant: sorrowful is disunion from the pleasant'. It is the sense of self that brings about these unions and disunions. Only in self-transcendence can be found the Peace. To be individualised is to be born, and to be born is to suffer, even if it be with the divine suffering of Prometheus.

The outflow of the Breath is therefore referred to as a curse, because it compels the Sons to exchange their blissful unity in Divine Mind for the sorrowful state of separateness and conflict. Yet their former state was one of potential rather than actual manhood; while the living process of tangible experience into which they descend to 'suffer and cause suffering' provides them opportunity for voluntary growth into the greater freedom of self-knowledge. But before the freedom of the Spirit can be expressed, before the limitations of concrete form be overcome and man begin to reach up from the finite to the infinite, the breath of life must journey through an almost endless series of physical forms, life after life. Only when we see the essential emptiness of a life process regarded merely as an extended sequence of repeated births and deaths, and we begin to seek the true purpose of our existence, only then can we use the weapon of our inborn freedom to cleave the bars of our material prisons and then transcend the limitations of our separateness by sacrificing the temporal to the eternal.

Because they are the self-conscious Sons with an inherent power of choice they are said either to 'obey' or to 'refuse' the creative impulse. But no unperfected spark of the creative fire can refuse the compulsion of the winds of the Spirit when they blow. This gale of the Spirit, the *pneuma* or Breath of the Brahman, carries the golden host of souls to embodiment whether they will or no. When the moment is ripe for the descent of the Sons, descend they must; and any reluctance to descend can only manifest as delay in the extended time-scale corresponding to the metaphysical moment of the 'curse'. In fact, from the artificial viewpoint of an *ab initio* creation, there is no 'third' of perfected men capable of refusing the command of the divine outbreath; there are only the two types of Sparks of potential manhood, manifesting the modes of active participation and passive acceptance.

We have seen that this division is the result of the war between the subjective consciousness of the Father-Light and the objective energies of the Matrix or powers of darkness. To one half of the Sons the significance of life therefore seems to inhere in the subjective aspects of experience and they seek their fulfilment in the private inner regions of the psyche, in thought and imagination; while, to the other half, the objective aspects of experience are all important and they plunge deeply into the sense life, gladly accepting its vivid stimuli and leading the hosts of souls to birth as if to a feast that they would share with others. Yet both modes are present in each Son, for each is an integrated organisation of Light and Shade; one mode is dominant while the other is recessive.

The out-looking of each Son is determined by the four functional modes of perception, the Lower Four; and because of the mixing brought about by the circumgyratory outflow, each Son chooses one of the four as a function through which to express his dominant mode. The other three functions then either support the dominant, or are relegated to the background where they manifest the qualities of the recessive mode.

Neither of these two modes necessarily lead men to seek their transcendence, for both types of men are usually content with their over-valuation of either the subjective or the objective aspects of life, and each thinks his own type superior to the other. The source from which both have come and the goal to which they must both ultimately return is a perfect balance of Light and Shade, Subject and Object, out-looking and in-looking.

To achieve that goal we have first to find the means of balancing the inharmonious forces within us, forces which tend to make us over active in some part of our lives and inert in others, which make us swing from emotional involvement to intellectual detachment, and from function to aesthetic. Our path to psychic wholeness therefore demands that we pay particular attention to our undeveloped functions. Contrary to the rule of worldly aims which exaggerates our unbalance by exploiting our most developed functions to their full, we should rather accept the suffering involved in learning to perform just those acts which come least naturally to us. The coldly detached 'intellectual' must unleash his feelings, while the manual worker must learn to use his mind. Such a process is, however, dangerous and should only be undertaken with proper guidance.

We have spoken of the blissful state of the Sons of Divine Mind before they descend, embryonic men in the womb of life, and we have spoken of the attractions that seem to lure them out into independent existence, the creative adventure into a world where they will attempt to re-establish their lost harmony. But the ambivalent world that lies before them is also full of dangers, and there are many men who fear its challenge. The nostalgic memory of the bliss they have left behind them is too strong, so that the outer attraction fails to draw them fully into the current of life. They are subject to a reluctance, a doubt as to whether they need follow the course of the macrocosmic sun over the threshold of the equinox into fully independent manhood.

Such reluctance to accept the flow of life is often thought to be a 'spiritual' characteristic, and indeed those who fear life may be devout religionists and even ardent ascetics, but it is in no sense spiritual to refuse participation in the divine outpouring, an outpouring which strives towards perfection through a long and painful process of growth.

The goal of the spirit is not a mere return to its source, unaltered by all that it manifests. It seeks a rich harvest of experience, and seeks it through those Sons who are the experiencing selves of men. The compelling drive of the Spirit has raised up our bodies, temples built without hands, the seats of the immanent divinity and the sacred vehicles of all religious practices; but the Spirit is itself inherently free from compulsion. 'The Spark, the so-called husband of the soul, is none other than a spark of the divine nature, a divine light, a ray, an imprint of divinity'.[1] Our essential being is that Spark, given, as it were, a lease of separate existence for the period of manifestation. We cannot refuse participation in the growth and decay of the physical body, for there there is very little freedom, but in our higher being the presence of that Spark which makes us men enables us to choose whether we will give ourselves to the realisation of the divine effort or whether we will preserve our separate egotism with a hard shell of selfishness.

Whether from fear of life or from desire for its pleasures we can refuse to be cooked in the boiling pot of the world, but if we so refuse to blend our being with the life of those around us, instead of striving by the power of our freedom to raise ourselves and others to participation in the higher unity, we condemn ourselves to ultimate annihilation in the final conflagration of worlds and men.

[1] Meister Eckhart. Sermon XXXI

We have become men, or more truly we are still animals in the process of becoming what men should really be. Unless we make use of our opportunity for further growth into full manhood, we must continue to suffer and cause suffering until the term of the universe is complete. The road to perfection is through growth in the inner life towards the Spirit and not through regression in nostalgic longings for the lost beatitudes of infancy.

Those rosy memories of childhood are illusory images that but faintly mask the terrors of the deep from which we have emerged, the nightmare terrors which haunt our psychic 'deeps'. If we refuse to grow upwards into Spiritual manhood and insist on remaining identified with the forms of our evolutionary childhood, the Great Mother from whom those forms have sprung will again devour them, for she is Death. The same maternal love that nurtures an infant can emasculate a youth and destroy his power of growth if the mother does not release her hold. It is this devouring love that peoples our nightmares with bears, witches, octopuses, spiders and the greater cats. We have to be born again into the inner life, a birth which carries us out beyond the Mother's grasp, whence we can look back on her with the freed vision of Man. Only then can we accept with love the smile that Death casts upon our form, and only then can we find within ourselves the true balance of the male and female elements of our being.

(6) *The older wheels rotated downward and upward . . . The Mother's spawn filled the whole. There were battles fought between the Creators and the Destroyers, and battles fought for Space; the seed appearing and reappearing continuously.*

Under verse 4 we described the 'older wheels' as being the archetypal patterns which pre-exist the phenomenal universe. The verse now speaks of the older wheels rotating downwards and upwards. This is not a reference to the movements of material bodies but to the cyclic flow of creative energy which gives rise to, sustains and then withdraws from the phenomenal forms.

This flow of living energy plunges down to the uttermost limits of the universe and returns upon itself. So long as the Cosmic Day continues, the river of life follows its endless course, cycle succeeding cycle in the eternal recurrence of extended time. Then, when Night comes, Life rushes back to its source, existence returns to non-existence, until the next Day dawns.

The downward and upward movement can also be described in terms of the variations in psychic emphasis which occur as the focus of the divine attention becomes increasingly out-turned or extroverted, stress being laid on the objective aspect of experience; this is followed by a withdrawal into a correspondingly introverted state in which the stress of atten-tion is on the subject.

The rotation of the Wheels is, in fact, another manifestation of the rhythm of the Great Breath which is at the root of all Cycles, from that of the great Cosmic Day down to the little days of man and even lower. Universes, Solar Systems, Races, Men and even atoms and electrons thus have their Days and Nights, their ever-recurring pattern of equinoxes and solstices. It is this same seasonal cycle that causes, for instance, the alternations in the climate of human thought, so that periods of crass materialism are succeeded by periods of soaring, if unbalanced, idealism.

In speaking of eternally recurrent cycles we do not mean to imply that events repeat themselves mechanically, but that beneath the small areas of life in which we are free to exercise our powers of decision lie vast systems of cyclic order, cycles that are regularly recurrent in general, though infinitely variable in particulars.

We have seen how the 'innumerable sparks' (V. 2), which are reflections of the one Light in the waters of creation, become individualised centres (Laya centres) through which the creative energy comes to manifestation. Their sheer multiplicity derives from the properties of the Matrix, so that as an aggregate they are her 'Spawn'. The symbol may seem grotesque to modern readers, but a mass of frog-spawn, for instance, with its countless little black dots, each surrounded by an egg of jelly, all separate yet all connected together and floating in masses in the water, is by no means an inappropriate symbol for the point-like egos, each in its separate vortex of form and all floating within the substance of the Matrix.

The Space of the Matrix is filled with the energy which flows out and returns through every one of these individualised Laya points. By the power of the third Logos the energy is caused to 'rotate', thus separating the creative moment from the withdrawing moment so that the forms built up by the first are preserved from being destroyed by the second. Thus the forms exist for a period as objective phenomena until the destructive moment overcomes the creative and the life ebbs out of the forms and they 'die'.

This compound life-death energy thus circulates throughout the universal space. On the downward flowing arc of its course it manifests as the power called anabolism; it creates and builds up forms. On its upward arc it manifests as katabolism; it destroys forms and causes them to vanish. From the interplay of these two aspects of the one Life arises the transformation of energy or metabolism which sustains forms in being for greater or lesser periods according to their level and scale.

This interplay of the creative and destructive aspects of the one energy is the great battle of life, the struggle to achieve a relatively stable existence, between the conflicting forces of growth and decay, the 'Creators' and the 'Destroyers'. Carried outwards on the creative tide, the seeds of life (the Elementary Germs, VI. 2) grow their outward structures of appearance; then, as the forces of withdrawal balance and then overcome the forces of creation, the forms reach maturity, they decay, and finally return into non-appearance.

This is the general pattern of the creative cycle. Within this great cycle, however, there are smaller cycles of coming and going, growth and decay, birth and death. Throughout the universe the characteristic structures of each level come into existence and pass out of existence in accord with the periodicity of their particular life cycles. Whether we speak of physical forms of the animal, vegetable and mineral kingdoms, or of the subtle inner structures of thought patterns and feeling which support the outer appearances, all, according to their nature, some with a quicker rhythm, some with a slower, are born, raised to maturity, collapse with the withdrawal of the forces which sustain them, and are then born again as the circling power changes from its inflowing to its out-flowing mode and causes the reappearance of the seed that had seemed to disappear.

The Battles between the Creators and Destroyers also signify the conflicts between adjacent levels. As we have already stated, each level stands in the relation of creative subject to the one below it, because the higher send forth the Light and Desire-energy, while the lower have in them more of the Mother and are Destroyers inasmuch as their 'matter' eats up or absorbs the energy. The Battles between them refer to the exchange of energy that is always going on; sometimes the upper, subjective, or spiritual level being dominant and sometimes the lower, objective, or material one.

These conflicts are always going on at all the levels and on all the scales of the phenomenal universe. We can see them, for instance, in what we term psychic conflict when the mind is in conflict with the desire nature, or the desire nature with the world of physical things. In this latter struggle, sometimes the desires succeed in moulding the outer parts to their bidding while sometimes the outer parts are victorious, and desires are thwarted by a hostile world.

The battles for Space stand for the conflicts between the forms on any given level. As the forms increase under the creative impulse they inevitably come into conflict with each other. They trespass on each other's fields, and the stronger or more highly charged with Desire-energy drive out or dominate the weaker, just as, for example, the strongly hunger-charged image of food drives out of our mind the weaker images which till then had been occupying our mental 'space'. Here we have that struggle for survival which is such a feature of the lower levels and is so familiar to us on the physical plane. In all the four lower levels this process goes on, the stronger forms driving out, killing, absorbing, or enslaving the weaker ones. We can see it on the mental and desire levels as on the physical, for does not a dominant system of thought or a powerful desire-complex either drive out from the field of consciousness, or else absorb, or render subordinate to itself, any other thought or desire system that may be in the field? If allowed to exist at all, the weaker ones are made to serve some subordinate purpose of the stronger system and are thus taken captive. If this is not possible, if there is too much conflict between their natures, then it is war to the death, and the weaker system is altogether refused a place in consciousness.

Such slain systems, whether of thought or desire, do not, however, disappear from being altogether. Killed though they may be as far as the conscious life is concerned, they enter the dark depths of the psyche there to work mischief underground. There are interesting parallels to this process in the traditions of old conquests on the physical plane, for do we not read again and again, for example in Ireland, of the conquered races being 'driven underground' and forced to inhabit an underworld of caves and the interiors of mountains, where they became enchanters, fairies, or ghosts, and work harm to their conquerors by their skill in magic arts?

Truly this is what happens to the slain forms in all the lower levels. They vanish 'underground', but from the depths of the psyche they work strange magic. Their energy is not destroyed but merely driven below the surface whence it irrupts into the conscious mind in all sorts of mysterious and magically illusive ways, manifesting as strange but irresistible compulsions, irrational fears, and even hallucinations, which disturb the peace of the victorious thought or desire systems. This is true even on the physical plane where, in some form or other, the slain come back to haunt the slayers as ghosts. In many mysterious ways we men are haunted by the spirits of the forms we have murdered; and blood which has been spilt (and not merely human blood either) cries to the heavens for vengeance which, in the end, the heavens or *kārmic* Powers always grant. In retiring from the plane on which they were manifest, the ensouling principles of such slain systems draw nearer to the source of their energy, and so become stronger till they burst forth again in a new manifestation to renew the struggle with their fellows, perhaps on more favourable terms. This is what the verse terms the Seed or *Jīva*; ensouled forms appearing or re-appearing continuously. The process of re-incarnation is thus seen to be not an arbitrary institution laid down for man alone, but a process that is inherent in the nature of the lower levels of the cosmos and that, like all else within the cosmos, can be studied and its laws ascertained within our own hearts.

(7) *Make thy calculations, O Lanoo, if thou wouldst learn the correct age of thy small wheel. Its fourth spoke is our mother. Reach the fourth 'fruit' of the fourth path of knowledge that leads to Nirvāna and thou shalt comprehend, for thou shalt see. . . .*

There are many people who are disposed to think it a matter of great significance to know our present place amidst all these mighty Cycles, as if there were some consolation to be drawn from knowing just how far distant in the remote future may lie those promised eras of social peace, material plenty and natural spirituality foretold by the myths of tradition. There are also not a few persons attempting to follow the inner Path whose main preoccupation appears to be with knowing just 'how far' they have gone, at what 'stage' they have arrived. These questions are equally futile whether pursued on a cosmic or a personal scale.

Let us, then, try to understand what is the actual significance of an Age, and why so many disciples of the Path are apt to lose themselves in calculations and in reveries of the unattainable future. But we must first recollect that our own standard of time perception is determined by planetary positions within our physical environment and has therefore no absolute validity. On other worlds and in other states of being, such as our dreams, the experience of time is different.

We can say that an Age is the period during which the flow of the circling river of life falls with particular emphasis on one aspect of a sevenfold cycle, the emphasis on one causing the whole complex to be modified by its qualities. Then the stress falls on the next in turn. The lower the wheel, the more materialistic will be the qualities, and the higher, the more idealistic. Whether we can calculate their periodicity or not, such regular variations of attention can be observed on all scales from the small cycles of our individual lives to the greater cycles of communities and nations. From this fact, and from the confusion over the word Spirit, the unwarrantable conclusion is often drawn that the world will be 'spiritualised' (whatever that may mean) when, in the ordinary course of cyclic sequence, the point of psychic emphasis is carried 'up' to the 'higher' and, presumably, more 'spiritual' levels. Such is the power of words to mislead! We have only to consider for a moment to see that any cyclic force that is expected to carry us up on the upward component of its current to less materialistic psychic states will inevitably carry us down again on its downward component. Whether we are carried as straws on the current, swim with the current, or struggle against the current, all our movements will be in the dimensions of time. No movement in the temporal flow can of itself lead us to our liberation or to our salvation in eternity. Death, which in most ancient traditions is synonymous with Time, releases us from our bodies, but not from Time, for though in the after-death state the time scale may differ from the one we know here, it is still time. The only direction in which we can find release from the constant flow of cyclic events is across the stream. Our gaze must be fixed neither forward into the future nor backward into the past, but on the one fixed point of certain reference, the present moment. The current may carry us where it will; but so long as we keep headed for the other shore we shall eventually reach it. Without effort, however, nothing will be achieved; and effort is peculiarly the property of the present. Whatever is to be achieved is to be won now or never at all. The inner goal of the Spirit is not placed in some far off cyclic event destined for the human race whether men like it or no; it is here and now, 'closer than the jugular vein', and our efforts to find it must be made where it is.

The fourth spoke of the cyclic wheel is said to be our mother —mother earth. It is the fourth, lowest, and middle of the seven-aspected cyclic chain of events which 'descends' from dimensionless 'Sparks' to the mineral earth, and then starts again from the earth to build up an 'ascending' series through plants and animals to men. It is also the 'fourth' of the minor cycles which are included within the great evolutionary Cycle, for the materialisation of all aspects of the cosmic process follows a similar pattern. All the forces of the cosmos which begin to be externalised at the fourth macrocosmic level are, as it were, concentrated at the fourth or lowest stage of the material universe. And just as the unmanifest powers turn outwards and downwards at the higher 'fourth', so they begin to turn upwards and inwards at the lower 'fourth'.

From a material viewpoint we lie at the very bottom of the manifest creation; and such historical records as we have may well make us wonder whether changes of emphasis of the Life-wave have ever produced any very marked increase or decrease in those human lusts and passions by which man's materiality of outlook may be gauged. Nor do we find anything better when we pass to less material worlds, for those who have not learned to control their desires during their physical life are not less, but more at their mercy after death.

Here, our thoughts and desires may and do run riot without necessarily leading us to indulge them in action, whereas there, without the inertial resistance of the body, a man may be utterly ruled by them.

This fourth spoke of the wheel has correspondences with the fourth Cosmic level which is the level of the Higher Mind or level of individuation. This means that on this physical wheel Mind has great effectuating power and dominates the pattern of the whole; it also gives us the power to adhere at will either to spirit or to matter. Contrary to what might be expected from the terminology used—bottom, lowest, etc.— life in this physical state has very considerable advantages for anyone following a path of spiritual discipline (*sādhanā*). This is the world of effectuation or action (*Karma Bhūmi*), and unless we take advantage of our embodied state to raise ourselves above the compulsive power of our desires and perfect ourselves as men we shall certainly not be able to do so after death.

Again, we might expect that, having achieved as much as is possible on this physical level, we should then pass upwards, conquering the problems of each level in turn, until, as the verse puts it, we win the fourth fruit of the fourth path of Knowledge. This is the type of spiritual progress envisaged by people who think overmuch in terms of cycles. The Teacher knows this, and it is as if he were teasing the *Lanoo*, or disciple, by deliberately confusing the fourth spoke of the cyclic wheel with the fourth path of knowledge, for though the two have some connection they belong to scales of quite different dimensions.

These Four Paths are known to Buddhists under the names of *Srotāpanna*, he who has arrived at the Stream; *Sakridā-gāmin*, he who returns but once; *Anāgāmin*, he who returns no more; and *Arhat*, the perfected; and each of them is further subdivided into four. Hence the reference in our text to the fourth or final fruit of the *Arhat* path which is the path of full knowledge. They have also been referred to in Theosophical writings as four Initiations, which indeed they are, since each

U

one of them marks the awakening of a new and higher grade of consciousness. Only when the fourth fruit of the *Arhat* path is gained does the disciple stand forth, a liberated soul, a master of the Wheel, a Teacher of gods and men.

It seems as if H.P.B., too, has enjoyed the joke, and, by leaving the remainder of the verse untranslated has kept secret the Key to the way out from the whole ponderous business of her Wheels, Chains, Globes, Rounds and Races, which is that when any man by virtue of great efforts reaches the fruit of the fourth path of Knowledge and becomes the *Arhat* he will comprehend, for he will see that his essential Self is not bound to the wheel of cyclic return.

Though the cycles of life-in-form go round and round unceasingly, yet he himself is not, and in truth never was, within those cycles, nor does he get older with their passing. He is the *Sthānu*, that which 'stands' beyond all cycles, the Being in which all cycles go their way, the mystic centre of the Wheel of Life round which all things turn yet which itself moves not. The Wheels revolve, the Cycles come and go unceasingly, but not for him.

> 'No need hath such to live as ye name life;
> That which began in him when he began
> Is finished; he hath wrought the purpose through
> Of what did make him Man.[1]'

For him are true the triumphant words of the Buddha:

> 'Countless and sorrowful the births that I have wandered through, seeking the Builder of these Houses of Life. Now art thou seen, O Builder. Never again shalt thou build House for me. Broken are all the beams and sundered lies the ridge-pole. My mind is set on the Eternal; extinguished is all Thirst.[2]'

There are many people who reject the path to this world-

[1] *The Light of Asia.*
[2] *Dhammapada*, 153 & 154.

transcending Knowledge as if it were altogether too high and dry for them. They prefer to remain within the Cycle, always looking ahead for the coming of the new *Avatāra*, the second coming of the Christ, the next Buddha, the Messiah, the end of the world, Armageddon, the Supramental Descent, the Seventh Round—the list could be extended indefinitely, and none of these events have ever come in the expected manner. Such people believe that they, with the followers of their faith, will be redeemed by a particular event in time; and they fail to see that what comes in time must also go in time.

Nevertheless, perhaps even such an expectation of the impossible is better than the mere intellectual perception, unsupported by action, of,the truth of this transcendental path. This is where the connection lies between the fourth wheel and the fourth path, because the knowledge of the non-identification of man's Self with his body has to be won and effectively experienced on every level of his being. It is only here, on this Fourth wheel, that the path to the transcendence of all wheels can be begun.

This is not to say that this fourth wheel of ours is the only sphere of experience in which effortful practice (*sādhanā*) of the contemplative way is possible. The *Anāgāmin*, he who returns no more, is the type of the traveller of the inner path who, while not having reached the goal, has achieved such a degree of human development that even after the death of his physical body he, unlike all other men, can yet act purposively, and thereby continue to follow his chosen path without the need of returning to birth.

The cycles from which we seek freedom are not, however, the cycles of planets, stars and galaxies, nor of social, intellectual and technological progress, nor even of death and rebirth. All these are like milestones along the path we travel and mark our position on the road's interminable length. Nothing outside ourselves is the cause of our bondage, therefore we are not bound by the seven states of material experience, represented by the seven wheels, so much as we are by the modes of the psyche corresponding to the lower four Cosmic levels. These latter are the background and driving mechanism both of the material universe and of our own being. Our problem is, therefore, to find the fulcrum point within ourselves by virtue of whose presence the driving mechanism is able to move us, and whose discovery will enable us to separate self from not-self.

Basically this point is the ego-centre, the false assertion of independent will. But in stating this we have said nothing plainly meaningful, for very few of us have any direct comprehension of what is meant by the true Self or the false. We have so identified ourselves with our automatisms that they constitute the limit of our lives. We live within a small spiral of mechanically habitual and repetitive patterns of thinking, feeling and acting, with our animal heredity of instinct replacing the higher human intuition. Inside this endlessly extended spiral we spend our lives, treasuring as most precious the very mechanisms that shut us in. Sometimes, because the mind is free in its essence, it breaks its bonds and ranges free, but when it returns with its illicit findings, they have to be rendered harmless lest they should disturb our basic assumption that we are here to enjoy ourselves—an assumption that no natural or man-made catastrophe, however horrible, seems able to shake. We have become the spiral of self-referred events, and within this spiraline course we sleep and wake from day to day—if our waking may be graced by that name. When we die, we leave behind only the physical element of the mechanism and, after a short time of rest, take up another physical body as the vehicle of our mechanical integration.

Our course after death in such circumstances is not a high flight into the sphere of the true Self but lies on a lower orbit on which the subtle mechanisms of our habit integrations never leave us. Because of this we never really die and are therefore never really reborn. Like snakes we shed a skin only to gain another. We have become automatons; and so long as we continue to identify ourselves with the same habitual and mechanical patterns of behaviour they will never leave us. Incarnated in the body of habit, we travel through one material rebirth after another. Indeed, it is the false self, or ego-centre, in man which is more truly the bottom of the universe than is the 'matter' of his environment. For matter, in whatever state, is a reflection of some aspect of the divine harmony, whereas the lower or false self contrarily asserts its eccentric separateness from the harmony, and, like a cancerous growth, adds to itself from the psychic energies derived from sense experience, energies which are properly the nutriment of the soul.

And so we plunge from Air to Earth and back again, cultivating the fields of sense experience. There is no lack of guides whose voices urge us to leave this repetitious procedure, if we would but listen to them. They urge us to pass from the study of the outer worlds of sense to the study of the inner truths. Then the cyclic power which imprisons us within the coils of our personalities will unwind itself and, in its aspect of redeemer, will lead us out from the cycle of birth and death, out from between the earth and water of the Matrix, out into the blissful Light of the Spirit.

Either we must 'calculate' our true and time-transcending position amongst the cycles, or we shall be compelled to add birth to birth in an endless series of ultimately purposeless repetitions.

No mere nostalgia of the soul brings liberation from the compulsion of the cyclic ascents and descents which are the reincarnations of man. Nostalgia is an emotion of weakness, a longing for the past instead of an acceptance and transcendence of the present. So long as we reject the unpleasant component of experience, our memories will be distorted, the sorrow of life will fade into shadows, and the past will be suffused with a rosy but deceitful glow, childish dreams of the heaven that 'lies about us in our infancy'.

The soul whose dynamism of return is founded on nostalgic

longings for perfection no more wins his heaven worlds than does the exile when he returns to his home. Sooner or later the projected images of childhood fade and the stark reality beneath them looks out from the gaunt visage of age.

STANZA SEVEN

Being the last of seven Stanzas from
The Book of Dzyan

1. *Behold the beginning of sentient formless life. First, the Divine (vehicle), the one from the Mother-Spirit; then the Spiritual; the three from the one, the four from the one, and the five, from which the three, the five and the seven. These are the three-fold, the four-fold downward; the 'Mind-born' Sons of the first Lord; the Shining Seven. It is they who are thou, me, him, O Lanoo; they who watch over thee and thy mother Bhūmi (the earth).*

2. *The one ray multiplies the smaller rays. Life precedes form, and life survives the last atom (of form). Through the countless rays proceeds the life-ray, the one, like a thread through many beads.*

3. *When the one becomes two, the 'three-fold' appears, and the three are one; and it is our thread, O Lanoo, the heart of the man-plant called Saptaparna.*

4. *It is the root that never dies, the three-tongued flame of the four wicks. The wicks are the sparks that draw from the three-tongued flame shot out by the seven, their flame; the beams and sparks of one moon reflected in the running waves of all the rivers of earth.*

5. *The Spark hangs from the flame by the finest thread of Fohat. It journeys through the Seven Worlds of Māyā. It stops in the first and is a metal and stone; it passes into the second, and behold— a plant; the plant whirls through seven changes and becomes a sacred animal; from the combined attributes of these, manu, the*

thinker, is formed. Who forms him? The seven lives; and the one life. Who completes him? The five-fold Lha. And who perfects the last body? Fish, Sin, and Soma.

6. *From the first-born the thread between the Silent Watcher and his Shadow becomes more strong and radiant with every change. The morning sunlight has changed into noon-day glory. . . .*

7. *'This is thy present wheel', said the Flame to the Spark. 'Thou art myself, my image and my shadow. I have clothed myself in thee, and thou art my Vāhan (vehicle) to the day "Be with us", when thou shalt re-become myself and others, thyself and me.' Then the Builders, having donned their first clothing, descend on radiant earth and reign over men—who are themselves. . . .*

LIFE

Up to this point the Stanzas have been telling us of the structural cross-beaming of the great seven storeyed building which is the universe. The idea of solidity has been exteriorised as the Element of Earth, an Earth which is the external garment of energy worn by the Sparks of divine awareness and which carries the impress of the empatterning powers of the seven Archetypes.

The first verse of this seventh and last of the Cosmogonic Stanzas is a recapitulation of the whole process up to this point. Its purpose is to remind us of all that has gone before and to stress that the life which is so obviously present in our bodies, but which seems so lacking in the mineral substance of our earth, is in fact inherent in every level of the universe and in every atom in existence. From top to bottom the universe is living being.

The stanza then goes on to distinguish between those aspects of the cosmic pattern which are man's self-conscious essence, and those which belong to his form. The stages by which this living process gives rise to man's psycho-physical vehicle are only summarised. their fuller treatment being reserved for the second set of stanzas on Anthropogenesis.

(1) *Behold the beginning of sentient formless life. First, the Divine (vehicle), the one from the Mother-Spirit; then the Spiritual; the three from the one, the four from the one, and the five, from which the three, the five and the seven. These are the three-fold, the four-fold downward; the 'Mind born' Sons of the first Lord; the Shining Seven. It is they who are thou, me, him, O Lanoo; they who watch over thee and thy mother Bhūmi (the earth).*

The Life of which this stanza speaks originates, like all else, in the Ever-Darkness. It is the inherent power in the Absolute Godhead to evolve, to grow, to develop and to live. It is 'sentient' because life and consciousness are inseparable; and it is 'formless' because neither can it become objective to the senses, nor is it in itself the forms to which it gives rise and which it invests.

'Life', we were told, 'pulsated unconscious in Universal Space' (I. 8); but, as we have pointed out, this 'unconsciousness' is not to be understood as a dull insensitivity. The Life of the Great Mother, the Matrix, is only unconscious in the sense that it does not know, not in the sense that it does not feel. And it is this throbbing, sensitive life that infuses every Spark or focal centre in existence, from the atom to man's psychic being.

The verse takes us first to 'the Divine', the first 'Divine World' (V. 4), the 'One Egg' (II. 3), which is the limited Space of creation marked out by the Ray in the unlimited Matrix. This is 'the One from the Mother-Spirit', and this is 'the Ocean of Life' (III. 4).

Then comes the 'Spiritual', the second 'Divine' World (V. 4), the Spiritual or *Arūpa* universe, filled with the multitudes of archetypally ordered Sparks and Energies. The primary pattern of the Spiritual 'World' is, as we have seen, the trinity of conscious modes, the Three, their complementary, four spatial qualities, the Four, and the fivefold qualities which characterise the sensible universe, the Five. These are the qualities exteriorised by the Three, Five, and Seven 'strides' of Fohat (V. 2), to become the conjoined 'Threefold, Fourfold', consciousness-in-form, 'downward' into the world of externalised things, 'things' which are born of the Universal Mind, the Mind of the first Lord *Svabhāvat* (IV. 5).

The differentiated qualities of the outer universe of form derive from the seven archetypes which are now shining outwardly as the effectuating powers or 'Fighters' (IV. 5). And it is these 'Shining Seven' which, like the 'Planets' of antiquity or their other symbol the seven stars of the constellation Ursa Major (*Saptarshi*), 'are' the multiple phenomena of existence, 'Thou, I, He'.

We are accustomed to apply the personal pronouns only to man; but the manifest universe is the body of Divine Man, it is personal through and through. In the last verse of this stanza the Primordial Flame is represented as saying to the Spark: 'Thou (the Spark) are myself (I), my image (He), and my shadow (It)'—the final illusory 'It' with which we think to condemn a 'thing' to insentience.

The same seven powers that watch over 'thee' also watch over the earth (*Bhūmi*) which is our 'mother' in the sense that it is the material source of our forms. On whatever level of our embodied being the same controlling powers preside over the phenomena of experience, for every grade of Spark is 'subject to and the servant of' each of the Seven (IV. 4).

This phrase 'to preside over' seems at once to take us back to a world in which certain Gods presided over market-places and others over battle-fields, an idea long supposed to have been abandoned as empty superstition. Nevertheless there *are* Gods, Angels or Divine presiding powers, both of market-places and of battle-fields, Gods, in fact, having a special and controlling relationship to all the phenomena of the Cosmos. Such Gods are entirely real; and the phenomena we know, as well as many more that we do not, owe their being and their peculiar form to the presidency or participation of those Gods.

Moreover it is on a knowledge of the Gods concerned in any given object or event that practical occultism depends for its power.

(2) *The one ray multiplies the smaller rays. Life precedes form, and life survives the last atom (of form). Through the countless rays proceeds the life-ray, the one, like a thread through many beads.*

In Stanza III. 3 the One Ray of Light dropped into the Mother-Deep, and in Stanza IV we saw how the One became the Many—'The one ray multiplies the smaller rays', or, as Stanza V. 6 puts it, 'From One Light Seven Lights; from each of the Seven, seven times seven Lights.' The essential unity of the Ray of the Father-Light, by interaction with the potential multiplicity of the Matrix, produces the many rays. And just as these countless rays are united on the one hand by the unity of the Father-Light which shines in them all, like the light of the one sun falling on different drops of dew, so on the other hand they are united by the life of the Mother which throbs in their hearts: the 'countless' Sons (IV. 6) 'expand and contract through their own Selves and Hearts' (III. 11).

These countless 'rays' are the metaphysical connections between each 'Spark' and the 'Parent Flame'. We must not allow the concrete symbols of the 'ray' and the 'thread' to mislead us into thinking in terms of such subtle-physical concretions as 'astral cords'. The 'Flame' to which each 'Spark' is linked has not got a spatial location like an astronomical sun, but is the universal background of metaphysical 'Light', the 'shoreless sea of Fire' of Stanza III. 7. Because each 'Spark' is a focus in that sea of Light, its connection is referred to as a 'ray'.

There are not two different sorts of 'ray', one of consciousness and the other of life, but there are two aspects to each 'ray' which are only theoretically separable. The separate 'rays' are derivatives of the primal Father and Mother poles of the universe, consciousness and life, and so carry both qualities to manifestation.

The symbol of many beads on a single thread is often used in illustration of the series of human reincarnations, but in this verse the reference is to the essential unity of the living light which shines in every focus, vortex, or organisation in the light, linking each to every other in a single harmony of being.

Life indeed both precedes form and survives the last differentiated atom or monadic integration. The whole cosmos is living with a life that is independent of the differentiations of forms to which it gives birth. When we say that a thing dies, we mean only that a particular mode of life has withdrawn or ceased to manifest; but its ceasing to manifest no more means that the life has ceased to be than the water of a dew-drop ceases to be when it evaporates in the sunlight.

Increasingly the material sciences teach us that life is a function of our physical bodies, something whose existence is entirely bound up with them, something which vanishes utterly with their destruction. This view is contrary to the mass of human experience. All humanity, 'from China to Peru', has felt that life is not a function of the body but something separate and beyond it. This feeling has sometimes found expression in the abstract symbols of philosophy, sometimes only in the concrete symbols of ritual cult and worship, but in all cases the symbols, whether abstract or concrete, have been but the expression of a knowledge which is none the less real because it is not mediated for us by our physical senses. Men in general may not have known exactly how or why life was thus independent, and their various philosophies were largely attempts to give some account of that how and why; but that it is independent has, we repeat, always been a matter of knowledge to the human psyche. Has been? No, it still is. The psyche knows now, as it has always known, that life is no mere function of physical bodies but is something transcendent and immortal. The psyche knows it; it is only the ego-mind which, by limiting itself in the interests of gaining command over the external physical world, has shut its eyes to a knowledge inherent in that of which it is itself a part.

The methodology of modern science, a methodology of great and undoubted power in its own field, depends first and foremost on the abstraction of and emphasis on certain aspects of the totality of our experience. Nothing that cannot be caught in the meshes of the scientific net is allowed to have any reality, and it is only very recently that a few scientists and philosophers have begun to see that what we catch in the waters of the universe depends on the type of nets with which we fish. Whales are not caught in shrimping nets nor tadpoles in deep sea trawls, and their absence from these inappropriate snares in no way affords a proof of their non-existence. Scientists catch their fish and put them to most spectacular uses, but they should not proceed, as they so often do, to disqualify other fishers and their catches because their findings do not, and cannot rightly be expected to, appear in the scientific nets.

The worst of it is that the practical applications of the discoveries of science, ethically dubious though many of them are, hold out such promises of freedom from physical hardship to a comfort-loving and somewhat frivolous world that people are led to take scientists at their own exaggerated evaluation and their methodology as the only rational approach to reality for the practical man. But the 'practical man' is himself an abstraction if not a myth. Man does *not* live by bread alone, and it is emphatically true that the road of science, shut off from the wider reality by the walls of methodological dogma, straight with the ruled straightness of all-dominating intellect, broad with the dead breadth of asphalt, and clean with the sterile cleanliness of a modern hospital, is a road that is heading straight for the disaster of racial neurosis, a neurosis whose first stages we are now beginning to see all round us.

Demon est deus inversus. The Gods whom we refuse to worship in their bright forms stalk the earth in grim and horrid shapes, so that the indifference to mere bodily life which should result from inner knowledge reappears amongst us in the form of callous brutality, and bodies are fanatically sacrificed in millions upon the altars of our selfishly chosen aims. Never can man for long remain content in the pursuit of mere ease and physical security. If we will not sacrifice our comfort to the bright Gods, those Gods in their dark, hideous and negative forms will wrench it from us, leaving us in misery. Nor should we raise useless cries of blame, for those Gods are not privileged beings who

> 'sit and smile in secret looking over wasted lands, plague and famine, blight and earthquake, sinking ships and praying hands'.[1]

Seated in our hearts, our brains, our feelings and our bodies, yes, even in our bones, nerves and muscles, in every level and sub-level of our complex many-mansioned being, they are our very selves. 'It is they who are thou, I and he, O Lanoo.' It is they who from within our human eyes, timid with fore-knowledge of death, gaze forth with a divine unwinking serenity to which joy and sorrow, life and death, are but a universal warp and woof, a serenity from which we are apt to shrink back in fear when we catch a glimpse of its deific calm, darkly showing within the eyes of some fellow being.

(3) *When the one becomes two, the 'three-fold' appears, and the three are one; and it is our thread, O Lanoo, the heart of the man-plant called Saptaparna.*

When the One Darkness manifests the two poles, the third term appears as the relationship between them. These three unite as the triune root of self-consciousness, the Three that are One, the great and all-embracing Mind of the universe (*Mahat Ātman*), 'the Three that in the world of form have lost their name'.[2]

The bright consciousness of the Three-in-one is the living

---

[1] Tennyson's *Lotus Eaters*.
[2] *The Voice of the Silence*

Light, the one and only Light that lights the whole manifested universe. It shines in the heart of every atom and every organisation of atoms, giving them their existent being; and in that its eternal presence holds together the succession of transient patterns, giving them their continuity, it is called the Thread.

The triune Light shines in every atom, but the full power of understanding cannot manifest in one 'Element'. Indeed, Understanding in itself can scarcely come to manifestation. It is rather that Mind needs a vehicle through which to achieve the understanding of itself; and it is its striving towards this achievement through its own living process that gives rise to man—the seven-leaved man-plant (*Saptaparna*).

In the 'heart' of the man-plant the self-conscious integration of Mind begins to shine in all its glory—begins, for the incandescent brightness of man's out-turned intellect is only a shadowing forth of the divine perfection of which he is capable. In the heart of our being, our one true Self, is the power of Divine Mind striving towards perfect self-knowledge, the power of love seeking its fulfilment.

The 'seven-leaved' plant, however, is the psycho-physical organism which grows or evolves, forced upwards towards the Light by the living power within its heart. It is seven-leaved because each of the 'seven' macrocosmic principles contributes its quality to the microcosm which is man.

The man-*plant* is thus not the central focus of man's self-consciousness, but the integration of living cosmic powers which make up the sheaths, vehicles or garments worn by the Self. When, for instance, we say that we are identified with our physical bodies, we do not mean to imply that we are subjectively united with the experiencing centres of the minerals, cells, and even complete organs, all of which contribute to the totality of our physical bodies. The same is true of corresponding structures on more subtle levels of being. These lesser integrations belong to their respective macrocosmic levels and scales, but collectively they form a living integration or 'plant'.

The difference between the 'man-plant' and its 'heart' may be understood in reference to the terms used in the preceding stanzas. The 'plant' or psycho-physical organism of man is built up of the six grades of Sparks of awareness, those Armies of the Sons of Light (V. 4), which stood at the 'Angles'. The 'heart' is then the seventh and central grade of Spark, the very self-hood of the divine Son.

Can we identify the seven leaves of the man-plant, the major contributions of the macrocosmic principles to our psycho-physical organism?

In the first place, we have already seen that the individual Ego is a focal point or differentiation in the Universal Mind. We have also seen that the Universal Mind is a three-in-one; its focal differentiations, then, each of them a point-mirror of the whole, will reflect this threefold structure. In other words, the human Monad is a trinity in correlation with the Cosmic Principles referred to as Father, Mother and Son. This is the self-conscious 'heart' of the man-plant to which all the modes of experience are related. But the leaves or human faculties, though deriving from and reflecting the same three principles, are the psychic determinants governing both the modes of perception and the structures which form the avenues of perception.

The human correlate of the Cosmic Father is our outward-looking will to live, to seek experience, to know, to conquer, to possess, to create and to transcend.

The Mother appears as those modes of the psyche which are receptive to and retentive of any inflow, whether coming from the supra-human levels or from the manifest field of experience. To this we owe the psychic receptivity upon which sense perception depends, the retention of sense data as memory, and the reproduction of memory images. The direct apprehension of knowledge by the 'feminine' intuition arises from this impressionable receptivity. So far from being a dubiously attested 'supernormal' faculty, intuition is the very ground of knowing to which it is as fundamental as is breathing to life. As a means of obtaining the inner knowledge it is, as Plotinus said, a faculty which all have, but few use.

As the relating factor between the Parental principles, the Son is responsible for all activity, whether intellectual, emotional, or physical. It gives both love and understanding, and it gives balance, harmony and reconciliation. As the macrocosmic focus of Mind, it is the principle by which we relate or order experience content into significant patterns, and, as such, is the root of what we term pure intellect. It is the synthetic or focal point of view itself, the point or atom called in the Upanishads 'smaller than the small', symbolically compared to the hundredth part of the tip of a hair, and yet a mirror focussing the whole. Its active function of thinking is not the gaining of new experience—that, on one level or another, is the function of intuition—but the relating of the elements of experience, the perceiving of their patterns, and the ordering of them into accord with our perception of archetypal patterns.

We have now to deal with the four lower principles which themselves arise, as we have seen, from the interrelations of the higher Three.

Just as the 'Ray' of the Father-Light limited and defined the area of operation within the Matrix, so our individual 'rays', our monadic natures, give us the faculty of selective attention which, by setting a limit to our activities, permits us to gain particular knowledge or to achieve particular effects.

From this faculty of selective attention comes our ability to differentiate between phenomena. Arising from this differentiation comes the unbalance in the desire forces of relationship which makes some forms seem attractive and others repulsive. Finally, these attractions and repulsions lead us to identify ourselves with particular forms. Thus we descend from the universal to the particular.

Such an analysis is, of course, but the barest outline abstracted from what is essentially a unity of experience. The man-plant

X

comprises the totality of man's manifest being, but it is these unseen, impalpable, psychic components which are truly of greater significance than their visible 'shadows'. Rarely, very rarely, does the man-plant blossom—as rarely as the mythical *Udumbara* tree.

We repeat that the man-plant is the totality of man's psycho-physical organism, and its leaves are most importantly the modes of truly human experience. It would be only too easy to relate the seven leaves to any of the well-known symbolic lists of vehicles, sheaths, envelopes and bodies—auric, mental, astral, etheric, etc. We must at least *try* to relate our symbols to common experience and avoid, as far as is possible, the lure of exotic terminology.

The 'Thread' of this stanza has reference to the Vedāntic symbol of the Thread-Self (*Sutrātman*), a controversial symbol with at least two planes of application. On the plane of the Universal Mind there is indeed one universal Light that sweeps through all beings as the wind sweeps through a pine forest. That is the higher Thread-Self, the one Self of all which gives continuity to all existing things. But there is also the lower derivative of this Thread which represents the continuity of experience related to a particular Spark or focus in the universal awareness.

This latter thread of continuity has particular bearing on the connection between the series of human incarnations. It represents, as we have said, the continuity or identity of a particular Spark—in this case the self-conscious heart of the man-plant, 'This is our thread, O Lanoo'. Yet in considering the identity of a particular Spark, we are faced with the para-doxical difficulty that there is no means of differentiating be-tween points in the universal awareness except with regard to the form series to which they are related. This does not mean, however, that there are no separate selves. Notwith-standing the all-embracing unity of the One Self, it remains true that on this physical level of experience your yesterday is strung on a different thread from mine; and similarly in the intermediate worlds, your previous incarnation is a bead on a garland that is different from mine.

The denial of the doctrine of the Thread-Self, said to have been pronounced by the Buddha, is not a denial of the fact of reincarnation but is directed against the false notion of a hard, unchangeable and eternally separate core of ego substance which might pass from one body to another, itself unchanged. That successive lives were connected in a thread or stream was not only never denied by the Buddha but was positively affirmed in many ways. In some Buddhist schools, indeed, this very 'Thread' appears under the designation *santāna*.

It is important to remember that our triple-aspected Mind, higher Self, individuality, permanent ego, or *Jīva*, is not a thing-in-itself but a focus of experience. The focus is individual, the experience is not. The human monad is thus not something eternally separate and shut off from its fellows, for behind them all is the unity of the Light and of the Wisdom. Nevertheless, like its cosmic correlate the Universal Mind, it is aeonic in duration, lasting, unless deliberately dissolved, throughout the Cosmic Day. It is the essential principle of individuation, the archetypal 'I', the Kantian transcendental self or unity of apperception. It is the central neck of the hour glass through which the sands of experience have to travel on their way up or down. By way of illustration we may observe that the matter of my physical body is one and, even in a certain sense, continuous with that of yours. It is only differentiated by the points of reference, you or me. So it is with the content of the Universal Mind which is one in essence and common to all, though similarly differentiated by reference.

(4) *It is the root that never dies, the three-tongued flame of the four wicks. The wicks are the sparks that draw from the three-tongued flame shot out by the seven, their flame; the beams and sparks of one moon reflected in the running waves of all the rivers of earth.*

Following on from the last verse we read that it, the threefold thread, is the root that never dies: 'The root of life was in every drop of the ocean of immortality' (III. 6). We must remember here that 'immortality' means duration throughout the aeonic period of manifestation. Every spark of the parent flame is in this sense immortal so long as the Cosmic Father-Mother duality maintains the web of power which is the manifest universe. Every existent Spark is maintained by the threefold thread which binds it to the universal background. The vortices of form around each Spark may change; the Spark as a focus may even be dissolved within the all-pervading sea of Light; but the triune Light which lights all Sparks is undying.

The simile of the spark must not be pressed too far. The separateness of the cosmic 'Spark' is not like that of a spark shot out from a bonfire—drifting away to be extinguished in the night. Every focus in the universal Light feels itself to be separated because the divine self-affirmation of the Logos is forcing it to look outwards into the vortices of form; thus it ceases to pay attention to the inner unity.

The lower or false ego-centre in man, the empirical ego, is not a separate entity, something objectively distinct, but is a mode of operation by and in Mind. The Self-affirmatory outward seeking of the Father-Light becomes the self-assertive search for personal advantage. Without this assertion there could have been no human progress. Indeed, the truly negative aspect of the ego only appears when it is used both in denial of universal spiritual values and in the preservation of the personality with the implied intention of gaining ego-immortality.

We are here using the word personality in the sense of the Latin *persona*, a mask—the mask of human attributes which surround the Spark of divine Mind and with which the Spark becomes identified. This use is not intended to deny validity to the other and higher application of personality to divinity when it is intended to evoke the sense of that plenum of life.

intelligence, power, beauty, and, above all, love, whose integral manifestation is most brightly constellated in the person of man.

Egotistic self-identification with concrete form seems to have led some people to think, by contrast, of the higher Self as a sort of invisible balloon attached to the backs of our necks by a fragile cord, a radiant though rather blasé being which is apt to give us up as a bad job and float off in search of a more promising anchorage. It is hardly necessary to say that this is nonsense, though the sort of nonsense that possibly derives from some misunderstood facts about human evolution. Dominated by separative desire we are our lower selves. Dominated by our perception of the universal harmony we are our higher selves. And this is as true of our physically embodied state as it is of any subtle state of being. Shining in us all, as it shines in all things, is the inseparate Light of Lights.

The three-tongued flame, the triune flame of the Universal Mind, is said to be shot out by the Seven—'The Primordial Seven, the first seven breaths of the Dragon of Wisdom' (V. 1). The flame thus carries the impression of the seven archetypal differentiations, with the result that the Sparks of that flame are similarly impressed. The Sparks then transfer those impressions on to the vortices of energy with which they are surrounded. It is in this sense that the Sparks act as wicks to draw the patterns of the archetypal flame into the four lower levels of form; 'The three-tongued flame of the four wicks'. Thus are produced the atomic (in the psychic sense) centres of the threefold consciousness on each of the four levels and on each scale. And thus does the universe come to be filled with lives.

Let us not concern ourselves with the dizzying vistas of macrocosmic scales and subscales to which these descending patterns give rise in the manifest universe. Their study is seldom rewarding, for it tends to make one base one's certainty on ephemeral sense data instead of on the inner and undying certainty of the heart.

It is enough to say that, like the World Tree of the Upanishads, the Seven-leaved Man-plant extends its ramifications throughout the whole gamut of worlds. Our being, feeble and insignificant as it seems, imprisoned here within the tomb of the body, extends in reality through the countless mansions of a universe of which what is known to our astronomers is but a surface film. Seated within this wretched bag of skin our hands reach out and grasp the furthest stars. In each sensation planets are concerned and in our hearts there shines the Sun of Suns.

Wherever and in whatsoever worlds man may be dwelling, his fundamental constitution is the same. There will be the three-tongued flame of his triple monad and the four wicks of his lower principles which draw forth and burn with that flame. As to his scale and placing we shall have more to say in the next verse. Here we are only to note that in all cases he will have his seven principles derived from the Cosmic Elements, the Inner Seven, shining through, and inherent in the Light of the Father, the Master-Light of all our Day.

In all separate vortices of form it is the same central subjective Light that shines, and therefore it is that the Flame burning in the wicks of our various bodies is likened to the one Moon whose beams are reflected in the rivers of earth, those running streams of forms, ceaselessly flowing and giving place to new ones in accordance with the causal or *kārmic* law.

Just as the image of the moon remains constant in the midst of the ever-flowing waters, so does the one Light shine steadily within the changing forms. And just as it is the same moon that is reflected in any number of rivers, so it is the same Light that shines within the countless streams of form that we term living beings.

It is for this reason that the Buddha so strenuously denied that the Light of consciousness (*Vijnāna*) formed any sort of concrete soul which could be said to transmigrate from one life to the next. If a river plunges through a subterranean tunnel to reappear at the other end of it, the image of the moon reflected in its waters has not travelled with it; nor, on the other hand, is it the light of a different moon from that which shone on it before entering the tunnel. It is in this sense that a trans-migrating soul is denied. The stream of form, both before and after the tunnel of death, though changing at every moment, is one in virtue of the *kārmic* pattern which links its successive phases. The Moon too is one, one in its own unitary nature.

If we look deep into the eyes of any of our fellow beings, there, in the depths, the same light is shining, the only Light that has ever shone or will ever shine anywhere at all. It is for this reason that the inner teaching insists so strongly that the disciple must banish all sense of his own separateness from others, since it is only when he can feel himself rooted in that one Light that he will attain his true being. Till then he is only what Hermes termed a 'procession of Fate', winding his slow way through the worlds, experiencing joy and sorrow as the road is rough or smooth.

(5) *The Spark hangs from the flame by the finest thread of Fohat. It journeys through the Seven Worlds of Māyā. It stops in the first and is a metal and a stone; it passes into the second, and behold—a plant; the plant whirls through seven changes and becomes a sacred animal; from the combined attributes of these, manu, the thinker, is formed. Who forms him? The seven lives; and the one life. Who completes him? The five-fold Lha. And who perfects the last body? Fish, Sin and Soma.*

As we saw in the preceding verse, the Sparks are always in-wardly united to the universal background by the thread of creative energy which flows through and sustains them. They 'hang' or depend upon this Fohatic power for their existence. Note that the verse uses the term Spark in the singular, for the journey of all the Sparks is in fact the journey of the one Spark, the Son or Divine Mind.

The seven worlds of *Māyā* are the same as the seven small Wheels of Stanza VI. 3, 'one giving birth to another'. When the Sparks are separated by the energetic vortices which surround them, the periphery of each vortex, its outward appearance, seems to be a thing in itself. This seemingly independent reality of the rim of the vortex is the illusion (*Māyā*).

The first world of *Māyā* is approximately the Fiery Dust of Stanza VI. 4, which Fohat builds into 'balls of fire'. These 'Worlds' or 'Wheels' give birth to each other most significantly in the sense that each stage in the evolution of forms arises from the living substance of the worlds below it. This is the journey of the Spark: into form, through form, and finally beyond form. It travels through Time and Space, descending from Spirit into Matter and ascending again to Spirit in its long pilgrimage of self discovery. The pauses in the journey are the periods of rest between the outbursts of creative energy. During these pauses the free energy which has been thrust into the level is assimilated in the production of relatively stable forms. These periods of 'whirling change' occur at each stage of the process and not only at the one mentioned in the verse.

As we have seen, the first outrush of circling energy produces the clouds of fiery dust. Then comes the first pause, the first of the 'Seven Eternities' (VI. 4), while the energy–filled clouds pass through the many whirling changes which result in a mineral universe, 'a Metal and a Stone'.

This distinction between metal and stone is primarily symbolic. To the whole ancient world the veins of shining metal seemed to have grown in the body of the dull rock. The very earth was felt to be alive and to have given birth to metals from her womb. The earth is indeed alive, for in the heart of every womb-like vortex of the atoms there shines a spark of life itself, a 'metal' in the heart of every 'stone'. The 'atoms' are a myriad living wombs within which the seed of life is growing. The invisible powers of the higher Sparks descend into every vortex and the visible periphery of form, the world of illusion, vibrates and throbs in harmony with the life of all. Thus the descending forces of life thrust outwards from the centre of all things.

The next pulsation or increment of energy brings an expression of the next higher order in the scale of being. This is represented by the Plant, an order of life which is able to build up and sustain its forms directly from the mineral world. How the first order of plant life came into being is a matter of no greater and no lesser significance than how the first atom, the first universe, or the first man came into being. The same forces which brought the mineral atom into being have brought plants, animals and men into being, and the same spiritual power that shines with incandescent brightness in the minds of men glows luminously in the hearts of atoms. But neither the Self of man nor the heart of the atom is 'material'; both are sentient, both are formless, and both are living. Every part of the universe is interdependent with every other part, and all are bound together into a meaningful whole by the purposeful and directed journey of the Spark from potential to actual understanding of its selfhood.

The components which are built into the cells of plants derive from mineral substances; but neither the power of life which thrusts down roots into the soil and thrusts up stems and leaves into the sunlight and air, nor the factors which determine the qualities of form, are in themselves mineral or even physical. These latter determinants no doubt have their physical correlates in seeds which, if interfered with, can produce mutations, but this does not alter the fact that those physical correlates had first to be produced by the unaided forces of life, forces which do not depend upon chance occurrences for their operation.

Let us again repeat the dictum of Stanza IV. 4: 'The Sparks of the Seven are subject to and the servants of . . .' all seven of the seven Archetypes. And let us also recall that every Spark of the divine Fire, no matter to what level its predominant characteristics belong, has its central heart or nucleus of awareness, a 'mental' content of ideal archetypal pattern, an impressionable surround of desire energy into which the pattern is projected, and the peripheral effects of the pattern which, in combination with other such organisations, may become apparent to sense perception.

This is the general pattern of the manifestation of all the orders of existent being. The determining patterns and their subtle correlates precede the production of physical forms. This does not mean, as some people have thought, that the inner worlds are enlarged and more exciting versions of this one. The original 'Plant' did not condense, full grown, from a misty counterpart some millions of years ago any more than a Californian Redwood tree did some thousands of years ago. Yet both sprang from patterns in the Divine Mind, just as Waterloo bridge sprang from the mind of its architect before its arches could spring from the banks of the Thames. The flows of life are directed by their prior patterns, and the resulting forms are sensible expressions of parts of the Divine Wisdom.

It is also necessary to note that the present ability of a highly integrated man to retain a large proportion of his conscious functions in the intermediate world of after-death does not mean that the men who now make up the human race were in a similar condition before their original descent into physical birth. We repeat that mankind in general began with a potentiality of growth into self-conscious manhood. If we are so foolish as to take mythological accounts of man's descent at their face value, we must believe that the history of the human race has run contrary to the whole of anthropological and evolutionary evidence. Nothing is to be gained by dreaming of the heaven that lay around us in our racial infancy. Our racial childhood was a bitter struggle in which we ourselves took part, and we have grown because conditions forced us to grow or perish. To some extent conditions continue to force us. When we fought together as boys we could do little more than give or get a black eye or a bloody nose, but now the race has come to manhood and, like men, we find weapons in our hands that can do irreparable harm. Again we must grow or perish, and our growth must be intentionally directed towards that greater maturity of the Spirit through which our still potential manhood can be made actual.

The Plant is now said to whirl through seven changes and become a Sacred Animal. The evolutionary 'changes' produce an animal organism capable of housing the Sons of the central Light, the self-conscious Light of Divine Mind. Cabbage-like though many of us are, the Stanzas are not implying that the body of man is a walking vegetable, nor are the 'seven changes' to be referred merely to the evolution of botanical species. Animals are as much (and as little) distinct from plants as are plants from minerals, yet the evolution of both animals and plants has gone on hand in hand in a way that the evolution of the mineral earth has not. The conditions under which the mineral elements were formed would seem to be entirely prohibitive to the production of plant and animal cells, but, given the proper environment, both orders of form spring up within a relatively short interval. Their evolution is interdependent, for, in one way or another, they feed upon each other; animals upon both animals and plants, plants upon the residue of both. In this interchange of life we see the 'battles fought between the Creators and the Destroyers . . . the Seed appearing and reappearing constantly' (VI. 6).

There are thus two aspects to the evolution of physical forms: a descent of the spiritual hierarchy into increasing materiality, and a corresponding production of forms which ascend from below—forms whose apparent reality is a shadowy illusion when contrasted with the inner powers they clothe. Yet the structural forms have to be brought up to a sufficient proximity to man before they can carry the projection of the higher or more intellectual modes of desire. There must be a certain affinity between degrees of form and degrees of consciousness before the two can attract each other and so come to fruitful union.

These two aspects have interesting correspondences, for the 'metal' in the heart of the 'stone' can also be read as a symbol of the human monad or *Jiva* in its vehicle of separated individuality on the higher mental level. Firmly rooted in this individuality the 'Plant' then represents the branched or differentiated sense life of the lower mental vehicle which is associated with the plant-like structure of the nervous system. With roots above and branches below, the sense life stretches out into the warmth of the desire life, there to support and be supported by the warm red blood-flows of the animal nature. Thus we see how the physical plant on the ascending scale, with its seemingly miraculous power of transforming the 'dead' earth into organic tissue, comes to symbolise the power on the descending scale which links the inactive awareness of the Self to the desire life.

Again the two primal poles of being, Father-Light and Matrix, meet each other, now as the descending and ascending components of the material evolution on earth. Wherever the two components meet, we find a cyclic interchange of consciousness and form. The desire forces which ebb and flow between them first flow outwards, leaving an emptiness or privation that demands to be filled. The organisms from which it flows out are then driven outwards by hunger in search of forms which they devour and whose desire energy replaces what has been lost. Sometimes the desire energy ebbs slowly away in the sheer process of sustaining the organisms, sometimes it bursts out in creative activity, sometimes the hunger is for physical food, sometimes for sense stimuli. The modes vary according to their level and scale, but the energy is the one living energy of divine desire, Fohat, the swift Son of the Divine Sons.

From the combined attributes of all the powers that come to manifest existence 'Manu, the Thinker, is formed'. *Manu*,[1] the thinking creature, is man, the only thinker in the universe, the only existent being capable of truly rational thought. In this context, Manu refers to the total psycho-physical organism: the mind at one end of the scale, the body, including

---

[1] *Manu:* a Sanskrit word meaning: thinking, wise, intelligent. It is a derivative of the same root as *Manas*: mind, intellect, in its widest sense.

the brain, at the other, and between them the subtle intermediary vehicles of the sense powers, recorded memories, and
instinctive forces which link the mind to the body.

Lest the negative associations of the word should devalue
the image of man as the 'Thinker', let us recall the words of
Stanza V. 2: 'Fohat is the steed and Thought is the rider'—the
Thought of the Divine Mind. Without the divine shining of
mind the form of man remains 'an empty, senseless Shell'[1]
The whole range of subtle and gross vehicles of Mind are
the production of Fohat's circular errands (V. 2), the Small
Wheels (VI. 3) or organisations in the illusory worlds of
appearance. Man's struggle to develop his power of thought
and so to master his vehicles no doubt begins with the knitted
brows and heavy down-turned pondering expressed in Rodin's
crouched figure of the Thinker. But thought is not forever
bound to earth. Carried by the leaping power of Fohat, man's
thought, like the Divine Thought, can take 'seven strides
through the seven regions above' (V. 2). Then indeed he no
longer crouches over the problems of tribal culture or their
modern equivalents, but stands balanced between Heaven and
Earth, 'here a world and there a world'. Without the guiding
reins of thought, Fohat, the divine Eros, be he never so divine,
can do no more than run his circular errands round and round
the cyclic wheels of time. Guided, he is the liberator; unguided,
he gives bondage.

Yet, as we have asked before, to what are we bound and
from what and for what are we liberated? We are bound by
compulsive desire forces that flow through us and around us,
seeming to give value and reality to the myriads of apparently
separate things; and it is from this compulsion that we seek
liberation. But just as man's body without a mind is empty,
senseless and meaningless, an animal and not a man, so, if the
existent self of man reunites with the Divine Mind and passes
beyond the threshold of manifestation, there is no longer a
man. Only when Manu the Thinker is formed does man appear,

[1] S.D., II. *Anthropogenesis*, verse 17.

and only when the perfect balance between the thinker and the vehicle of his thought is achieved, can man be liberated from compulsion and yet remain as man.

Who, then, forms the Man? The Seven Lives, 'The Primordial Seven, the first seven breaths of the Dragon of Wisdom' (V. 1); and the One Life, the Breath of the Darkness. The One Life furnishes the dynamic evolutionary urge, the thrust which is behind all nature; while the Seven Lives, the archetypal differentiations of the One Life, sustain the seven Small Wheels of illusory appearances which are the grades or stages of evolution leading up to man's physical organism.

The Tibetan word *Lha* means a spirit or god, and here refers to the functional powers which complete the psycho-physical organisms. Though a detailed analysis may in fact reveal a more complicated structure of sense organs than the ancients suspected, the symbolic number five has always represented the major modes of the sense powers. To speak of these powers as spirits or gods is apt to be misleading to modern men who associate the words with super-human beings, but these non-personal modalities of living powers are just what the ancient world meant by 'gods'—powers which provide man with attributes, yet at the same time rule him by determining the extent of his functions. These are the *Adhishṭhātri devatā* of the Upanishads, allegorised in the *Kenopanishad*[1] as the gods who can do nothing without the Brahma-power of which they themselves have no knowledge—'He who sees with the eye, but the eye does not see'.[2]

The Seven Lives and the One Life are responsible for the structural elements of man's form. Filling the form and determining the pattern of its evolution as a vehicle of sense and intelligence are the powers of the psyche, the fivefold Lha. In the total organism thus produced there is nothing as yet to distinguish man from animal. There is no freedom to choose, for instance, between acceptance or rejection of glandular

---

[1] *Kenopanishad* III.
[2] *Brihadāraṇyaka Upanishad* III. vii. 18.

stimuli and instinctive habit patterns (conditioned reflexes), and no freedom of selective attention. There is no power of rational communication, no perception of ethical values, no self-awareness, and no intentional transcendence of limitations —no understanding, no perception of meaning, nothing but instinctual power-drives, nothing worthy of the name of man.

What, then, are the inner powers that raise the totality of man to perfection? The verse gives the answer in purely symbolic terms: 'Fish, Sin and Soma'.

'Fish' represents the vast multitudes of silvery forms to which the Matrix, the Ocean of Life, gives birth; each form, a reflection of the one Moon 'in the running waves of all the rivers of Earth' (VII. 4).

'Sin', the Chaldaean Moon God *en-zu* (or *zu-en*), means 'The Lord of Wisdom', the knowledge or Wisdom aspect of the Divine Mind. This is the Moon of whose reflection in the Waters of Life we have just spoken. It is the power which manifests the slow unfolding of the divine wisdom in four successive stages, the power which is indeed not the originator of its light but shines by the power of the Father-Light, the Light pole of the Ever-Darkness.

'Soma', the fluid pressed from the magic lunar herb of Vedic ritual, represents the intoxicating power of the divine desire which urges the 'gods' to manifestation. The same desire energy is responsible for the sense of separateness without which there can be no manifestation; and this is associated with the separate drops of Soma that descended from the filtering cloth, the same symbol as the separate drops of the Heavenly dew.

Fish, Sin and Soma are thus three aspects of one power, aspects which 'perfect' the last body of man. Without a form, man is an unidentifiable spark, merged in the sea of universal fire. Without understanding, man is an unperfected animal. And without the living power of desire, man is an inert lump.

Each of these three is in itself a triad, for all things derive from and correspond to the trinity of Father-Mother-Son.

This is the triple mystery that each initiate must solve before he can become the perfected adept: the mystery of the triple consciousness, the triple form, and the triple power.

It is indeed the triune spark of Divine Mind within us that makes us men. Our self-affirmation is a spark of his Self-affirmation, our knowledge is a spark of his Wisdom, and our humanity is a spark of his Compassion. As a universal principle, There in Divine Mind lies the root of personality. As a spark in man, There lies our still unattained perfection. The personal divinity as an existent reality is the Divine Man in whom potentiality has been perfected as actuality. All such Men are one, yet they have not become the One. They exist, though they are not visible to these outer eyes. Their being is indeed the greatest mystery.

It is theoretically possible for the human race to grow to spiritual maturity without the compassionate intervention of these liberated Seers, but in actual fact this is not what happens. Both racially and individually we owe an incalculable amount to those Lords of Wisdom who have guided us in our struggle to become man. Sometimes their promptings are felt in our hearts, sometimes they speak to us through the images of dream, rarely they accept the limitations of physical form and teach us directly in the world—teach us of our origins, our present being, and our path to perfection.

Here at last is Man, to whose evolution the totality of universal power has contributed. The lofty calmness of Himalayan peaks, the wide expanse of troubled oceans, the stability of earth, the leaping flames of fire, the soft caress of air, the blind gropings of plants, the ruthless savagery of beasts; sun, moon and stars, and all the vastness of space, all that we see and feel around us as separate elements of the macrocosmic harmony, all, all are in the microcosm of Man. Has not some mystic declared: 'Thou canst not behold the Sun unless he already dwells within they breast'?

Thus the Sons of God are 'born on the Fourth' (VI. 5) into the lower worlds of illusory appearance. At the fourth macrocosmic level, the level of individuation, they were born as separate individuals, and from there they descend to meet the upward evolving series of forms at the stage represented by the fourth of the seven small wheels. At the higher 'Fourth' the one great river of Life divided into many lives, just as a great life-giving river of the world, a Nile or a Ganges, divides at its delta into numerous smaller streams before it joins the lower waters of the sea. And this is perhaps the greatest illusion of all, that each little stream of life thinks itself separate from the others, each existing in its own right. It forgets that the fresh waters of its spiritual heredity descended from the snowy mountains and flowed across thousands of miles of plains as a single great stream. It forgets that the precious burden of fertility-giving silt it deposits along its path is not its own life energy but is a sacred trust for distribution to the river's lower reaches. It forgets that the salt waters, ebbing and flowing in the tidal creeks of its physical form, flood up from the sea of the Matrix and drain back into it, losing every trace of recognisable individuality. Lost in the confused windings of its channel in the hot and steamy worlds of desire, it forgets its source and forgets its goal and is overcome by the fevers which infest all such swampy regions —fevers giving rise to illusory sensations of heat and cold, lust and despair. These are the worlds of the opposites, the worlds of multiplicity, the worlds of desire and of the fever of life, where all is sensation and all is swiftly changing contrast. Osiris trapped in his measured coffin floats down the Nile to the delta. Joseph in his coat of many colours—seven colours worked by the fivefold Lha and given by the Father, the One Life—is sold into Egypt, the bodily tomb.

The soul is never truly of these levels, but, just as the *Soma* was known as 'the guest in the jar', so is the soul a guest in the lower worlds, entering them to give and to take, to give its life and to gain experience, to suffer and to cause suffering, to learn, to love, and to hate; finally to rediscover its forgotten origins and to return through solving the mystery of self-

Y

knowledge. For all desire is the desire for experience, and all experience is a passion, a suffering, an acceptance of stimuli. The soul must learn to accept both and to transcend both.

At the level of the soul's birth the creative urge is expansively unashamed, but, balancing the descent, the contractive ascent of the feminine pole of being seeks to enclose the experiencer within the restrictions and limitations of form. This contractive force is the origin of the shame which led Adam and Eve to hide the nakedness of their creativity behind the leaves of 'Plants', their first coverings of 'skin'. Thus the expansive urge to create comes to be associated with self-gain and pleasure while the restrictions of form are identified with loss and pain. The soul's sense of separateness, backed by the self-affirmation of the Father-Light and compelled by the force of the cosmic desire, leads it to seek its fulfilment, not in a self-abrogating acceptance of all experience, but in the pleasurable experiences of expansive creativity only—the desires to do more, to feel more, to possess more and to know more. It aims at self-gratification through the gaining of what is pleasurable and the avoidance of what is painful.

In these worlds of contrasting experience every action inevitably gives rise to its complementary reaction. This is not an arbitrary bit of morality imposed at the whim of an irate Father-God, but is an essential law of the cosmos maintaining the harmony of being. The poise of the whole may never be disturbed by the eccentric movement of one of the parts without compensating forces flowing in to correct the balance. When we give ourselves to mere pleasure seeking and we try to avoid the compensating effects, the unbalance we thus set up within ourselves dims the windows through which the light of Conscience—knowledge of the pattern of the divine harmony—shines in upon the soul. And in dimming that light we shut ourselves more securely into the tomb of the body. Thus the immature inner life is starved of the vitalising influences on which it depends, and finally dies of neglect.

Let us not undervalue the experience of suffering, for it is the ever-present incentive to progress; externally, for instance, in medicine and social order, inwardly in spurring us to rise above transient phenomena. In all the manifest worlds of form there is no escape from the duality of joys and sorrows. The heavens of unadulterated bliss and the hells of pure pain conceived by exoteric religion are structures of fantasy, projected images of one-sided human longings and the fears that shadow them. Here, our experience is a mixture of sensational extremes, and 'here' is always the position we occupy in any world of form, gross or subtle. The integral attainment cannot be achieved with only one part of ourselves. Every level of the cosmos has contributed to our being and each level faces us with a problem we have to solve. This is why, for instance, the conquering of physical pain with drugs leaves the ethical problem of pain untouched, and why G. I. Gurdjieff stressed the necessity of conscious labour and voluntary suffering if one is to tread the path of harmonious development.

Not even the man who attains the unitary vision of the Spirit is freed from the dual nature of experience until his whole being is blended with the ultimate source. So long as compassion persuades him to remain within the worlds of form he suffers, not, it is true, from egotistic identification with phenomena, but by virtue of his acceptance of our suffering as his own. For in his vision there is no essential distinction between himself and the selves that are enslaved to phenomena.

It is not being suggested that we should attempt to reverse the accepted order of things, neurotically seeking masochistic satisfaction in pain—that, in any case, would still be to seek sensual satisfaction. We have to find a poise which keeps us inwardly undisturbed by the attractions of promised pleasures on the one hand and the repulsions of expected sufferings on the other. This sought-for poise is no dully sluggish and unresponsive torpor; it is more akin to the deep waters of the sea that maintain their calm, no matter how much tumultuous frothing disturbs their surface.

We have already seen how the human monad identifying itself with the (mental) forms and caught by the outgoing tide of Desire-energy, plunges deeper and deeper into the sea of 'matter' or outward manifestation until it identifies itself with a physical form or body. There its form is overcome by stronger forms (VI. 5) and it retreats once more to gain new energy by contact with its source. Its subsequent history will thus be a cyclic one, circling upwards and downwards between the fourth and the seventh levels. This is the cycle known to us as that of life and death; death being a withdrawal to the higher levels, to be followed by a new descent and physical birth.

If we consider a diagrammatic arrangement of the levels, we find the place of physical man to be a minute subdivision, almost at the bottom of the scale of being; above him stretch level after level of ever more rarefied materiality and heightened spirituality. Even here in this material universe, when we succeed for a moment in detaching ourselves from our all-absorbing personal pursuits and we open our perceptions to the vastnesses of stellar space, we are apt to be appalled by our relatively microscopic size. Our civilisations, our cultural attainments, our activities, all seem of less significance in relation to the universe than colonies of ants are to us. To think like this is to gauge man's significance by the dimensions of his physical body, and to do this is to fall into the trap. Man's physical size relative to the universe is only an index of his insignificance if we consider him merely as an aggregate of chemical substances.

It cannot be too often repeated that man's body is an animal vehicle through which he gains experience. So long as he wholly identifies himself with the body and its needs he is indeed of little more significance than an animal, but his true being reaches out beyond the confines of the material universe, for it is rooted in the all-pervasive consciousness of the Universal Mind in which is held not only the physical universe but also the whole gamut of scales and sub-s. les, subtle as well as gross, that constitute the totality of the manifested cosmos.

In terms of physical sense experience the size and the distance of sensible objects are related terms: the further away a man is, the smaller he appears to be. Similarly, to the detached view of the soul established in its higher being, the bodies that are its material wrappings on the different levels appear to get progressively smaller the lower they stand in the scale—'it contracts when the breath of the Mother touches it' (III. 11). Relative to the body the soul is gigantic; but this is a measure of its inner significance, not of its material size.

Indeed, the whole concept of dimension derives from the earthly and constricting modalities of form and is not truly an attribute of the soul, for the soul is both greater than the great and smaller than the small.

(6) *From the first-born the thread between the Silent Watcher and his Shadow becomes more strong and radiant with every change. The morning sunlight has changed into noon-day glory. . . .*

Considered as a macrocosmic principle, the Silent Watcher is the Father-Light (*Shānta Ātman*), the Witnessing Consciousness or ultimate source of the separated Sparks. Microcosmically, he is the human monad, he who presides over the whole series of separate incarnations.

When the Sparks of Mind first become aware of themselves as embodied beings, the psycho-physical organism is inadequate as a vehicle of expression; it cannot mirror the full range of truly human thought, feeling and action. The full correspondence between soul and body can only be brought about during the long ages of evolutionary development throughout which the 'Lords of Wisdom' or personal manifestations of the Divine Man—the 'Builders' of the next verse—overshadow and guide the building of the forms.

To the human monad these long ages of evolutionary change appear as a cyclic series of incarnations. The psychic

pressure from above or within produces the necessary mutations of form so that, as life succeeds life, the shadowy inadequacy of the body is exchanged for a sense of its bright reality
—'the morning sunlight has changed into noon-day glory'.
Because of these physical limitations during the earlier stages
of the evolution of form, the soul finds greater opportunity
for activity in the subtle inner state often referred to as the
Astral world. For this reason it feels itself to be more highly
developed in its subtle integration than it is in its physical
integration; and this has given rise both to the occult tradition
that the evolution of man preceded that of the animal and to
the myth that the human race was highly 'spiritual' before it
fell into physical birth. Spiritual beings there indeed are—the
'Lords of Wisdom' or 'Sons of Fire'—but man's psychic evolution on the racial scale only precedes the physical evolution
in time in the sense that he tucks his 'astral' tail inside his pants
before the physical one disappears. The determinants of the
physical evolution are indeed always inwardly prior to their
outward effects. There could be neither hunger nor fear if
there were no prior inner will to survive and then to transcend
the dangers of the outer field of experience.

As the physical body improves as a means of expression,
so the relative stability of the physical world replaces in importance the glittering but unstable fluidity of the subtle world,
and 'the thread between the Silent Watcher and his Shadow
becomes more strong and radiant'.

We must remember here that this 'radiance', this 'noon-day
glory', refers to degrees of outwardness or manifestness. The
Stanzas regard the original source of all as Darkness; and the
lower we go in the scale, the further we get from our source,
the less there is of Darkness and the more of Light. But what
is Light to us is Darkness to the Seer, and *vice-versa*. As Words-
worth puts it, it is with trailing clouds of glory that we come,
a glory that lies about us in our infancy, but which, with each
new descent to a lower level and with each putting on of
form, fades away 'into the light of common day'.

The twilight of the Cosmic Dawn gave place to the morning sunlight of the early Day. Now that we have plumbed the very depths of manifestation, it has changed yet further into the radiance of the 'noon-day glory' in which the magic play of *Māyā* goes on till the Day draws to a close, and, in the calm evening atmosphere of tasks accomplished, we see the setting sun herald the night of peace.

The strength of the 'Thread' between the Watcher and his Shadow is an index of the degree to which an integral personality has been achieved. Loss of personality can be a very real danger to 'primitive' peoples in whom the process of self-identification has not gone much further than bodily functions. To those of us who are trying to break down and detach from the vast structures of identification we have built up around us such people may seem to be fortunate, but they are not. Such loss of personality, when it occurs, is of the external integration only and leads merely to rebirth in the vortex of the tribal womb.

The connecting 'thread' of the 'first-born' is as tenuous as a wisp of incense smoke; a gust of passion can sever the body from its Watcher, leaving the animal what it was before. Only after many births of purposeful growth does it become strong and radiant. And then its shining light pervades our being and its threefold strands of living fire will support our efforts, if we strive upwards to our undying source.

(7) '*This is thy present wheel*', said the Flame to the Spark. '*Thou art myself, my image and my shadow. I have clothed myself in thee, and thou art my Vāhan (vehicle) to the day "Be with us", when thou shalt re-become myself and others, thyself and me.*' Then the Builders, having donned their first clothing, descend on radiant earth, and reign over men—who are themselves. . . .

This, said the Father Flame to the Spark, is thy present creation. This is the sphere in which experience is to be gained through the long ages of the Day. Within this Wheel or universal system, the organisation of which is now complete, the separate streams of life will flow throughout the course of what is termed their evolution.

As we have seen, there is a deliberate ambiguity in the use of the word Spark in the singular, for the Spark is the Universal Mind of which the multitude of Sparks, the human souls, are the sons, the Son-Suns of Stanza IV. 6. It is, as we have often said, within the Universal Mind that all the truly manifest processes take place. 'No man cometh to the Father save through the Son',[1] that Son who is himself the Vine or World Tree of which the individual souls are the branches or leaves.

'Thou', the Universal Mind, 'art Myself', the Father or Light, 'my Image', reflected in the waters of the Matrix, 'and my Shadow', the mask of external appearances. The Universal Mind is the Three in One. The Light of the Father has entered the Mother and gone forth into outwardness as the radiant Son, just as the life of our own souls goes forth into the image we create and project. In the Son the Father has become manifest, the former serving as embodiment, clothing or vehicle (*vāhan*) of the latter. Within that Son the Light of the Father goes forth upon its creative adventure, ensouling all that is, wandering, a pilgrim of eternity, through the long winding circles of time's maze, till the Day 'Be with us' comes, the mystic Day of unity at the end of the manifestation. At that 'Day' the Universal Mind, having gathered together once more its scattered limbs, the 'others' into which it has differentiated, will once more re-enter the Great Mother and become 'thyself and me'.

As we have seen above, the same teaching that is true of the Universal Mind must also be true of its sons, the human egos, which are the individual differentiations of the Universal Mind and its correlates in the septenary of human principles. Just as the Mind, the Three in One, gathers up its scattered limbs, the many simultaneously existing individuals, so does the triple human monad gather up at last its own sons, the countless successive incarnations in which it has wandered.

[1] *Gospel of St. John*, XIV. 6.

Each human personality is a son of his individual father or monad, and, with certain exceptions to which we need not refer, each such son returns at death, a prodigal son, to the father who sent him forth. When we say that he returns, it is not meant to imply that he is preserved intact as a personality within his father, for much that is mere temporal dross is purged away in the fires of death. Nevertheless, his essence, all that is of lasting value in his experience, is gathered to the father and serves as a basis for the next adventuring forth into birth.

At the mystic Day 'Be with us' the Soul stands once more face to face with, and indeed enters into, the Great Soul, the one Life of all. He thus becomes 'Myself', for all separateness vanishes, and yet, since that Life is the life of all, he at the same time becomes all 'others' too. If it be asked whether at that time any 'others' still exist, it is replied that the Day 'Be with us' has an individual as well as a collective sense. Cosmically it is no doubt the day when the manifested system of separate lives re-enters the unity of its source, but, long before that consummation, the Day 'Be with us' arrives for him who can finish the course and, having mastered all the worlds of sorrow and separation, stands on the Shore of Light. It is at this moment that the Soul is faced with the great choice, the choice for which he has been preparing himself through many lives of renunciation. Beyond and in front of him blazes the sorrowless white Light of the Unity. No barrier stands between him and it, for he has earned the right to enter in. Behind him are all the illusions of separation and plurality, illusions that he has passed through and knows to be unreal. He gazes on the Light and knows that in it is true Being, stainless and sorrowless for ever. Once he has entered it, he himself becomes that Light, the light of absolute wisdom, and in it there are neither Days nor Nights, neither world systems nor men who dwell therein. These things are not, and he now knows they are not; in that one Light they neither have been, are, nor will be.

'Now bend thy head and listen well, O Bodhisattva—

z

Compassion speaks and saith; "Can there be bliss when all that lives must suffer? Shalt thou be saved and hear the whole world cry?" [1]

For enlightenment is twofold or has a twofold aspect. The great teacher Ashwaghosha writes: 'In the one Heart of Reality we may distinguish two aspects. The one is the Reality in its intrinsic aspect, the mystic Void, the other the Reality as the ocean of birth and death. *Each in itself constitutes all things,* and both are so closely interrelated that one cannot be separated from the other.' [2]

The worlds are the Light and the Light is all the worlds, yet in the worlds the Light is deeply hidden, and in the Light the worlds (as such) are not at all.

The choice lies open, nor, should he go forward, can any cry of blame from us who are not reach his ear who now forever is.

Nor should we underestimate the magnitude of the choice. It is easy for those who are still in some large measure attached to the life of plurality to imagine that they themselves would not hesitate to sacrifice the bliss of unity in order to remain in touch with the world of suffering. But such imagining is void of meaning, for it is not till all trace of attachment to the world has been burnt out in the fires of yoga that any will reach that further shore and be confronted with the choice. Only he whose soul has soared upwards through many lives, he whose flame-like spirit has burnt its way through all that stands between itself and unity, is able to stand on that topmost peak of being; and none that has not done so can gauge the intensity of the divine thirst that draws him in to the Peace. Behind him is the tremendous thrust of many lives of intense effort and aspiration, driving him like a spear-point ever onward. The great bow which long ago he strung and drew has launched him like an arrow, flying straight to the very heart of Reality.

[1] *The Voice of the Silence:* The Seven Portals.
[2] *The Awakening of Faith in the Mahāyāna* (slightly altered from Suzuki's translation).

What is there that can stop that onward flight and hold him poised and motionless upon the edge of Bliss? Only one thing, the divine force of Compassion which speaks in his heart and reminds him that, though he himself has conquered all illusions, there are still all the 'others' who, like himself in the past, still battle with the bitter waves of the sea, crying to Gods for help no Gods can give. Even now he can turn a deaf ear to that cry, telling himself that it is but illusion—as indeed it is—and that in truth, as he now sees, there is no bitter sea, no struggling lives, so self, no others; no, neither are nor yet ever have been.

This is the last and most subtle temptation of all, and only he who throughout has followed the path of love and compassion will be able to resist that voice, for it speaks the truth, yet not the whole truth. The uttermost truth is indeed, as Nāgārjuna proclaimed long ago: 'there is no difference at all between *Nirvāṇa* and *Saṃsāra* (the world ocean). That which is the limit of *Nirvāṇa*, is also the limit of the worlds. Between the two we cannot find the slightest shade of difference'.[1]

It is the same unthinkable Reality that manifests both as the bliss of Unity and as the sorrow-laden worlds of separate beings. To choose the former and to shun the latter is the last snare of ignorance.[2] When Light and Darkness are in truth but one, what profits it to choose the Light when our countless other selves still wander in the Dark? May not the wisdom and world-mastery that has been won be held in manifestation as a beacon in the night for those whose need is great? The bliss of Unity and the sorrow of separateness are not two but one. Shall not, then, he who sees that oneness sacrifice the bliss for the sake of his other selves who see it not and to whom all is

---

[1] *Mādhyamik Kārika* XXV. 19 & 20.
[2] We repeat that it is not for us who are still far from that Light to point fingers of facile criticism at those who choose the Unity and 'go on', for the choice and its alternatives are far beyond our comprehension. Nevertheless we can but cleave to the path of our own teachers and pray that, when our time comes, we too may make their choice.

therefore dark and grievous? Shall he not himself remain in, though not of, the worlds of separation to hold out a helping hand to those who are both in and of those worlds? And at the same time, shall he not repay the debt he owes to those who helped *him* on his upward path?

Thus speaks the voice of compassion in his heart on the great Day 'Be with us.'

> 'Now thou hast heard that which was said.
> Thou art enlightened—choose thy way.'[1]

Let us now leave the question of the individual attainment and return to more universal considerations. The One Life, as it prepares to ensoul the separate forms in which it will wander through the labyrinth of Time, utters the prophecy of final redemption and return. It is that One Life that is the Life of all; and it is for that reason that the ultimate home-coming of all its scattered members is assured. Wherever they may wander, and into whatsoever deep pits of ignorance they may fall, never, never can they go beyond the embrace of that One Life in which they live and move. Hence it is with these words of benediction and assurance ringing in their hearts that the Builders of individual facets of that life set forth on their adventure, and, clothed in their first subtle clothing of the intermediate region, descend onto this physical earth and there rule as the inner Rulers of the men who are their own lower selves—men who are themselves built up from the innumerable modalities of the one living Spirit. Each man, each part of man, and each sub-division of every universal principle which contributes its properties to man, is a facet of the divine experiencing, and each is a fraction of the One— 'The Beams and Sparks of One Moon reflected in the running waves of all the rivers of earth'.

Into the Earth the Light of Lights descends, and from the Earth it streams back towards its source. This is the radiance

[1] *The Voice of the Silence.*

of the Earth. Filled with the light of Spirit it is now radiantly visible to the eye of Spirit, the inner Ruler of Man.

From one point of view the Builders are the Divine Kings and Teachers, 'culture heroes', who, in the early stages of human history, descended to guide the hosts of younger souls. But from a still more important point of view they are our true Selves, the sparks of the Divine Creative or Imagining power which, seated deep within, fashions all experience for us. It is they who create or build the very texture of our experience and then rule over us, their own projections. The world is a structure of creative imagination, and it is they who are its Builders, each with its sovereign power, yet all being facets of the Universal Mind, restrained within its shining Divine Net. It is useless for us to set up our personal imaginings, or rather fancies, against the structure of that divine Building. Even here, when imagining becomes creative, as in true art, the private will is in abeyance and has no personal control over what is fashioned. So it is with us. We may idly imagine a world where life shall not be followed by death nor evil actions by their bitter fruits, but that imagining will be of no avail. Within us are our Rulers, our true Selves: as they imagine, so shall the structure be. For them the freedom of creative life within the Soul of all; for us the discipline of obedience, the effort to make ourselves into plastic instruments by which that vision may be made manifest. They are our Selves: in *their* imagining lies for us freedom, happiness and peace. Our very life is lent to us by them, and to them it returns each night of death. It is only through him who is 'one with his Father', him whose personal self is but a vehicle for his Father's will, that the Father's divine power can manifest freely with all its wondrous freedom. When that occurs, as it has now and then occurred, we gasp and idly prate of Gods, not knowing that beyond all Gods is Man, the heart of each of us, Ruler of all that is.

Thus has the One Spirit or *Ātman* multiplied itself, saying 'I am one; may I be many'. And so that Spirit, having become the many separate selves, wanders Odysseus-like in many strange disguises and plunges into countless new adventures.

> 'For all experience is an arch wherethrough
> Gleams that untravelled world whose margin fades
> Forever and forever as we move.'[1]

Then, in the end, weary of journeying, those Selves give ear once more to the Voice which, though overlooked, has never for a moment ceased to sound within their hearts. Those memories of which Plato spoke well up in the depths of the Soul, at first faintly and sporadically, but then with an ever-increasing vividness until, in comparison with their spiritual light, the whole outer universe grows dark and empty. Then it is that a great detachment (*vairāgya*) from the projected image comes upon the Soul, and it is seized with a passionate and quenchless thirst for Home. Slowly and with hesitating steps that yet grow firmer as it proceeds, it sets out upon the homeward Journey, taking with it the garnered treasures of its experience.

The day 'Be with us' is a metaphysical event within that simultaneity which is the true being of the Universal Mind. For those who can see, it is a present reality; for the others, it cannot become known until the cycles come to an end and only the ever-present remains. 'Every man', says the Upanishad, 'goes to the Brahman at night', and so he does, but he brings back, at the most, a faint sense of narcissistic contentment —'happy I slept'. So it is with the unawakened souls when it comes to that Day. For them, when the brightly sun-lit field of out-turned experience grows dim, the inner darkness remains blank nothingness. Those who have never thought of themselves as being anything but a flow of sensations and memories are factually nothing but what they think themselves to be. At the Universal withdrawal their outer coverings of form are dissolved, the 'Sparks' vanish that have never truly lived, and they return to their source. Such 'Sparks' have failed

[1] Tennyson's *Ulysses*.

in their task; they have never become self-remembering, awakened individuals, consciously uniting within themselves the Above and the Below.

The path of the soul as an experiencing being circles between the higher unity, the Above, and the lower separateness, the Below, acting as a uniting agent between the two. Joined to its source in the Universal Mind the soul has no separate being and no experience of separate parts. Joined to its physical body of sense it looks out from one location upon the extended content of the same experience. For the soul is a focal point in the light of Consciousness, and through it the trans-individual divinity garners the experience of its multiple modalities. Thus the Divine looks from itself into itself and experiences the flowering of its own infinite potentialities.

This is the outward-looking mode of the divine experience. The other, inward-looking, mode lies in the return of the soul to its source where all forms vanish and only the bliss of total unity remains. And whereas the outward flow from unity to multiplicity is the flow of separative desire, whether divine or human, the inward flow of return to that unity is the flow of love, for all love is a self-negating in which two become one.

Our lives may spring from origins of which we have no ordinary awareness, but unless we strive to become aware, unless we listen to the secret message of our hearts, give our whole attention and all our energies to its realisation, the plant of the inner life will make no growth. Each of us has befouled himself in the pursuit of egotistic aims, and it is by our own efforts that we must be cleansed; the energies we have stolen for our own purposes have to be repaid. Yet, of the whole harvest of experience that we reap, good and bad alike, nothing is wasted if its lesson has been learned, for it is out of the richness of life that the soul must draw its strength, not from any weak refusal of experience. Nevertheless, significant though they may be as fields of experience, the material worlds are real only by virtue of the presence of the divine Consciousness that sustains both them and us.

'All things are perishing except His face.
His is the fore-ordainment
And unto Him ye shall return.'[1]

*   *   *

With the birth of Man on the shores of the Ocean of
material existence, whose tremendous content, shining with
the light of all-pervasive consciousness, both attracts and repels,
fascinates and terrifies, and with the promise of a last Home-
coming, we reach the end of this Cosmogony as handed down
to us. It is in this last promise, sounding even now within our
hearts, that lies the ultimate security of all our deepest values.
If we and all these worlds were mere chance products, then
Life could have no meaning and no value.

If we have read aright the Stanzas' message, it is that this
great universe and all that it contains was not sent forth merely
to be rejected. It is no great abortion that should never have
been born, but a divine harmony in which each part is linked
to every other. Seen in the Truth, it is a shining being, the
unity of God spread forth before Him on the web of Time
and Space. The study of it is the study of ourselves.

He who experiences the whole is Man. Cosmogony is
Man writ large upon the Heavens. Its truth is in his heart.
We do not speak of such potential men as we are now, though
even we, alone among all beings, have in our hearts the power
to grasp the cosmos in our fists, to fuse again the mass of
scattered splendour into a gleaming Pearl within the heart.

They who have formed that Jewel, the Treasure hidden in
the Darkness of the One, They are the Perfected Man or
Men of whom the Stanzas tell. Unseen by us they walk upon
the Waters of the Cosmic Ocean, neither sinking in their
depths, nor yet forsaking them, alone to the Alone. One with
his Source, such Man does not abandon in their darkness
those who still flounder in the bitter waves of sorrow; forever

[1] *Qu'rān.*

he holds out a hand to those who turn to him for guidance and for comfort. How should he leave them, for he knows they are himself?

Dwelling in the worlds of transient form, he holds in being the Sight of their Foundation. By him have all the opposites been reconciled, yet not dissolved, but held within his heart. For him the worlds and heavens were sent forth. He is the goal to which our steps should lead.

What should we call him but Eternal Man?
'Shine on us from afar, Moon of the mountain fringe'.[1]

---

[1] From a Japanese *No* play included in Adams Beck's *The Garden of Vision.*

I. GENERAL INDEX

II. INDEX OF NON-ENGLISH TERMS